Beyond Words

A Memoir Story

For Lisa,
With hope and healing.

Gayle

GAYLE A. HUNTRESS

ISBN: 1492956341
ISBN 13: 9781492956341
Library of Congress Control Number: 2013919221
CreateSpace Independent Publishing Platform
North Charleston, South Carolina

For Jack, Carm, and Beth

I would not have been a poet
except that I have been in love
alive in this mortal world,
or an essayist except that I
have been bewildered and afraid,
or a storyteller had I not heard
stories passing to me through the air,
or a writer at all except
I have been wakeful at night
and words have come to me
out of their deep caves
needing to be remembered.
But on the days I am lucky
or blessed, I am silent.
I go into the one body
that two make in making marriage
that for all our trying, all
our deaf-and-dumb of speech,
has no tongue. Or I give myself
to gravity, light, and air
and am carried back
to solitary work in fields
and woods, where my hands
rest upon a world unnamed,
complete, unanswerable, and final
as our daily bread and meat.
The way of love leads all ways
to life beyond words, silent
and secret...

—VII (excerpt) from the poem "1994" by Wendell Berry.

Prologue

After spending the morning following a complicated set of directions about what to pack and how and when to arrive, I finally turn off a dirt road, onto another dirt road, onto a long rutted driveway. My little car bumps along the dirt road. It's hot. The windows are open, and I can see a thin film of dust on the windshield.

There is man dressed all in black standing on the side of the road. When I get closer, I see it is actually a woman. She's wearing black army fatigues that hang low on her hips and a fitted black T-shirt. She purposefully walks partway into the driveway and holds up her hand. It's not a wave. It's the sign for stop, but stronger than that. She's saying "halt" with her whole body. She strides over to my window. I smile at her. She does not smile back.

"Hi, I'm here...I'm here to register," I stammer out.

She looks at me from a face that is serious, but not unkind.

"Are you ready to die?" she asks.

Her question catches me completely off guard.

"Excuse me?" I ask.

"Are you ready to die?" she repeats. "Let go of everything you think you know. Are you ready to die in that way?"

I consider the question. I think about the last seven years and trying to fix myself—to remove this feeling of brokenness and go back to feeling the way I used to. I think about how nothing has worked and how tired I am of trying, always trying, to be OK again.

"Yes," I say quietly. "Yes, I'm ready to die."

At the end of the long driveway, which is more of a road itself than a driveway, I do finally reach an official registration table. Again, the women are all dressed in black. They are like the woman on the road—all unsmiling and serious, but not unkind. You can tell the participants because we're all dressed in colors and are glancing around nervously. They've asked us to maintain silence by not talking unless absolutely necessary. I feel like my own skin is itchy, and I don't know what to do with my arms. I set up my tent in the circle with the others, glad to have something to do. I follow the same steps to set it up that I always have: in car campgrounds, in fields, near lakes and high peaks, sometimes miles from civilization. I stake it to the ground, pulling it taut, then raise the poles. I could do it my sleep. The left one is slightly bent where I tripped over it years ago, and it takes an extra twist to make it lock into place. When I tripped over it, I was drunk. Out-of-my-mind drunk—the kind of drunk you can only get when you're car camping instead of backpacking and have the luxury of taking a thirty-pack and a cooler with you. I was doing what all my college friends did then: drinking to have fun. It was considered a good time. But for me it was more than that. I drank to stop having a bad time. I drank to forget, to take the sharp edges off of the feelings. It didn't make them go away. It just made them blissfully dull for a while. If drinking had made my pain go away entirely, I'm sure I would have slipped into full-blown alcoholism and enjoyed the ride. But instead I just dabbled and experimented and was able to do it under the guise of having a good time.

As I stick the pole into its grommet, I notice that it's got a miniscule tear on one side. I'll have to remember to repair it when I get home. I've had enough total equipment failures over the years to know the best way for gear to take care of you is to take care of it. The tent was new once—a pristine top-of-the line, three-season tent named after the highest peak in Maine. Now, I can barely read its name, rubbed off by wear. Katadin.

I count the years back on my fingers to when I first saw it lying on the hearth Christmas morning. Nine years. My first Christmas home from college. The last Christmas we were all together. It was unwrapped, but there was a card taped to the outside that read:

So you can take home with you on all your adventures.
Love, Mom

It was by far my biggest present that year. I was thrilled by it, and it hadn't even been on my ask list.

When it's set up, I crawl inside and sit cross-legged and inhale the slightly musty scent of nylon that is unique to tents. They all smell pretty much the same. It's the smell of adventure and of being nomadic and the smell of beautiful and wild places.

I was thirteen when I went camping for real for the first time. Three years later I went on my first canoe expedition, and the smell of a tent got embedded into my soul. Our small group of campers traveled to northern Saskatchewan for fifty days and during that time went weeks without seeing any other people. Every few days when an airplane passed, a high droning dot in the sky, we'd all stop paddling and look up because it was an event.

We joked that expeditions were an exercise in moving from one form of discomfort to another. And it was mostly true. We were always too hot, too cold, hungry, aching, bored, or just plain tired. But the discomfort was just part of it. We had rules against complaining. There was even a name for it: "expedition behavior." It meant that if you were uncomfortable, most likely everyone else was too, so for God's sake, talk about something else or don't talk at all. On that trip and the ones leading up to it, I learned what it was to have something be hard and keep going anyway. Quitting simply wasn't an option. On those trips we only had ourselves and each other and couldn't call for help if we wanted. This was years before cell phones, and even if they had been available, there definitely wouldn't have been service where we were traveling. I'll bet there still isn't.

It didn't matter how long the day was, how much your shoulders ached, how badly your face swelled from black fly bites, or how many more miles you had to carry the eighty-pound canoe because the riverbed had dried up. Even a broken arm or leg wouldn't mean rescue—we'd just have to keep going to the nearest place to call out for a float plane to fly in. It's a lesson I've learned well. Forge ahead. Don't talk about it. Power through.

A woman nearby drops something, and I hear tent poles clattering together, and she curses quietly. Everyone is still trying to be quiet. What did they call it during registration? Respectful silence. Necessary silence. Something like that.

I'm still sitting cross-legged in my tent, but this is an entirely different kind of discomfort than wilderness travel. I'm not too hot, or too cold or hungry or tired. I'm uncomfortable with the same feeling that's been inside me for seven years, preventing me from really being present anywhere. I try to name what the feeling is; that's what June would ask me to do if I were in her office. I try to picture her enormous sage-green couch, her wooden rocking chair, her kind face.

"What's the feeling?" she'd say. "Tell me about it; tell me where it is in your body and what it feels like."

"Fear," I'd answer. "Right here, in the center of my stomach."

Everything here feels foreign and weird. I kind of want to pack up my tent and leave it's so strong. It seems like theater—all the women dressed in black and the silence and that woman in the driveway asking me if I was ready to die.

What the hell was that about?

I'm not ready to die. Not at all. I came here because I'm ready to live.

Part I

Chapter One

The first thing I remember is sitting on a quilt next to a pond. My head is in Mom's lap, and I can see Jack holding a fishing pole. Dad is shirtless and helping him cast. It's hot and I have to close my eyes against the sun. It's so bright. I can hear buzzing insects flying all around us. They are dragonflies. Mom shows me one that lands on her arm.

"It won't bite. They are nice," she says.

The dragonfly has emerald eyes and a blue body, turquoise with flecks of red. Next time one lands on me, she brings the camera slowly to her face and takes a close-up of my arm and the brilliant bug. I watch it for a long time. Its wings are transparent, with complicated patterns etched into the surface. Its tail moves with a regular rhythm, up and down, up and down, pulsing out life like a heartbeat.

Now that I'm older and almost eight, I'm pretty sure that memory pond is Paige Pond, across the street from my house. To get there, I have to walk down the road 115 steps and then squeeze through the gap in the big metal cow gate. Or, I can take the shortcut over the ledge underneath the big maple and get to the gate quicker. The roots of the big tree curve and twist out of the ground over the ledge, and I can climb down the steep bank on them. Last year Jack climbed to one of the high branches in the corner of the yard and tied a thick rope so it hangs down. You can stand on the top of the ledge and swing way out, over the road. Or you can swing like Spiderman back and forth. Mom found us doing that and covered her eyes.

"This is so scary. I can't watch this!" she said.

She says that a lot, usually when we are playing the most fun games that involve ropes and being up high or jumping off things into piles of leaves or snow or dirt. She has a plaque in the kitchen that one of her friends gave her for Mother's Day. On the plaque are little cartoons of kids doing all sorts of dangerous things around the words, "Never Watch Your Children At Play."

I ask her if I'm breaking the rule when I swing on the rope, the rule where we're not allowed to pass the big pine tree at the edge of the driveway without permission. Because actually, I pass the pine tree in the air if I get a really good swing. She says no, it is OK. As long as I'm touching the rope, it is OK. When I'm not swinging, I can go anywhere I want within the acres. An acre is a big thing, and there are eleven of them that are ours. The edges go from the pine tree in the front yard at the edge of the driveway, up around the orchard to Route 32A, and then way back into the field. There's a stone wall covered with poison ivy, so I don't play on it, but that's one side. The creek is the last side, down in the hill next to Sally and Louie's house. They're old and all their kids are grown up, and they're really nice and let their dog, Connie, come up and play with us. I think Connie misses the kids, because she spends most of her time at our house, except at night when Mom shoos her out of the kitchen during supper so she won't beg. From the big window next to the kitchen table, I sometimes watch Connie walk herself home. I think she looks sad, so sometimes before she goes, I slip her a little piece of chicken or hamburger under the table.

The field going down to the creek and Sally and Louie's has a slope that is perfect for sledding in the winter. Except at the bottom of the hill, if the snow is really good and you make it that far, you have to bail out before hitting the barbed wire in front of it. It was left there from years ago from when there used to be cows in the field. If you make it through the rusty barbed wire, there is a stone wall right behind that. I think it's good that Mom stays inside and doesn't sled with us, because it would probably be another case of it being too scary for her to watch. Plus, she has hot chocolate with two big marshmallows in each cup waiting for us when we get inside. Sometimes she throws in one extra as a "thank you" if we've taken off our snow pants and mittens and laid them out by the woodstove carefully instead of just piling them all in a wet heap.

I wish I could remember being born. Mom says I was born on a crispy day in the fall. Her belly was so big she couldn't sleep, and just as the sun was coming up, she saw a red fox in the side yard from her bedroom window. It had frosted during the night, and the fox looked bright against the white of everything else. At that moment, she said, she knew she was going to have girl and that the girl was going to have red hair. She was right, although I was so ready to come out into the world that I was almost born in Paxton at the fire station in the back of the Volkswagen. But they made it to the hospital, and before Dad could even park the car, I was born.

We don't have the Volkswagen anymore. I'm sad about that because it was a punch-buggy and if we had it, I could sit in the back seat and punch Jack and Carm in the arm whenever I wanted because we would be riding *in* a punch buggy, and I'd get all the points. But maybe it wouldn't be so good because then Jack could do punch-buggy-back, and my arm would hurt, even if we were just going to the Big Y in Ware. Now, the family car is a Pinto with sides that look like wood and insides that smell like old bananas. It has to be a station wagon for all five of us to fit. Jack and me and Carm ride in the back seat, but Carm still has a booster seat because he's little.

Sometimes Dad takes us out in the Cadillac when it's summer. Most of the time it's parked in the barn with flowered sheets over it to protect it from the bird poop. But when it is nice, he takes it out into the driveway and washes the whole thing and puts the top down. The car is painted metal-yellow so when he rubs polish on it with rags it looks like gold. It used to belong to my grandmother, so it's old and smells like leather inside. I can lay down flat in the back seat and still have room to put my arms all the way up and still not touch the armrests. He drives us to Janine's Frostee, and Mom wears a scarf tied around her head to protect it from the wind. When she does this, Dad calls her "Jackie O." This summer my brother is trying to beat Chuck Turner down the road to see who can eat the most brown derby sundaes before school starts. Derby sundaes are like banana splits but with brownies under the ice cream. So far Chuck is winning with twelve, but it's only July. On the way home from Janine's, Jack and I huddle down in between the front seat and the back seat. It's warm down there and protected from the wind, and when it gets dark out, we tilt our heads back and look at the stars. It's neat to ride in a car and see the whole sky all at once going so fast but having all the stars stay in place.

Dad takes me and Jack to Pastor Ewing's house to pick out a new kitten. There are seven in the litter, and they are in the kitchen, all rolling around in a cardboard box lined with an old pink towel.

"We can take them out in the yard," says Pastor Ewing. He is wearing a blue work shirt and jeans that have a rip at the knee, and he looks more bald than normal. I wonder if he just puts his robes over whatever he's wearing when he goes to church and we can't tell, even if he's wearing ripped pants. That would be so unfair because I have to wear stupid tights and dresses.

Pastor Ewing carries the box out to the backyard and turns it over beneath the clothesline. There seems to be more than seven, and they are everywhere, rolling around and trying to climb all over each other. Jack sits right down in the middle and picks up two, one in each hand. I sit next to him, and he hands one to me. It's so little and can sit in both of my palms. It licks my thumb. Another one tries to climb up Jack's knee, and he pulls it into his lap.

"Which one should we pick?" I whisper. "How do we know which one is the best one?"

"I dunno," he says. "Dad said we could only get one to replace Pooh Bear."

Pooh Bear was big and black, but I don't remember him that much because he died two years ago when I was only six. He was old. Mom and Dad had him before they had any of us, even.

"Should we choose by color?" I ask.

"No, I think we should choose by the one that runs around the most," says Jack.

We each take as many kittens as we can into our laps and watch the rest. There's one that is trying to climb up Dad's pant leg as he's talking to Pastor Ewing. It's a gray tabby with white sock feet.

Dad bends down and puts the cat back on the ground.

"I'm not a tree," he says to the kitten. "Go climb on those shrubs over there." He points at us.

The kitten swishes her tail and runs over to Jack, who scoops it up. "This one," he says. "This one is the best one."

I nod. "Definitely the best one."

Pastor Ewing tells us we have a girl cat and gives us a shoebox to take her home. When we get there, she runs in zigzags and slides on the wood floors, and Mom names her Scamper.

I like how animals get their names for what they do or how they look. It makes more sense than people names that come from other people in your family or names your parents just think sound good.

I was named after my great-grandmother Gaynor, and I think there's something wrong with my name because everyone calls me "Gay," and sometimes older kids laugh at me. I know that the word gay is in the last line of the Kookaburra song we sing in music, and it's also a song I hate because sometimes kids sing my name extra loud and look at me. I sometimes wish I was named something with a Y like Cindy or Mandy or Tracy, but Gay is what I'm stuck with.

⌒

Sometimes Dad takes me to work with him in the big green van that says *Sedum* on the front in yellow letters. He's a landscaper, and so the back fits the riding lawn mower and has racks on the side with shovels and rakes. It always smells like gasoline and dirt in there, and I kind of like it. We usually go to the bank in Ware, and he shows me how to pull out the weeds and dig holes where he will plant yellow pansies. I always hope one of my friends will come to the bank while I'm there and see me working with my dad, doing real landscaping. I keep asking if I can drive the lawn mower, but Dad says not until I'm ten. Until then I have to ride on his lap and maybe just steer it now and then. Sometimes when he mows our yard, he hooks up the wagon to the back, and we get to ride, all three of us. The wagon is a brown rust color with a few spots of red and says *Radio Flyer* on the side. The handle broke off two years ago when I was six, so now there's just rope to pull it. Dad ties it to the hitch and puts the mower on the fastest speed. The best is when he goes over the bump in the side yard and then up the dip on the side of the driveway, and the wagon tips over, and we all end up in a pile. It's so fun.

When he's not mowing the lawn, he's pulling weeds or planting flowers or trimming the hedges with the giant scissors. He's outside a lot. Mom is in the kitchen a lot, cooking and doing dishes and talking and laughing on the phone. Sometimes the curly white cord gets totally wrapped around her, and when we need something, she has to twirl around to untangle herself. After we're done working at the bank and if I've done a good job, we stop at Goddard's on the way home. Dad stops at the wall of little mailboxes in the store, and Ruth smiles big and hands him the mail from the under the barred window that makes it look like she's in jail. I go over to the candy counter next to the cash register and stand for a long time. There's a lot to choose from, and I can only get one thing. I think hard if it's better to get a Charlestown Chew or Hubba Bubba. The Charleston Chew is the biggest candy bar, but the bubble gum lasts the longest, and you can blow bubbles with it. I choose the gum, then Ruth comes out from behind the mailboxes to the counter so we can pay for it. At Halloween we trick-or-treat at Goddard's, and Mr. Goddard lets each kid pick one thing from the rack for free. It's the best stop for sure since all the rest of the houses around the common give "fun size" candy, which really just means it's extra tiny, so there's nothing fun about it.

The other best place to get candy is Butler's next to the baseball field and tennis court. I'm allowed to go alone on my bike if Jack comes with me. Usually Chuck does, too. We get the watermelon Jolly Rancher sticks that turn your mouth pink, and if you suck them just right, they get sharp at the end, and you have to be careful not to cut your tongue or get mad and poke your brother. My other favorite is Big League Chew. I haven't been able to fit the entire package of shredded gum in my mouth all at once, but I keep trying. Mr. Butler doesn't get mad if you take forever to decide, and he also will pump up your bike tires for you using the air pump for cars with the red hose that pings. He fixed my chain once when it broke, and the next day Mom sent me down with a plate of cookies for him. I stopped and ate one on the way there because they were just out of the oven and still warm, and I couldn't help it.

When I was little, before I knew how to ride a bike, I used to cry and follow Jack and Dad to the barn when they went on rides. It wasn't fair. I wanted to go.

A few times they went without me, but once Dad asked, "You really want to come with us, huh?"

"You're too little," said Jack.

I cried harder and held on to Dad's leg.

"Maybe there's a way," said Dad. He rummaged in the workbench and found an old towel he used to check the oil in the lawn mower. He folded it and wrapped it around the top bar, securing it with duct tape. "Ta-da! Kid seat just for you."

He helped me up, and I put my legs on either side like a horse, but the towel slipped and I slipped with it, going over to one side. Dad caught me around the waist.

"Try it like this instead." He lifted me so both my legs were going the same way.

"English fancy style" he called it. Dad got on the seat behind me and did a few circles in the driveway. My knuckles were white from holding on tight to the handlebars. Dad's hands were outside of mine, working the brakes and gears. It was scary, but I kind of liked it. Any moment I knew I could fall off, but it was all right because Dad's arms were right there on either side of me.

We rode out of the driveway, off the crunchy gravel, up the hill, then down towards the center of town—past the sand pit, past the cemetery, moving almost as fast as a car. I looked down at Jack riding his own bike next to us. I was so high up, going so fast. My hair whipped behind me, and I could hear Dad breathing hard going up the hills.

All that summer it became our after-dinner adventure. Carm had to go to bed, and we went everywhere, coming home just when the sun was getting close to the tops of the trees.

We ended the ride the same way every time, by speeding down Sessions Road into the curve of our driveway. The bike got wobbly on the gravel, and sometimes I screamed for fun. Dad hit the brakes and we left a peel mark, like Dukes of Hazard. Jack sometimes spun out his back wheel in an arc, just like a real dirt bike.

"Cool," Dad said.

The next summer, Dad taught me how to ride myself. He took me out to the barn, and I watched as he used a wrench to put the training wheels back on the bike—the same bike that Jack learned on. It had a blue banana seat with flecks of sparkle in it and a red frame. There were rainbow plastic streamers attached to the handlebars when it was new, but when I got it, there were only three left on the right side and one on the left. I knew right away that I would end up pulling them all out, one by one, until there were none left. I'd try not to, but it would happen automatically, with them just hanging there waiting to be pulled out. Dad flipped the bike down from the workbench, onto the concrete.

"Sit on that and see how it feels."

I climbed on. The bike tilted to one side and rested on one of the training wheels. I shifted in the seat and it tilted to the other side. Back and forth like a clock.

"Good, that's good," he said. "Someday soon you'll ride without the training wheels, but now they'll keep you from tipping over, see? Pedal. Give it a try."

I pushed down with my foot, and the bike inched forward. I pushed harder. Since I was resting on one training wheel, I turned right, towards the parked car. The bike lurched to a stop. Dad had grabbed the handle behind the seat to stop me.

"Why don't we try in the driveway? There's more space." He helped guide the bike outside and gave me a push. It was harder on the gravel to pedal.

Pedal. Tilt to the other side. Pedal. Back and forth.

"You're doing it, Sissy Jupe! Go!"

I love it when Dad uses my special name. I once asked him where it came from, and he said he just likes the word "Sissy" since I'm a girl, and the "Jupe" part comes from his favorite dog when he was growing up. She was a beagle named Jupie.

"Dad, you named me after your *dog*!" I said.

"Of course." His eyes were squinty so I knew he was teasing me.

"That dog was one of my favorite things in the whole world when I was a boy. And now you are."

"Am I more favorite than Jack and Carm?" I asked. I was teasing him and squinting my eyes, too.

He made a look like he was thinking really hard. "You are without a doubt my most favorite, most special daughter I ever had."

"And your only one," I reminded him.

"Still my most favorite one," he said.

In the springtime all of the snow melts, and what's left is broken branches and sticks and rotten leaves. Dad goes to work in the green Sedum van doing yard cleanups for people. Then he comes home and works on our yard until Mom calls dinner from the back porch. We get to play outside in our boots after school, and everything gets muddy. After it rains we carve out rivers with sticks in the driveway and make dams with the mud and pea stones. Everything smells like mud outside, and it feels funny to be outside without a winter coat. On a warm day with dull sun, I just wear a T-shirt, my favorite one with the neon cats on it, shorts, and winter boots. It feels even stranger to wear boots with shorts.

We make a long series of dams and a chain of small lakes in the driveway with sticks and our plastic beach shovels. In a coffee can, we carry stones and mud from one dam to another that needs reinforcing.

Soon, Dad's green truck rolls down Sessions Road, coming home. One pass of the green van and all of the engineering would be ruined, so we stand in front of our work and wave our arms. He sees us and parks on the road. He watches us for a few minutes from behind the windshield, then gets out and brings one of his big shovels, the kind with a little shelf for your foot that you can stomp on. He comes over to where we're making a deep pool and an enormous dam right in the middle of the driveway, scraping away at the gravel with our plastic beach shovels. He's smiling.

"Let me help. Quite the production you have going on."

With three shovelfuls he makes a hole that would have taken us the rest of the day to finish. We look up at him, our shovels still poised in the air. He is so tall and strong. A hole that deep, dug that easily is amazing. We scramble to divert the water into the new mega-lake, overjoyed at our good fortune. He watches for a while, then throws the shovel over his shoulder and whistles on the way to the house.

Later, Mom makes us take our boots off in the shed and go directly into the bath before dinner. We all leave wet stocking footprints to the bathroom. I hear my parents talking through the open bathroom door.

"They are making a disaster of the driveway. I think we produced three gophers instead of children," says Mom.

"I know," he says. "Isn't it wonderful?"

For the next two days, he parks at the end of the driveway, and Mom drives across the lawn to keep our work intact so we can keep building. When the water stops flowing and the ground becomes hard a week later, Dad fills the wheelbarrow with gravel and fills in the holes and has us use a metal rake to smooth out all the dams.

The whole time he comments on our work.

"Wow, that's a big one."

"Look at all the water that one held."

"Quite the production."

One windy day after the ground is drier, Jack gets the kite out of the barn. The kite has scary octopus eyes and wild tentacle streamers. We take turns running through the sloppy ground, mud spattering our backs, until it's in the air. The wind picks up and grabs at the kite, taking it higher and higher. We let the spool of string fly through our hands until it gets hot, letting out more and more string. We reach the end of the spool, and the kite is high, way above the trees. Still it tugs, wanting to go higher. I find a small spool of string on the workbench, and we tie that to the end of the kite string, and up it goes. Soon, it runs out, but I can hardly make out the octopus eyes in the bright sky. Carm is hopping around us, wanting a turn.

"Let me! Let me try!"

Jack lets him. Carm is so excited, he keeps bouncing from foot to foot as he holds it.

"Stay still, Carm, or you might let go!"

I run inside and get the spool of purple string from the basket near the telephone, where the tape and rubber bands and broken pencils are kept. I run back to the field, and Carm is still holding the string with one hand, stretched out against the pull, and is pointing at the sky with the other. Jack is standing quietly behind him, holding on to an end as backup. We tie the purple string to the end of the white string and let the kite pull away. Higher and higher it goes until it is just a small, black dot.

"Jack, do you think we should pull it in? Will an airplane run into it?"

"No, it's not that high. See?"

He points up and I see a jet plane way up above the dot. Still, it is a marvelous thing to be holding on to a tugging string with a kite impossibly high like that.

We start getting cold, standing in the wind, and we take turns winding up the string. It takes forever. Our hands hurt from the winding and the cold.

"What would happen if we just cut the string and let it go?" I ask.

We are thrilled by the idea of putting something out into the world. We'd lose the kite, but it seems worth it just to have the thrill. We talk about the kite going to Wisconsin, to California, over the entire ocean to China but keep winding anyway. I pull the string in, hand over hand to the ground while Jack winds as fast as he can. We reach the end and can't get the knot undone; Jack bites it and it breaks.

He holds the end and looks at me and looks at Carm.

"Mom would miss the purple string, but we got that back. So, let's do it."

We discuss it and decide that we each get to hold on, Jack first, then me, then Carm, and on the count of three, we'll all let go. We hand-slap promise to all do it at exactly the same time, no holding on to be the last one.

"One."

"Two."

"Three."

We all let go and whoop, and I feel the string slide through my fingers. It is gone almost instantly, pulled up into the sky. We shade our eyes against the sun and watch the kite dot disappear. For a long time we stand there, thinking we still see it; a small dot against all that blue. But it's gone. Off to fly with the airplanes. Off to Wisconsin and China.

Chapter Two

" **L** ook what I made for you!"

Mom had been working at the sewing machine for weeks with pieces of pink fuzzy fabric. After measuring my head three separate times, she holds up the result.

It is a fuzzy pink bonnet with floppy stuffed ears to make me look like a rabbit. The ears even have white on their insides. A satin pink ribbon secures the bonnet and ears around my chin. I put on my pink pajamas with feet, the ones I got for my eighth birthday. Pink pipe cleaners twisted together and taped under my nose are the final touch.

We are going to deliver May baskets for the church to the "shut-ins." Mom said they are the people who have trouble leaving the house because they are too sick or too old. Each basket has some cookies and flowers and candy in it. Mom lets me have a handful of Hershey kisses for my very own. I eat three and put the rest in my pocket for later.

My job is to jump out of the car and carry the basket up to the door. Then we ring the doorbell or knock on the door. When the person opens the door, they are usually wearing pajamas or a bathrobe and look really surprised. Some even put their hands on their cheeks like a cartoon person being surprised. Everyone smiles and I have to turn around to show off my rabbit costume. We say "Happy May Day!" and go to the next house. Sometimes for extra flair I hop a few steps if they are still watching.

Mom hums when we drive to the next house and turns to me. "It's fun helping people, isn't it?"

"Yes," I agree wholeheartedly as I unwrap another Hershey kiss.

Dad and Jack lift the wooden roof rack onto the minivan. It's painted brown and is supposed to match the wood color on the sides of the car, but it really doesn't. I guess it's better than the things that look like hamburger boxes that people put on cars, but not by much.

Dad packs it with all the suitcases we won't need until we get to the cabin in Wisconsin, and Jack's fishing rods go on top. The rest of the bags for the four-day trip that we'll use in hotels and while visiting Aunt Alice and Uncle Chris and Gram Avi go in the van with us. When we're packing and bringing load after load to the car, Dad sometimes rubs his face and stops talking and then goes into the bathroom for a long time. Then he comes out and gives orders to everyone in his loud voice.

When we're finally all loaded up, I sit in the middle seat, and Jack and Carm sit in the big seat in the back. We drive for hours and stop at the Quality Inn and sometimes the Holiday Inn, which is fancier and sometimes even has a pool. When Dad gets tired of driving, he hooks his thumbs underneath the steering wheel and leans his head back against the headrest so he's looking at the road down his nose. Mom taps his knee.

"Do you want me to drive for a while?" He always says no, and Mom goes back to looking at the maps.

Before the trip we all get to pick out one activity book, the kind with the invisible ink marker that smells like pineapples. You can write on anything and it doesn't show up, even on your hand. But when you color in the boxes for Mr. Mystery puzzles or Jailbreak, the answer appears. This year, Jack said he didn't want one because they were for kids. I asked if I could have his, but Mom said, no, one book would be enough to get me to Wisconsin. It's not really true, because one activity book has to get me there and back, and it takes four days, so I can only do five activities a day. I put little checkmarks next to the page numbers when I'm done with them.

If the road isn't too bumpy, I sometimes read, but I have to be careful not to get carsick. Mostly, I just look out the window at the other cars and the trees going by. I ask Carm if he wants to play school. I think about asking Jack, but I know he won't want to. He's got his Walkman earphones on and is tapping on his armrest. I take a page out of my notebook and think of adding problems, like what Mrs. Benowski gave to us. In my best printing I make ten problems and draw a line at the top and write "name" underneath it.

I hand it over the seat to Carm.

"What do I do now?" he asks.

"First, you write your name at the top, see?" I point to the line I drew. It takes him forever to write it.

"Now what?" he asks.

"Now you write in the numbers for the adding questions here," I say, pointing. "And while you're doing that, I'll correct other papers." I leave him to his work and turn to a fresh page in my notebook and fit as many checkmarks on each line as I can make.

I feel a tap on my shoulder.

"I'm done," he says, handing the paper over the seat.

"You have to raise your hand," I say.

He raises his hand.

"Yes, Carm?" I say.

"I'm done," he says. I take the paper, and he's written the number eight and some ones for all the questions.

"These are all wrong!" I say, making angry x's with a red crayon.

"You said write numbers!" he protests.

"No, you have to write the *answer* numbers," I say. "You have to add them!"

Jack leans over and pulls one of his Walkman earphones off. "Give him a break, Gay! He's only in kindergarten. Jeez."

I show Carm how to make the numbers on his fingers, then count them all together.

"OK, that's easy," he says and takes the paper back.

After two papers he starts handing them back faster than I can correct them. I forget to ask him to raise his hand. I wish I had the calculator with me, the one with a crack in the middle from the office desk. He gets almost everything right, and by the time we pass the "Welcome to Illinois" sign, I stop correcting and just write 100 at the top of each one with a smiley face.

I pull the netting over my head and adjust the green cardboard container tied around my neck. Mom tied the purple kitchen string around each container so that we could pick blueberries with both hands. She had us each stand in the kitchen in a row and measured so that our container hung down right above our belly button.

The white netting keeps the birds from getting the blueberries before we can. Mom says the birds could pick the bushes clean in a few hours. Jack and I discuss whether we could train flocks of birds to pick blueberries for you, but we decide not because their brains are birdbrains, which means tiny and dumb. But I wish it was possible, because it's August and it's hot under the netting and I'm getting static head from when it rubs around on my hair. We get to go swimming afterward, but my container is only half full, and Mom says Jack and I each have to pick three quarts. Carm can just do two. I think about stealing a handful from his bucket when he's not watching.

After what seems like forever, Mom says we can go home. All of the Tupperware containers she brought are full. I haven't finished filling my third quart, but she says it is OK. Our fingers and mouths are stained purple from picking and eating the berries. When we walk home, the cicadas are making their summer sounds from the field. I run from one side of the road to the other, finding the snapdragons. The fat buds are the best. I poke them and they explode. A small firework of seeds pops out, and the bud curls in on itself like popcorn. Each time, it is a surprise, and I never get bored of the surprising pop between my fingertips.

I want time to pass by faster so it will be next week already. Next Friday and Saturday is the Hardwick Fair. I'm old enough now to go off on my own this year, which will make it the best. I won't have to wait for Mom to go to different booths. It can take us hours to get from the Search the Hay game to the Beanbag Toss. It's awful. I try to be patient, but I end up standing there in the middle of the common, holding her hand, watching all the other kids having fun with their parents, and she's just standing there, talking and talking. One year the fair was happening around me and I was missing it, so I threw a pretty big tantrum right there on the common. Afterward, Mom made me sit under a tree for a time-out and said I couldn't have any more sugar that day. She said I had had enough, but I think she said it just because of the tantrum.

The morning of the fair, I put on the clothes I saved all week to wear: my summer shirt with the lemonade picture and puff paint on the front, jean shorts, and my sneakers with my best socks—the ones that are mostly white, with no holes or worn-down spots. I fold the map and put it into my back pocket. It's a map of the common that I made with colored squares for each of the booths. I know where they will be because they are in the same place every year. I made a dotted line in pencil for my path that shows how to get to all the best booths over and over again, like a circuit. I eat my cereal fast and find Dad in the yard and tell him I'm ready to go. He says it's only seven and the fair doesn't even start until ten, so I'll have to wait.

"Your brothers aren't even up yet, Sissy Jupe," he says.

"I can fix that!" I yell, then run into the house to jump on their beds.

Just before school starts, we'll go to Sally and Louie's for the sunflower contest. Mom had the idea because she read about it in *Yankee* magazine, and it showed a picture of a huge sunflower field in Canada that was so big it looked like an ocean of yellow flowers. She asked people to plant them back in May. It was decided that everyone would bring potluck picnic, and Myron, as the oldest, would be the judge. Myron is my godfather's father, so it's kind of like he's related to me but not really.

He always shows up wearing an old top hat and a dusty jacket with two flaps in the back that he calls "tails."

We bought our seeds at the Farmer's Co-op in April from a huge spinning display of all kinds of vegetable and flower seeds. We planted them in the back of the house in a bare patch of dirt so they'd get the most sun.

When they grew taller than me and had yellow petals like a bonnet around their brown faces, Mom asked, "Do you know that when they get big, their faces will actually move and follow the sun as it moves across the sky?"

"That's not true!" I said. "Plants can't move!"

"Just wait," said Mom.

When they are tall to my chin and turn from green to yellow, I watch them closely when I'm out playing. They aren't moving. But when I come back hours later when the sun is setting, I see the head has turned towards the back field and the setting sun. It must either move really fast when I'm not looking or really slow, so slow I can't see it happening. I really thought Mom was kidding. It seems like magic that plants can move.

I fill the brown plastic jug that we use for Kool-Aid with water, carry it outside with both hands, and pour it on the ground at the foot of the six plants. I still can't tell which one is going to be the biggest. I ask her about them moving fast, and she says, no, they move so slow we can't see it when it's happening. She shows me another picture from the magazine of the fields in Canada and points out how all the faces are all turned in the same direction.

Late in the summer, Mom helps me decide which two are biggest, and we cut them off halfway down their thick stalks with a sharp knife from the kitchen. We load them and a potato salad into the wagon and walk down the hill to Sally and Louie's.

I think ours is huge, bigger than my head, but I see it's pretty small when we lay it out on the picnic table with the others.

"Ah, well. Maybe next year," says Mom.

The adults have the same argument (that's not really an argument) about how to measure the ones with the curved faces. I can tell they're not really mad because they are laughing when they're pretending to yell. Do you measure the whole curve or just the width as if it were flat? If you measure on the curved part, it adds at least another four inches. Just like last year, we can't decide, and Myron bangs his measuring tape like a gavel and calls, "Order! Order!" and proclaims that there will be two awards, one for the flat measure and one for the curved measure. He measures each one, and Mom writes the inches on a piece of cardboard with a magic marker. Bob carries out his from the back of his truck, and it's enormous, like an oversized platter that you would put a whole turkey on at Thanksgiving. He wins the award for the flat measure, and Sally wins for the curved. Mom made actual ribbons for the winners out of cut up pieces of satin. She takes out her camera and snaps a picture of Sally and Bob holding their ribbons and sunflowers up high. She lets Jack and me be in the picture, too, and we do one nice one with us smiling and standing and then a second one making funny faces.

Afterward Bob lets me hold the prize sunflower. I can barely lift it.

"Do you want to know my secret?" he asks.

I nod seriously. He bends towards me and whispers, "Water them every day, and put a few tablespoons of whole milk into the water. Also, talk to them."

"Are you joking with me?" I whisper back.

"No, really, talk to them. Say nice things. It helps them grow. I tell mine how pretty and strong they are. Like you." He winks at me. I think he's telling the truth about the strong part, but for the pretty part I think he is joking, and my face turns hot and I look down at my sneakers.

I don't have to look up because Sally calls us to eat, and we gather around the picnic table. Mom calls for grace, and Myron stands at the head of the table and takes off his hat, and we bow our heads. I'm starving and I hope it's not a long grace; I secretly open one eye so I can look at the stack of sweet corn and the cake with sunflower-yellow frosting in the middle of the table. I want to stick my finger into it, and maybe nobody would notice since everyone's eyes are closed. I squeeze my hands together harder so I won't do it. Myron thanks God for the good summer and good ground and for friends and family and asks that we keep following the light, His light, like the flowers know how to do.

Mom squeezes my shoulder, and I know what she's doing. Through her hand she's saying, "Remember when I told you about the sunflowers and how they moved and followed the light. Remember that."

I remember.

"Amen," we all say.

"Amen," Myron says again and flips the top hat back on his head like a trick. "Let's eat."

⟜⟶

We make two big piles of leaves right next to each other and jump back and forth between them. I like to bury myself all the way and then burst out like a leaf monster and throw leaves everywhere. Jack made up a game where you stand in front of the pile and just fall back without bending your knees. It's hard to keep your body straight, but when you do, you seem to fall forever before poofing into the leaves.

Dad is wearing his red plaid coat, the one that has snaps up the front and is quilted inside. One cuff is ripped, and the bottom seam is frayed. He wears it every fall to rake the leaves and to stack the wood in the shed.

"OK, that's enough, kids. Time to pack them up." We groan and pretend we're too tired to get up. Dad uses his loud voice. "Now, kids." And we get up. Dad fixed the piles where we made it messy, so they are big and tall again. It is so tempting to jump into them. Dad can tell I'm getting ready to and gives me his I'm-watching-you look. I give him my most innocent smile, where all my teeth show.

Carm holds the trash bags open, and Jack and me carry armloads of leaves over and dump them in. When they are full, Jack ties the tops. Then Dad puts them all in a row against the side of the house and leans three sections of picket fence to hold the bags against the foundation. The fence is missing boards in some places, and Dad says to be careful because there are nails sticking out.

"Dad, this is what people mean when they say they talk about a nice house with a picket fence, right? It's just that our fence is red instead of white?" I ask.

He looks at me with a confused look on his face and then bursts out laughing. I don't get what is so funny and ask him again. He laughs harder, then I start laughing just because he is.

When he finally stops and wipes his eyes with the sleeve of his shirt, he explains that usually a picket fence is put around a house, not against it to hold in leaves as insulation against the cold and drafts in the winter.

When we go inside later, I hear him telling Mom about it when I'm in the bathroom. I can hear them both laughing and decide it might be my favorite sound, the sound of Dad's deep voice and Mom's springy one laughing at the same time. It's weird sometimes what adults think is so hilarious. But I guess it's like when they don't understand what Jack and Carm and me think is so funny even though we explain it to them.

When it's winter, we all move into Jack's room because he has bunk beds. Dad closes the doors to all the rooms at the front of the house and puts towels under the doors to keep the draft out. A draft is cold air that comes in the cracks of old houses. There are also drafts around the windows, and when the wind blows hard, it sometimes moves the curtains. It's because of all the drafts that we share Jack's room. It's fun, kind of like a sleepover. And it's less scary for monsters at night if you know your brothers are in the room with you. Jack gets the top bunk because it's his room, and Carm and me have the two beds on the floor. You can also tell whose bed is whose by the sheets. Jack has Voltron, Carm has He-Man, and I have My Little Pony. We also have Charlie Brown sheets that we take turns using when ours are in the wash. I sleep below, and there's fabric-like paper attached to the bottom of his bed. I'm not supposed to, but sometimes I can't help poking holes in it with my fingers. When I lie in bed, I look up at the holes I've put there before and also look at the glow-in-the dark stars on the walls and ceiling. I make constellations out of them. I only know one constellation, so I name them with numbers. Big Dipper Four is my favorite.

In the summer, when we can hear the spring peepers, we will all move back into our own rooms. I like having a different place to sleep for part of the year. It's like the leaves turning or going back to school or Christmas trees—there're things that tell you what time of the year it is and what to expect next.

In the spring when I am in my room, I can see the streetlamp at the top of Sessions Road. I can see the circle of light from my bed at night. It's nice to have something that is light to look out on when it is so dark outside. The streetlight goes off automatically in the morning, so it's not on when we wait up there in the morning to catch the school bus. On school mornings, Dad gets us out of bed and makes us have hot cereal in the winter, but when it's warm, we get to choose cold cereal. After we eat, we get dressed, and he sits in the front room, reading.

When he calls out, "The bus went up," it means he heard it pass on Route 32A, shifting loud on the uphill climb towards Eagle Hill. We have fifteen minutes from that point to meet it after it has gone up the road, picked up the Webbs, and then turned around on the town line, and come back for us. We have to get out backpacks and lunches and put on our shoes or boots fast and get out the door. Just as we are leaving, Chuck Turner usually meets us at the end of the driveway and walks up with us to the top of the hill. We play tag while we wait, and sometimes Dad volunteers to be "it" and growls like a monster while he chases us. In the winter, I get to wear my pink moon boots with the Velcro, and we play on the enormous pile of snow from the plow. We stomp out paths and stairs in the snow bank and can stand almost level with the Sessions Road sign. We take turns in the lookout spot until we see the bus cresting the hill way far off down the road. We climb down and shake the snow from our boots and pick up our backpacks. Dad and the bus driver, Mr. Roy, say something about the weather when the door folds open for us, and then Dad stands at the top of the hill and waves to us until we can't see him anymore.

Sundays are the most boring days. We go to church in the morning and have to put on scratchy clothes. Mom and me fight about me wearing a dress. I hate dresses and stupid tights that touch me all over my legs in a clinging way. I want to wear pants like the boys do. Sometimes she wins, and I cry and put on the dress. Sometimes I throw a big enough fit and get to wear my nicest corduroy pants instead. Then we go to church and sit in the pews and have to sit still and be good. Partway through, all the children go to the front of the church for children's time. Pastor Ketchum comes down the stairs and sits with us and tells us a story, and then we go to bible school. We eat orange cheese crackers and drink fruit punch out of little paper cups with flowers. Then we color pictures about Jesus and Mary and the disciples, which are like Jesus' friends that follow him around wearing dresses. Pants didn't get invented for a long time after that. I'm glad I wasn't born then, because then I'd have to wear dresses all the time like Jesus did.

After church, there is a coffee hour, and Mom talks forever to everyone, and we all get bored and start poking each other and kicking at the folding chair legs until Dad takes her arm and says, "The natives are restless. We should go."

At home, Mom makes birds-in-the-nest and English muffins with grape jelly. A bird-in-the-nest is bread with egg fried in the middle of it, and besides grilled cheese, it is the best thing that Mom makes. Dad reads us the comics that come in color on Sundays in the newspaper and does funny voices. I can read most of them myself, but it's better when he does it. Then we all have quiet Sunday family time, and Mom and Dad take a nap. Since it's family time, we're not allowed to have friends over or go anywhere. If Jack and Carm don't want to play, I have to make up my own games. I like going to Stagecoach Rock and playing *Little House on the Prairie*. Stagecoach Rock is a boulder next to the barn. There's a flat space right at the top that is just like a seat, and you can let your legs dangle down. I have a jump rope with only one handle that is my reins. When I sit there, I can see the team of horses out front and the prairie grasses going on forever as we go west to find the fine piece of land where we will homestead. We'll have a cow and a house made out of mud and straw and get water from a pump that is outside. Dad showed me how to use the compass I found in one of his desk drawers, and I found out that Stagecoach Rock even faces west. Sometimes in the summer, I sit there after supper and watch the sun go behind the trees, and the sky turns all the colors, but mostly reds and pinks.

Besides *Little House on the Prairie*, I also like to read the other books that come in a series, because you can finish one and then keep reading about the same characters. It is like one really long story, and each book is its own adventure. My favorite right now is Betsy, Tacy, and Tib. It is a series that Mom read when she was a girl and gave to me. It's about three best friends in Minnesota who live in farmhouses right next to each other. They get in trouble together and go on adventures. I can't imagine having two best friends, because you can really only have just one best of anything. But I like how they have fun together and are inseparable. I had to look up that word in my blue *Webster's*. It means "always together" and "not separate." It would be neat to have two best friends at the same time, I think, and maybe someday I will.

Another kind of good friend to have is an imaginary friend. I had an imaginary friend until last year when I got too old. Her name was Mimi, and she lived in the bathtub in the downstairs bathroom behind the red-and-blue paisley shower curtain. I'd go in there and talk to her, and she kept all my secrets and never told anyone. I miss her sometimes. Jesus is also kind of like an imaginary friend, but he can't play games with you. He's just there with you, watching along with your guardian angel. In Sunday school I learned that God sent his son, Jesus, so we'd always be loved, always, no matter what. Jesus was born in a stable to Mary, who wears blue dresses and was the wife of Joseph. She was a virgin, which is a good thing. One of my favorite Madonna songs is "Like a Virgin." I'm not sure what a virgin is, but it has something to do with making babies. In her song, Madonna seems really happy about being like one. It's funny how Jesus's mother is called Mary and Madonna and also there is a singer called Madonna, and they are both virgins or like virgins. I'll need to remember to ask about that in the next Sunday school class.

I pump my legs, and the chains of the swing creak when I swoop down then up again.

"I can get higher!" I shout.

There is a raccoon tail tacked up near the ceiling, and I reach out with my sneaker. I get two raccoon points if I can touch it. Jack already has ten, but his legs are longer, so it's not really fair. The tail has been there forever. I think it came with the barn. The barn was built when I was two, and I think I remember the party, but I'm not sure. On one wall there's plaster and white paint, and everyone who came to the party signed their names. Just about everyone I know is on that wall. Even the band signed its name and drew a cartoon of themselves. They're called the "Band that Doesn't Give a Sh*t." The little star is supposed to be an "I," so technically they wrote a swear word on the barn wall, but since they're a band, I guess it's OK. I wonder if they were bad, like the scary band on TV with big curly hair and painted white faces. They wear spikes on black clothes and do bad things like swear and play the music really, really loud.

When it's nice out before the screen door is in, I can run from the barn, through the shed, directly into the kitchen. If I get enough of a running start, I can surf the foot rug in front of the door halfway through the kitchen. Mom hates when I do it because she says I'll break something, but I haven't yet, so I think I'm all right. The door is held open by a bent wire attached to the wall below the shed window. The crook of the wire fits around the latch of the door—something you can't do with a doorknob, so I guess it's good we have latches instead. I can tell if somebody lives in a rich house if they have doorknobs and carpets that are attached and cover the whole floor. Our house isn't one of the fancy ones like they show on TV that have sidewalks out front. The only time I see TV houses that are like ours is when Dad watches Bob Villa fix things on *This Old House.*

I asked Mom if Laura Ingalls could have lived in our house or maybe visited it because it is so old. She said no, Laura Ingalls lived in Minnesota. But our house was standing then, a hundred years before then, even. It was standing when there were redcoat soldiers and a revolution was about to happen. It is the oldest house in the town. Mom and Dad bought it when it was falling apart, before I was born, and restored it. They said it needed an extra lot of love. I've seen pictures of it then, when they got it, and in some places there was no floor, and we couldn't live there at first because there was lead paint and holes that children could fall through. The windows were broken, and there were no shrubs or pretty trees around it. It looked like an old haunted house that you see in Halloween books. But it doesn't look that way now. Everyone who comes to visit talks about the fireplaces and the wide wood boards in the floor. There are seven fireplaces, but only the one in the woodstove room works. The rest are stuffed with insulation to keep the heat in during winter. The wood floors are rough, and I can walk three baby steps in some of them before stepping on a crack. All the doors have black iron latches instead of knobs.

It takes me twenty-seven seconds to run around the house and barn, but if I cut through the shed and skip the barn, it only takes me fourteen. Jack can do it faster because he's not afraid to jump over the stone steps. He's not afraid of anything, and he's the best at all the games because he is eleven years old. It's not really fair. I thought maybe when I got older I might get better than him at some things, but no matter what, he'll always be two years bigger and faster than me.

Mom and Dad love to tour people around and tell them the history of the house and how they had to take all the guts out and rebuild everything from the ground up. They talk about how they uncovered all the walls and beams from layers and layers of plaster and paint and found beautiful wood underneath. This is my favorite part. I like to think of Mom and Dad pulling down the walls and finding out what was underneath, like a treasure. They talk about the first pastor, David Whyte, who the house was built for and how his name is carved in one of the old windowpanes that looks like it is melting from age. The style of the house is called "colonial saltbox," which means a short roof on one side and a long, sloping roof on the other. There's a chimney that all the fireplaces share going right up the center of the house, and carved mantels are around the fireplaces. When people look at the house, some ask about secret passages and the Underground Railroad. Dad says we are too far north for the railroad in Massachusetts. When I was little, I thought it was an actual railroad under the ground, but it's actually just a group of houses whose owners helped slaves get north to freedom, and all those houses had secret rooms. It got me thinking about how old our house is and maybe there is a secret passage we just have never found. I look for them all the time and press on the different panels in the wall, and I just know that someday I'm going to press the right one in the right order, and the wall is going to slide back and reveal a secret room, like the Batcave. I've even looked in the scary basement made of rocks with dirt for the floor and hanging spider webs and pipes everywhere, but still haven't found any. If I find one, I will keep it a secret and use it to play hide-and-seek and not tell anyone except Dad.

Sometimes Dad gives a yard tour and talks about the different plants and trees and takes the orange shears and makes a bouquet as he walks around the gardens. If the people are staying, he puts the bouquet in the blue vase in the guest room, and if they are leaving, he wraps it in wet paper towels so they can take it with them. It seems to make them really happy, especially the women. Dad said pretty much everyone likes flowers, but women especially like them. He gives Mom pink bubbly carnations every September for their anniversary, wrapped in a ribbon with a letter written on thick paper that feels like fabric. For their first date, at college, he asked her out by putting a pink carnation in her mailbox with a note. He says he wanted it to be a rose, but he couldn't afford it, and a carnation was the best he could do. Mom seems pretty happy to get the carnations every time now. Sometimes she cries a little when she opens his letter. I don't know what she would do if she got roses.

Mom puts Beau Monde seasoning on our eggs and grilled cheese sandwiches. She calls it "gourmet." Chloe is over for lunch one day and asks why the sandwiches taste funny.

I tell her what Mom tells us: "It will expand your palate. Just keep eating. You'll get used to it."

Chloe makes a face, and Mom laughs, then touches her and says, "Sweetie, I'll make you another one."

Mom hums as she puts another sandwich in the pan. I think she might like Chloe the best out of all my friends because she's always putting her arm around her and asking me how Chloe is doing. When we were in first grade, Chloe's dad had an accident and died. Chloe lives in a tiny house with her mother and sister. There are always lots of animals there, and her mother raises chickens. I like going into the hen house, into the dusty air to get the eggs from the hay. A lot of them have poop on them that we have to wash off in the cold sink outside the door, very carefully, with an old scrub brush. That's one thing they don't sell in stores: eggs with poop on them. Chloe also has a big, black shaggy dog named Valerie and a little Chihuahua called Judy. I don't really like dogs. I don't like how they bark and jump all over and put their nose into your crotch. Dogs are the rudest animals ever, I think. Once Mom came to pick me up, wearing her favorite white wool coat, and Valerie jumped up on her, leaving muddy footprints all over. Chloe looked as if she was going to cry. "I'm so sorry. Your coat. I'm sorry."

Mom raised her palms up flat in an "Oh well" and said, "Coats can be washed."

There are some places where you call people on the phone and order food, and they will bring it to you. I have seen it on TV commercials for Dominos, where you can call and a man in a baseball hat will come to your door with a pizza. You can also get Chinese food in white folded containers with a little handle. On TV they use the containers left around in a room to show if someone has been really busy or really sad. The same people who can get pizza and Chinese food delivered to their doors also get their mail in a mailbox at the end of their driveway instead of at the post office. I asked Dad about it, and he said that most people in America live in places where those things actually happen because there are more people clumped closer together. We don't live in that kind of place. We live in Hardwick, which is a rural place, and that means not many people, but lots of cows. I asked him what else you can get delivered in a city, and he said in the really big cities, like New York, you can get just about anything. I've been to Boston before, and it was neat, but seeing people everywhere that I didn't know made me nervous. There were traffic lights on all the streets and corners, not just the three lights like there are in Ware. Everyone was walking really fast on the sidewalk or in their cars, honking horns. The trees looked sick and there wasn't any grass. It would also be sad to live in a place where there wasn't lots of green around with a yard and trees and flowers. People didn't look very happy or stop to say hi to each other or wave. It's so weird that people live in places where they don't know everyone. I think it would be lonely and scary.

Last week we went to a party at the Robinsons' swimming pond. The adults had beer in a big metal pumper barrel that was covered with hay and ice. Us kids got Kool-Aid and hot dogs. My Dad and another dad played splashing games with everyone in the pond, and then we made sand creatures. Most of the dads stood in a circle by the beer barrel and laughed a lot. At parties my dad always plays games with all the kids before he goes and stands with the men. It's just like when we go to restaurants and have to be on our best behavior. When we start getting fidgety and poking each other, he stands and says, "I'm taking the wild Indians out for a walk." Taking us for a walk is a secret code for going outside to have fun. We usually go to the back of the parking lot. Sometimes we throw rocks into the dumpster or play hopscotch on the cracks, or Dad makes up a monster game and chases us. Sometimes he laughs so hard he falls over, and that makes us laugh even more. By the time we go back inside, the food almost always comes.

Dad walks in the front door, and we swarm him.

His eyes are squinty, and I know that he's going to say he has a surprise even before he says, "I have a surprise."

We follow him outside. He opens the back of his green landscape van, throwing open the doors.

"Ta-da and abracadabra! I stopped at a tag sale!" he says.

"Ducky! Ducky!" says Carm. Closest to the door there is a faded yellow duck with wheels and a seat you can ride on. I read the label on the side, and it says *Little Tykes*. Dad places it on the ground, and Carm starts flapping his arms and quacking. Soon he is riding it and pushing it in little circles around the van. It doesn't work very well on the gravel, but he doesn't care. I would have taken it onto the smooth floor of the garage, but he is little. I'll show him how later and maybe take a ride on it myself. It is for babies, but it looks fun.

For Jack there is a real pool table, which is also called billiards if you're fancy. He and Dad pull it out and, since the legs are shaky and one has a crack in it, they set it on two sawhorses in the garage. It comes with one straight pool cue and one that is bent. Jack immediately puts the balls into the wooden triangle and starts playing. I have never seen him play pool before, but he knows how to take the white ball and use it to smash the pyramid of other balls. He always knows stuff like this. Since there is only one straight cue, we take turns, and he shows me how to prop up the cue on my knuckles and shoot the white ball towards the stripes; that is my color.

"Why don't you just hit the ball you want to into the hole?" I ask. "Why do you have to do it with the white one? It would be a lot easier. Like this." I show him. "See? That's so much easier, right?"

Dad laughs and Jack snatches the cue back.

"Because those aren't the rules, dummy. You have to play by the rules."

Dad ruffles my hair. "Come with me; there's one more thing just for you."

He reaches into the van and pulls out a trash bag that has something big and square inside it. He pulls off the bag like a magician doing a trick.

"A dollhouse!" I shriek. "A dollhouse!"

It's not like the Victorian one that Allison has—the one with the porcelain figures that we have to play with very, very carefully. This one is a modern house. The walls are made of thick cardboard and painted to look like bricks. Everything is made of plastic. I've never seen anything so wonderful. The furniture is all packed in separate plastic Ziploc bags and looks like the kind of furniture real people use today—a square sofa and round kitchen table, a fuzzy shag rug. The family is packed separately. The dad is dressed in brown pants and a blue shirt, and the mother has a polka-dotted house dress. The teenage girl has short blonde hair and bell bottoms. And the little boy, although I decide he is a girl and is exactly my age, is wearing jeans and a T-shirt.

The dollhouse is by far my favorite toy ever. I save money to buy things for it. My best purchase is ten books, with real covers and paper pages you can open up. The little books are perfect for writing secrets, but I have to use a very sharp pencil and squint to make the letters small enough. Who, even a pesky little brother, would think to check the bookshelf in a dollhouse for my secret messages? Since the books don't have titles, I make them up according to what I am reading at the time.

Right now there's *The Secret Garden, Pippi Longstocking, The Bobbsey Twins, Anne of Green Gables, My Side of the Mountain,* and *Ramona Quimby.*

With the dollhouse, the best game is "Flood" or "War Invasion" where the whole family has to pack everything they own into two Sucrets cough drop boxes and get out of the house. They debate for a long time what to take. Everyone agrees they will need a blanket and two plates to share. But then the mother always wants to take the blue porcelain platter—it is her favorite thing. The dad wants to take the gun he borrowed from G.I. Joe. And the sister, who is a teenager and a bit of an airhead, insists on her makeup case and hairbrush. The whole family rolls their eyes at her, especially because she has plastic hair that doesn't even need brushing. But the little boy-girl always says they need the books. All of them. She insists. She refuses to go unless they bring them and throws a tantrum, even though she is much too old for that. She gets her way, and they pack up the books. They tie the Sucrets boxes to the cart made out of Legos and trudge off down the upstairs hallway to unknown dangers and adventure. But the little girl isn't scared because wherever they go they will have their books. They can read to each other around the campfire, trade the books for other books, and when things get hard, escape in their heads to the people and places in the stories. They will be OK.

Chapter Three

"Wake up, honey. Wake up. That's right, open your eyes."
Dad is sitting on the edge of my bed in his bathrobe, patting my arm. It is still dark out.

I sit up.

"I have something to show you," he says. He takes the afghan from the end of the bed and wraps it around my shoulders and lifts me into his arms.

"Ooh, you're getting almost too big to carry," he says when we get to the stairs. "Can you walk?"

I nod and I follow him into the driveway. Jack is already standing there. He looks silly in his pajamas with his sneakers on. I am barefoot and the stones in the driveway make me take small, wincing steps. The three of us stand by the curve in the driveway, the one that the plow man always forgets is there and takes chunks out of the lawn each winter. Now, in the late spring, the edge of the grass is still muddy from being run over. Above us, the hydrangea is just beginning to bloom, and its white flowers look like they are made of glow-in-the-dark plastic, like the stars on Jack's bedroom ceiling.

"Do you see it?" Dad points up into the sky.

Up above the top of the hill where we wait for the bus, beyond the roof of the Pitzis' house, there is an orange dot just above the tree line, fuzzy in the early morning darkness. It has a trail of fading orange behind it. It seems to be moving, but just barely. You can tell by the way it is getting closer to the pinprick star in front of it.

"Do you see it? That's Halley's comet. We had to get up early to see it because it will only be in our hemisphere for a few hours."

"What's hems-sphere?" I ask.

"It's all the space around the world. Like really high up in the sky above us. The comet is a big fiery ball of rocks and ice, and it travels around space in a big circle. It only comes around every seventy-five years. Cool, huh?"

We all do the math. I have to do the adding with a stick in the dirt in the driveway, but Jack does it in his head.

"Eighty-six. I'll be eighty-six next time I see it," he says.

"I'll be eighty-four. I think," I say, unsure of my math in the dirt.

"Yup, you're right, kiddo," Dad says.

"How old will you be, Dad?"

"Too old to count," he says without hesitating. "I won't see this again. But you will."

"Why not?" I ask.

"Because I won't be around anymore."

I think about that for a minute.

"Where will you be?" I ask.

"Um. Well, I'll be too old then. I won't be alive anymore. But don't worry," he adds quickly, "that will be a long, long time from now. When you are old and all grown up yourself. Probably when you have kids of your own."

"Oh," I say. I can't imagine being grown up and having kids of my own. It is too big of an idea. But even harder is imagining a world in which Dad doesn't exist, a world where he isn't. Is that even possible?

I move closer to him and wrap an arm around his leg and lean my head into his waist. The honey-sweetness of the hydrangea floats down around us. It smells like summer. I bury my nose in his bathrobe, and it smells like winter, like wood smoke and wool blankets. Summer and winter, together.

"Are you ready to go back inside?" he asks.

"No, not yet. I want to wait and watch Halley's comet get to that next star," I say.

Jack stretches and yawns and says, "I'm going back to bed."

We listen to his feet crunch back down the driveway as we gaze into the sky.

After a few minutes, I ask, "Dad, what you said about not being here someday—was that true?"

I want him to say no, but I know that he won't. Unlike other grown-ups, he always tells me the truth. He doesn't answer right away, though. It takes so long I am just opening my mouth to ask again when he takes a loud breath.

"Yes, it is true. Everyone and everything dies at some point. Even me."

"Like Pooh Bear cat?" I ask.

"Yes, like Pooh Bear," he says.

"But it won't happen for a long, long time, for years and years, when I'm old and all growed up?"

"Right," he says, "for years and years."

⌒

"Have you finished your bathroom jobs?" Dad asks.

What he means is have we put our dirty clothes in the hamper, brushed our teeth, and peed. We all nod.

"Did you take your Flintstones?"

We all nod again. I can still taste the metallic, salty sweetness of Dino between my teeth—purple is my favorite.

"Did you swing on the towel rack?"

This is a trick question. And we shake our heads instead of nodding. And it is true, we didn't swing on it tonight. But we do most nights even though Dad told us not to. The rack is attached to the wall opposite of the sink, and it is the perfect height to play parallel bars on if you put one hand on the edge of the sink and one hand on the towel rack. You can lift yourself up and swing your legs like gymnastics and do air running. But we do it too much, and Dad has already replaced the screws and the drywall twice. We aren't allowed to do it anymore.

"OK, into bed, then!" He throws up his arms, and we all launch onto his and Mom's big bed, clamoring for the best spot.

As usual, Carm ends up on his lap, Jack on his left, and me on his right. We all snuggle our feet under the covers and lean against Dad. He's wearing a wool sweater, and I pull up the sheet as a barrier so I don't have to feel the scratchies on my cheek.

He opens *The Bobbsey Twins' Mystery at Meadowbrook* and starts reading from where we left off at chapter eight, called "A Log Cabin Clue." Nan and Bert and Freddie and Flossie just found something suspicious that will probably lead them to solving the mystery.

Dad says next year he'll read to us from the Hardy Boys, who are two brothers who solve mysteries, too, but he thinks it might be too scary for Carm right now. I don't like scary things, so I'm kind of glad we're waiting. But the Bobbsey Twins aren't scary. Each book happens in a different place, such as at the seashore or in the country, and the kids always have a mystery to solve, and they have a grand time. They also have a "swell time" and a "gay time" and use neat things we don't have anymore, like "icebox" and "rumble seat."

I like how the two sets of twins are always together in the books. I think it would be awesome to have a twin, like a best friend who was also your sister. Carm was born with a twin, but the twin died when Carm came out. I don't remember him being born, and I asked Carm if he remembers his twin and he said "no." I guess there's no way he could because he wasn't even born for a day. The twin's ashes are buried beneath the dogwood tree in the front yard. Every spring it blooms white flowers, and Mom goes out and weeds around it and straightens out the little circle of stones on the ground around the trunk. Since Dad is a landscaper, the yard has lots of shrubs and flowers and small trees everywhere, but the dogwood is my favorite. It is an entire tree with big flowers, not like an apple or a cherry tree with just little blossoms. Carm's twin's tree is still small, and it only has a few flowers, but there's another dogwood on the side of the house that is huge. After the flowers come out and turn a little brown, they start falling off, and when it's windy, it looks like it is snowing. I like to stand under the tree in my shorts, pretending it's freezing, making my eyes go soft so I can see the white petals fall with all of the spring green behind it.

⁓

"How are you feeling?"

"Awful," I say. "I have a headache. And I barfed three times today."

Dad puts his big hand on my forehead, and it is enormous and covers half my head and feels so heavy and cool.

"Where does it hurt?" he asks.

I point to my temples.

He sits on the edge of the bed and with his pointer fingers rubs both my temples around and around.

After a while he asks, "Is that better?"

"A little," I say. "Will you bring me some more ginger ale?"

He leaves to go and get it, and I hear him and Mom talking in the kitchen.

When he comes back up, he asks, "Do you want me to bring some laundry in later?"

I nod, then hear him starting a load in the bathroom. After it's in the dryer awhile, he'll take it out warm and overturn the basket on my bed. Under the blankets I get to feel all the warmth come through, and then he stands there and sings while he folds it. The rule is that I have to be very still so that I don't mess up the folded piles. He'll sing my favorite today, I bet, because I'm sick.

You are my sunshine
My only sunshine.
You make me happy when skies are gray.
You'll never know, dear, how much I love you.
Please don't take my sunshine away.

When I'm still and quiet and warm with Dad right there above me, I always fall asleep.

⁓

One of the most exciting things happened on Tuesday. I was working on my five times multiplication when the principal's secretary, Ms. Hanson, came to the door of the classroom and motioned Mrs. Hurly over. I was in the row closest to the door, so I had no trouble hearing her say, "I need the Huntress girl."

I was already standing by the time Mrs. Hurly got to my desk.

"You should take your jacket and bag with you. You're having an early dismissal today."

I went to the back of the room and got my jacket and backpack. Ms. Hanson had already gone back to her office, so I walked alone through the quiet hallway to the principal's.

Mom was there, and she winked at me.

"Oh, there you are. Hurry up, or we'll be late for the dentist."

I didn't have a dentist appointment that day. I was just there for a cleaning last month. Confused, I followed her out to the minivan, which was parked in front of the school. Dad was in the driver's seat, and Jack and Carm were in the back. They were all smiling at me.

"What's going on?" I asked.

"We're playing family hooky!" said Mom. "We picked up Jack at the junior high school and then came to get you. We're going to the city to see a show."

"Like a movie?" I asked.

"Better," said Dad. I couldn't imagine anything much better than when he had taken me, and just me, to see *101 Dalmatians* with him on a Saturday last winter when the rest of the family had the flu. He had bought me my very own popcorn plus an entire box of Junior Mints that I didn't have to share with anybody. It was just the two of us, a "Dad and Daughter Date" he called it, and I couldn't wait to go on another one.

"It's a play," said Dad. "On a stage. It's only in Boston for this month. Mom called this morning and got last-minute discount tickets. It's about cats and is supposed to be fantastic."

"Cats?" I asked. "An entire play about cats? That sounds kind of dumb."

He reached behind the seat and squeezed my knee.

"There's singing and dancing and costumes. Trust me, you'll like it."

I pulled the sliding door of the minivan closed, and we were off. Partway there Mom handed us all sandwiches out of the red Igloo cooler. She had Jack get his white buttoned church shirt out of the bag in the back seat and brought a flowered blouse for me to put on over my T-shirt and tuck into my corduroy pants. I had never been to a show that required a new outfit before. We got to the city with all the stoplights and lots of people on the streets. Mom read off the directions when we drove, and Dad said a swear word when he tried to turn down a road that said it was one-way. We parked the minivan in a big garage that was the same one like they had at the airport. Twice Mom made us check that all the windows were closed and all the doors were locked. There was a huge crowd in front of the theater even though it was a matinee. I learned that meant the show was in the afternoon instead of at night.

Mom came back from the box office and said she could only get two seats together, and one of them was partially behind a pole. They decided that Dad would sit behind the pole because he was tall and could crane around it, and Carm would sit with her in the double seat. Jack and I would have to sit alone. I didn't like the idea, but Mom and Dad kept saying how great it would be, and I needed to be brave. The theater was bigger than anything I had ever seen. Our entire house could have fit inside it. A chandelier the size of a car hung from the ceiling. Everything was red and plush and thick. Dad and the usher helped Jack and me find our seats. I was right on the aisle. It wasn't so bad. If I turned around, I could see Dad's tall head behind me, and that made me feel better. The usher said I could go and sit with him until the show started. It was only a few minutes until the lights blinked, and Dad said to go back to my seat. For a terrible moment after I sat down, everything went dark. But then I remembered. Jack was four rows in front of me, in the middle. I could picture the back of his head in my mind, his ears sticking out a little with his short buzz cut. Mom was on the other side of the rows with Carm in the seat next to her, way in the back. And Dad was almost directly behind me, eight rows between us. I was in the dark, but my family was all around me, sprinkled in with the rest of the audience even though I couldn't see them. I thought I would be scared, but I wasn't. Then the curtain rose, and the music started.

It was unlike anything I had ever seen before. Hundreds of people seemed to be on the stage at once, singing. The music filled the space. I could feel it through my feet, up through the thick red carpet. I could feel it underneath my ribs, through the cushioned red seat. The people on stage were dressed like cats in colored tights and fuzzy vests, with whiskers and everything. They leapt and twisted and sang. There was not any talking, but the songs said the words.

At intermission I waited for Dad to come and get me from my seat in the crowd. He bought us a can of ginger ale to share, and he and Mom shared a tiny little bottle of wine—the smallest I've ever seen. We stood in the lobby and sipped our drinks. At first we all talked over each other, then Dad made us go one at a time and say our favorite parts. Even Mom and Dad seemed excited. There were hardly any other kids there. I saw one girl, and she was wearing a lace dress with a big bow around the middle and black Mary Jane shoes. I wished I was wearing my better shoes. Lots of people were dressed up. Mom took me to the ladies room, and there were two rooms, one with the toilets and another room before that with couches and mirrors and a thick rug. After we used the bathroom, Mom gave me some lipstick to put on in front of one of the big mirrors. We stood there with the women in long dresses and skirts, and she showed me how to blot, which means press your lips together on a Kleenex.

I was excited when the lights blinked, and I gladly found my seat again. I felt a shiver when everything went dark and the curtain rose. I thought the second half could not be nearly as good as the first half, but it was. When I thought things couldn't get any better, something else happened on stage. A cat person swung through the air on a rope, or an entire junkyard rose up out of the stage. After one song all the cat people ran into the audience, and it was scary at first. I thought they should have stayed on stage where they belonged. They all went right by me because I was on the aisle, but one stopped and got down on her hands and knees. She pawed at my knee, just like how Scamper touches a piece of string. I sat very still and didn't breathe. I only moved my eyes. I didn't want to scare her away and at the same time wished she would go back on stage. I could tell it was a woman underneath all that makeup by the way she moved and that underneath the cat costume she was very beautiful. It was almost terrible to be close to something so magnificent, this person who was also a cat. I knew it was all pretend, like Halloween costumes or the Easter bunny, but it all seemed so real, like I was in their world. Then, she turned and swished her tail and ran back to the stage.

At the end, Mom surprised us and got the cassette tape of all of the music from the show. I was thrilled. I could hear the songs again whenever I wanted. We slept in the car on the way home, and when we got there, I immediately put the tape in the brown plastic Fisher-Price tape player and turned it at loud as it would go. We all put on our pajamas and danced in the upstairs hallway to "Jellicle Cats," pushing off the walls with our feet like they did on stage.

The song "Memory" was much too slow and sad, and I didn't like it, but Mom said we all had to listen to it all the way through to calm everybody down so we could sleep.

⟶

Before school starts Mom takes me to Wilton's in Ware. It's in an old factory building near the river, and it smells like mold. I hate the changing rooms because they just have flowered curtains up that droop in the middle, so people can see in on either side. I think someone threw up once on the carpet because that room smells like vomit. When I was little, I liked to crawl under the round racks of clothes and look at people's feet. I liked the feeling of knowing I could see everyone but they couldn't see me. Mom would always pull me out and make me go try on things. I'm too big now to go crawling around under the racks, but I still think about it.

My favorite pants are the corduroy kind because they are softer to wear than jeans. They come in all different colors, too. I like pink and purple the best. Sometimes I pick out tops that match exactly, but Mom says a better way to match is to choose patterned shirts that have the pants color in them, instead of all the same color. It doesn't make sense to me. If little flowers or polka-dots match the pants, wouldn't more color mean that it matched even better? Sometimes I just give up and let her buy my clothes. As long as they are not scratchy or stiff, I'll wear anything. Some of my friends get excited about clothes and make a big deal when they come to school wearing something new, but I think it's silly.

The one thing I do get excited about is sneakers. I love going into Bresslar's on Main Street and smelling all the new leather. New sneakers are so white and bright. I love the way you have to put your foot on the metal measurer and Mr. Bresslar slides the triangle up to see how much you have grown. He gives it one more tap and says, "Room to grow. You're not done yet!" then goes and gets the right box. My favorite shoes are the Kangaroos that have a zip pouch on the side to carry things. You can put in a quarter or a secret message or a folded dollar even, if you have it. I also love the Velcro that Kangaroos have instead of laces. They make a ripping sound when you pull them apart, but nothing actually rips. My last shoes I stuck and unstuck so many times that the Velcro wore out, and they started flopping on my feet. I tried to duct tape them back together, but then it was hard to get my foot in and out. When Mom saw it, she said it was time to get new shoes and please don't wear duct tape to school like that or else people will think we can't afford new shoes. It was kind of like the time at the Girl Scout Awards when Mrs. Thompson said we had to have our badges put on our vests for the ceremony, and I used duct tape instead of sewing mine on because it was quicker. Mom didn't know it until she saw me go up to get my award, and she said she almost died of embarrassment, but she also thought it was kind of funny. I was listening when she told Dad about it. He laughed and said, "That's our girl!"

⌒

When I come down to breakfast, there are streamers up around the light fixture, and the chair at the head of the table has the pink-and-blue Happy Birthday banner hanging on it. It's made of felt and has cake frosting stains on it. I think they're from Carm, but Mom said we've been using it so long they could have come from me when I was little.

I sit in my special chair and have a bowl and spoon all set out, plus an entire box of Corn Pops, which is a special occasion cereal. While I eat, I open my stack of cards and set them out in a row in front of me. I can't believe that I'm ten today. I thought that being double digits would feel differently, but maybe you only feel different when you turn a bigger number, like thirteen or sixteen.

Jack comes in and sits down, plunking his backpack next to him. Usually he's gone to junior high before I'm up, but today I got up extra early.

"Can I have some?" he asks, pointing to the Corn Pops.

I hesitate, but I don't want him to call me stingy, so I push the box to him. Maybe I'll put it away in the back of the shelf before Carm gets up. Jack pours a bowl and hunches over it, chewing fast.

"Your glasses are wicked dirty," I say.

He looks up and squints at me through the film.

"Oh, yeah," he says. He goes back to eating.

Ever since he started junior high he seems sad. After school, instead of playing with Carm and me or having Chuck over, he has to do homework. He has math called "Pre-Algebra" that is really hard. I looked in his room at his textbook, and the problems have letters in between the numbers.

"Can I clean them for you?" I ask.

"What?"

"Can I clean your glasses?" I say again.

"Whatever. Sure." He takes them off and hands them across the table to me.

I take them to the sink.

"Don't use soap," he says around a mouthful of cereal.

I run the water hot and rinse them, then dry them with the corner of the dishtowel.

Jack drains his bowl and wipes his mouth with the back of his hand and takes the glasses from me. He presses them back onto his face and picks up his bag, pausing at the door.

"Enjoy ten while you can," he says. "Happy birthday."

⌒

"We're going on a mystery birthday trip," Dad announces.

"Where?"

"If I told you, it wouldn't be a mystery."

We drive on Route 9 through Ware into Belchertown. Dad parks the van on the common in front of the Belchertown Bike Shop.

I look at him. "Here?" I ask.

"We're buying you a bike. A ten-speed for a ten-year-old," he says.

The man in the shop leads us over to the girl's bikes. There are three to choose from. The best one is bright red and says *Royce Union* on the crossbar. The crossbar curves down; that's how you can tell it is a girl's bike. I touch the curved handlebars. They are soft and covered in black foam.

"You like that one?" Dad asks.

I nod.

I am allowed to "take it for a spin" around Belchertown Common. The bike man is careful to show me how to work the gears and brakes.

Once I try to stop, like on my old bike, by going backward on the pedals and instead of braking, they just pedal backward. I remember and squeeze the brakes and almost fall over. I hope they didn't see.

I ride in a circle back to where they are standing.

"It looks a little large," says the bike man.

He pulls a little tool out of his pocket and lowers the seat.

"Give it another spin."

I ride again around the common. It feels weird to have them looking at me. I try really hard not to wobble or fall over.

When I come back, braking carefully, Dad asks, "You like it?"

"Yes!" I say. I still can't believe that bikes come in this red color or that it is going to be mine.

Dad pays; it is expensive. I can tell by the number of bills he hands over. The men shake hands, and Dad loads the bike into the back of the Sedum van.

All the way home, I keep turning around in my seat to look at it. It looks especially red and new lying in the middle of all the dirty gardening tools.

I will ride that bike around town, and Mr. Butler will notice how new it is next time I go to get candy. I'll ride it to Little League and beat Jack going up the hill on the way home. Maybe I'll ride all the way to Chloe's house or all the way to Ware to Janine's to get ice cream.

Dad catches me looking at the bike in the back of the van.

"You like your bike, Sissy Jupe?"

"I love it!" I say. "I'm going to ride all over the place."

"It won't be long before you start driving cars."

"Is it much harder than riding a bike?" I ask.

"No, you'll pick it up fast. You'll be fine at it."

Chapter Four

"This is my pancreas," Dad says and draws something that looks like a kidney bean. The little white notepad he has brought up from the kitchen phone looks tiny in his hands, and he holds the pencil stub with his two fingers. He stopped reading early tonight, and Jack and I are on either side of him, Carm on his lap in the middle. I lean my head on his shoulder so I can see better.

The way he is drawing now is so different from when he drew for me in his office with the drafting pencils at the slanted drafting table. Then, his hands moved fast; the pencil moved back and forth quickly. He reached into the tray on the top of the slanting desk and grabbed one pencil, then another. They had letters and numbers on the sides and were different thicknesses: 2B, 4H, 6B. He told me that the numbers and letters meant that the pencil made a different kind of line, and he needed each one when he was making up a yard plan for a house so it looked right. He took an 8B and made thick, dark lines, up and down. It was the thickest pencil in the tray. Then he took a 4H and drew a circle in the air two inches above that. With a 2B he touched the circle and started making curvy lines coming out of it.

"A rabbit!" I exclaimed.

"Oh, you were quick that time. I tried to trick you by starting with the tail, but you were too quick."

I beamed then.

But I don't yell any guesses this time. Dad is being serious.

"My pancreas is in here, in my belly." He points to his belly, and Carm immediately looks down at his.

"No, not yours, Carmie." Dad gives half a smile and points to himself to make it clear.

Carm squirms around and pokes him in the belly button.

"Dr. Nardi is going to cut off this part here." He makes a dark line on the right side of the kidney bean, up and down, up and down, until it makes a little dent in the paper. His voice sounds far off. I wonder if I should go and get him the 8B since he wants to make a dark line.

"And after Dr. Nardi does that, then I have to stay at the hospital for two weeks. The doctors just have to take out the sick part, the part that has the cancer, and they will leave the rest of it. I'll be gone for just a little while, and then I'll come back home and get all better. When I'm in the hospital, Mom might bring you into the city to visit."

I want to ask if maybe we'd see one of the fancy shows on the stage again, but it wouldn't be any fun without Dad there. Then I think about how the doctors will have to get to the pancreas and Dad's belly—standing around him with his body open like when there are doctor shows on TV. It makes me dizzy, so I push the thought out of my mind. Two weeks is a really long time.

Carm squirms around again and reaches up with his small hand to rub Dad's scratchy cheek.

"Pan-crease," he says, trying out the word.

"That's right, Carm," says Dad. He closes his eyes for a second and pinches his lips together and swallows hard, like he has something stuck in his throat. "That's right. Pancreas."

⌒

I'm sitting in the window seat that looks down over five basketball courts made of cracked blacktop with weeds growing in jagged lines. Five black men are playing on half of one of the courts, and two white men are passing a ball back and forth to one another. I can hear the ball bouncing even from up here. We pushed the number seven on the elevator, so we must be seven stories up here.

I have never been in an apartment before, except for Gram and Gramp's condo in Florida when Jack and I spent practically an entire Christmas vacation leaning over the balcony counting the red cars. We got to 164 before we switched to blue. But this is Boston. This is a real city. And a real apartment we are borrowing from friends. Mom said it is a Godsend to have somewhere so close to the hospital. I have been to the city four times before: to see the *Cat's* show, the Children's Museum, and the aquarium. Plus in school we took a field trip to the Freedom Trail to see the red painted line on the sidewalk that followed Paul Revere and George Washington and all sorts of important men when they did their revolution. But those were just visits. This is like playing house in the city.

I try to concentrate on my book, *Little Men*, but the basketball sounds and the view from the apartment window are distracting. I finished *Little Women*, and Grace at the library said I might like this one, too, but I don't think it is quite as good. Jo March, in *Little Women*, missed her dad when he was away in the army. At least I get to talk to my dad every day while he's in the hospital. His hospital number is taped up next to the phone, and every day right after dinner we are all allowed to talk to him for two minutes each because it is a long-distance call. He always sounds far away, but it's better than not hearing his voice at all. Later, we get to go see him, but only for little while because Mom says he's recovering.

This morning Mom ruined our lunches, which she said she did on purpose, by taking us into the bakery across the street from the apartment building. There were big men with white aprons that talked loud and asked you what you wanted. It smelled like bread and almonds, and the windows were steamed up. Stacked on trays there were hundreds and maybe thousands of tiny cookies, doughnuts, and pastries in all sorts of colors. We couldn't decide, so Mom got a small box of the tiny cookies, one big cookie called an elephant ear, and two little chocolate cakes stacked together with whipped cream inside called a whoopee pie. That one was the favorite of all of us, and Mom said we could all go back tomorrow if we're good and each get our own. If I lived here, I could actually walk to the bakery. I'd probably walk to school too. Or maybe even take the subway called the "T" that you have to use special tokens to ride, like an amusement park.

The apartment building has a small courtyard, and when we arrived yesterday, I took the wrong door from the lobby and walked into it instead of outside to the street. The door locked behind me. I pounded on it, but nobody came. I knew Mom was waiting for me out front. There was high black iron gate on one side of the courtyard that was also locked. It had intricate designs of leaves and vines twisting around the bars. After testing it, I climbed up and over, being careful of the sharp spikes at the top, then ran around the block.

"Where were you? This is the city; you can't go off on your own." Mom was angry.

"I got locked in the courtyard and had to climb the fence!" I said, whiney and breathless at the same time.

"In your dress?" she asked.

"Yes, of course," I said, confused at the question. She shook her head.

"What am I going to do with you."

Mom says it's time to go, and I put my book down, and we ride the elevator down to the lobby. I'm careful to go out the right door to make sure I don't get locked in the courtyard again. Out on the street, Mom points to the big building ahead and says that's Mass General, where Dad is. We walk to it and ride another elevator up to Dad's floor. Mom waves at a lot of people on the way to Dad's room like she knows them and even says their names.

Dad's room is at the end of a long hallway and is bright white. It smells kind of like the school lunchroom and floor cleaner. When we walk in the room, his face is turned sideways towards the wall, and he has tubes taped to his arm, and there's a machine beeping. He doesn't look happy or sad; it looks like he's just staring at nothing.

"David, we're here," says Mom.

He turns and sees us, and then his face wakes up and his arms open up wide, and we go to him. I want to launch myself onto the bed like we do at night.

"Careful!" Mom says to us. "You can get on the bed, but don't touch Dad's belly."

We give him hugs by kneeling on the bed and reaching under the tubes. Carm finds the remote for the TV attached to the wall and turns it on. Mom says she's going to check in with the nurses and will be right back. When she's gone, Dad says his bed is like a spaceship. He lets us all press the buttons on the side that make his head and legs go up and down. Jack and I work together and make it so his feet are in the air and his head is downward. He fake yells for help using the voice like an old lady.

"Help, help," he says, "you're going to pop my stitches!"

We all laugh, and Carm points to the red "plus" button on the side of the bed.

"Adding," he says, and before we can stop him, he pushes it. A nurse who is black comes hurrying in and takes one look at Dad with his legs in the air and us huddled around the buttons laughing and trying to make him go down. I think we are going to get in trouble, but she just smiles and presses the bed back to normal and says, "Oh, Mr. Huntress, I can see your kids got the same sense of humor that you do."

Dad came home from the hospital on Tuesday. He now has a thing around his waist that looks like a Walkman but it's to give him medicine whenever he needs it. Two men in a truck came to install the air conditioner and the hospital bed on the same day. They wore blue polo shirts with the word *MedTec* in embroidered letters on the chest. That morning, Mom packed up an entire bookshelf of gardening books and a stack of blueprints into boxes. To make room, Jack helped her move them into the garage. Afterward, she folded up the drafting table flat and moved it to a corner. I hauled the big Hoover out of the hall closet and passed it back and forth across the green carpet. Scamper's hair was embedded

in it. It took a long time. I hated vacuuming, but Mom had asked, and I
was trying to be extra good, so I didn't whine or try to do a bad job on
purpose so she'd take over and do it for me.

"That looks like enough, "said Mom. "Let's have some Popsicles and
get in the pool."

The pool was dug last summer. It has a curved shape with wide steps
that Dad designed himself. Instead of a ladder there is a cut-out shelf
two feet below the edge called a "swim out." Dad said it is the latest
trend in pools. He had promised us all a slide, and it is by far our favorite
part, except I hate when water goes up my nose when I splash in. I play
"Shark" with Carm and always win because I am a better swimmer. I
love winning, and it sometimes makes him cry. I always feel bad afterward, but when it's happening, I forget I'm being mean until it's too late.

We eat our Popsicles on the deck, and Mom wipes the back of her
hand on her face. It leaves a dirt mark on her cheek, mixed with sweat.
I am sweating too. It is hot. We have been in a heat wave. Everything
on my body feels sticky. Last year when it was so hot, Dad made his
bread recipe for the Pitzis' Fourth of July party. The bread was shaped
like the Statue of Liberty. When it came time to eat it, he stuck a
lit sparkler where the torch was. Mom took pictures, and everyone
"oohed" and "aahed" like it was fireworks. It was good, but it wasn't
as good as his anadama recipe. That is brown, sweet bread with molas-
ses in it. Once when I was little, he told me the story about how it was
bread that needed lots and lots of kneading because it was invented
by a husband whose wife kept going out at night, leaving him with no
supper. So he had to make his own bread, and when he did, he was
mad and said over and over again as he kneaded, "Damn Anna, damn
Anna, damn Anna."

I asked, "That's a bad word, right?"

"Yes, but you can get away with it. See? Anadama, anadama, anadama," he said, pretending to be angry as he pounded the dough.

He had me wash my hands, and I tried it. Then we both held up
wooden spoons at the counter and yelled, "Where's my supper! Where's
my supper!"

Mom came in to see what the ruckus was about.

"Oh, is that anadama bread?" she asked.

"You bet," said Dad. "Where's my supper, woman?" And then he pulled her to him and kissed her. Their lips were touching for a long time. I think they forgot I was there.

⁓

Kathy comes every morning except on weekends. She is from hospice, which I thought meant she came from the hospital, but Mom said it was a group of nurses who came to help out families when someone was sick. She has the blackest hair I have ever seen on anyone, and she dresses just like a regular person except that she has a stethoscope around her neck and a name badge. I like it when Kathy is here. Mom seems to relax for a while and sometimes sits out on the deck and has a glass of iced tea and reads her book. Most days she falls asleep there, and Kathy wakes her up when she leaves. A few times she stayed and made us sandwiches, saying, "It's my lunch hour; let's be extra quiet and let your mom nap."

I like how she hums when she is in the kitchen. Kathy asks us each how we are doing, like we are grown-ups. I try to answer for real instead of just saying "fine."

⁓

The pastor brought over his answering machine for us to borrow, and we are the only ones I know that have one. When a phone call comes in, there is a tiny little cassette tape that plays a message and then records a message from the caller. Mom had to re-record the greeting message about ten times because we kept making animal noises like monkeys in the background, so it sounded like were at a zoo. She thought it was funny at first but then sent us all away to be monkeys outside.

When the phone rings now, we run to answer it like always, but Mom stops us and in a tired voice says, "No, just let the machine get it."

We hear Mom's voice on the tape say to leave a message, and then the caller's voice comes on, uncertain, with lots of "ums" and pauses. It feels like lying to not answer the phone when we are here and pretend we're not, but Mom said it is OK; the callers understand that we need some space. Almost every night someone from the church comes with a big basket or cardboard box with supper in it. Sometimes, if we're lucky, there are cookies or brownies in it. The people come to the door and carry the box into the kitchen and sometimes stay and heat it up in the microwave and put it on plates for us. They almost never stay to eat with us but instead give Mom a long, hard hug and leave. We put out the casserole dishes and platters by the shed door, and the next night the next person takes them away. There's masking tape on the bottom of them saying who they belong to.

At night when the rest of the family eats in the kitchen, I take my plate into the office where Dad's bed is. I pull out the hidden slide-out drawer and balance my dinner on it. The rest of the desk is covered with medicine bottles and papers and glasses of water and little plastic basins. It's cool in the room because of the air conditioning. And since it is all closed up, it smells the way my room does when I have a cold—like sneezes and cough syrup. Dad sleeps most of the time now. I haven't seen him get up since last Monday. That day we had fresh raspberries with dinner, and I asked if he wanted to try some. He said they looked delicious and I told him that I picked them from the bushes in the field. He chewed three and then grabbed one of the pink plastic basins off the table near his bed and spit them back into it.

"Yup, perfect, Sissy Jupe. Sorry I can't swallow them."

He looked sad.

"It's OK," I said. "They'll be out again in August. You can have some then."

He nodded, but he looked even sadder.

I walk in front of Dad, and he pushes down on my shoulder. I wonder if I'll ever be as tall as him. I'm already one of the tallest in my class, and Mom says I still have a lot of growing left to do.

We walk really slowly since Dad hasn't been out of bed in a few days, and he stops in front of the house. He bends down to grab a handful of dandelions that have sprouted up in the tulip bed. There are lots of weeds in places there usually aren't. He makes the face where his teeth are clenched together, lets out a breath, then sits down on the stone step.

He's wearing loose pajamas with his brown bathrobe open, hanging off his shoulders. It's strange to see him outside with slippers on.

"Dad, are you OK? Should I get Mom?"

"No, I'm fine. Just have to move a bit slower than I'd like to. Here, help me up." He holds out his hand, and I pull with all my weight.

He makes the face again but gets standing.

We make it the rest of the way around the house to the back porch, and he sits again on the step under the pear tree.

I sit next to him and tell him about Flag Day at school and how I hope my teacher next year is going to be Mrs. Brandon. His machine beeps three times, and he presses a button. I want to ask him what I've been thinking about. Nobody has said it, but I can tell from the adults' faces that something is really wrong. Dad is sick in a way that is different from anything I've ever seen, and every day he spends more time in the hospital bed and less time outside the room. Before I can stop them, the words are out of my mouth. The thing that I can't stop thinking about I say, and I don't even think I mean to.

"Dad, are you going to die?"

He looks surprised and then he gets the look on his face like he does when he moves in the wrong way. Right then I know what he is going to say, and I don't want him to say it. I want to take back the question—do a rewind and go back to talking about Flag Day. I don't want to know the answer. I don't want him to say it out loud.

His big hand covers his eyes, and then he is crying. Then I start crying even though I try not to. I bury my face in his shoulder. We sit there a long time, and then he uses his bathrobe sleeve to wipe his eyes, then mine. He breathes in big breaths and tells me to do the same. He takes my face in his hands so we're looking right at each other.

And he nods.

I don't know what else to do or say, so I lean onto his shoulder and put my hand in his. I still want to take back the question. I want to undo it. He squeezes my hand three times. It's our secret signal.

I love you.

I squeeze back twice.

How much?

He squeezes back, and I think my hand might break.

In the Bible there are miracles. Jesus walked on the Sea of Galilee to reach his disciples, and Moses parted the Red Sea, and Lazarus was completely dead and Jesus brought him back to life. Jesus and God also healed lots of people who were sick and blind. Sometimes when people really wanted something, like the stopping of a plague or for there to be rain for the crops after a drought, they made sacrifices. It is like an exchange. People in the Bible could bring a cow or a sheep or your own son to be sacrificed, then they got what they wanted. Although in the case of Abraham's son, God said, "Never mind, you've proven you would have done it, so you don't actually have to sacrifice him."

I try to think what God might want from me. I think that doing something hard might be impressive, plus praying a lot, over and over again. I decide to memorize all of the books of the Bible, in order, without mistakes. The books of the Bible are like chapters and are listed in the front of the Bible I got at Sunday school. It has my name on it in gold and gold edges on the thin pages. There are a lot of books, so it will be hard and a lot of work, and I'll do that instead of doing things like watching TV or reading, so it will be a sacrifice.

My prayer goes like this.

Genesis, Exodus, Leviticus…

Please don't let Dad die.

Numbers, Deuteronomy, Joshua, Judges…

Please don't let Dad die.

Ruth, Samuel 1, Samuel 2.

When I'm awake, I pray whenever I think of it. I know a lot of other people are praying, too, so God, I'm sure, will hear it. The church even had an all-night candlelight vigil when Dad was in the hospital. At least two people were in the church at all times praying and keeping candles lit. Sometimes there were more. Everyone took shifts of an hour, even through the middle of the night. That has to mean something.

The back of the pew starts to shake, and I look over at Mom. She is crying so hard that her back is bouncing up and down on the hard wood of the backrest. Jack reaches over and takes her hand and squeezes it, just like I have seen her friends do. When she leans forward to press a Kleenex to her eyes, he puts an arm around her and pats her back. I don't know how he knows to do that. He has always been older, but now he seems like one of the grown-ups. I wish he would put his arm around me, too. Carm is too little to come to the funeral, and I think he's in the back of the church in the kid's playroom now with someone. I'd like to be there, too, sitting in those little chairs, putting together a puzzle or reading one of the storybooks or even playing with some of the little kid toys, like the plastic bus that has spaces for all the round Weeble people.

I look down at my pinching shoes and scrunch my toes so they pinch more. The pain feels good. I scrunch my toes until I get a cramp in the arch of my foot. I focus on the cramp instead of the fact that I am in church. I forget that there are people overflowing the pews and standing in the aisles along the walls. Forget all the relatives that are sitting behind us. Forget this is my first funeral and forget that we are here to "Celebrate the Life of David C. Huntress," like it says in the program. It is a lie. This is not a celebration. I am not happy, and nobody else looks happy, either. We are not celebrating anything.

I keep scrunching my toes and try not to think about the days before this or the worst day. The worst day was when the Turners took us bowling in Ware, and all the adults were acting funny. Mr. Turner kept handing quarters to Jack and Chuck, as many as they wanted, to play the video games, and he kept looking at his watch and going out to the pay phone. When it was my turn, I just threw the ball down the lane and didn't care where it went. I had a knot in my stomach that wouldn't go away. We had stopped at Janine's on the way there, but I threw most of my ice cream cone away. I was too nervous to eat it. When we got home, Mom met us outside Dad's room and said that he died. I didn't think it was possible, because I was talking to him just that morning. I didn't know it could happen just like that. I pushed past Mom and saw him in the bed and knew it was true. It wasn't like he was sleeping at all, like sometimes people say when someone dies. He just wasn't there anymore.

I stood in the corner. People came and went out of the room, but I didn't move.

Gram Avi was sitting in a chair next to the bed, and there was black stuff smudged all around her eyes. Aunt Kathy got up and said, "Let me get you some water, Mom." Then, the phone rang and someone called to Gram, and I was alone with him. I went to the side of the bed and touched out my pointer finger to his hand. It was cold, and his skin looked yellow. His eyes weren't all the way closed, and it was scary. I put my hand all the way in his, and there was just no feeling there. I squeezed it anyway, three times. Our secret signal.

I love you.

He didn't squeeze back, but I knew he wouldn't.

Part II

Chapter One

There are all sorts of books that Mom reads now that I never saw before: books that have doves and hearts and pictures of sunlight on the covers, and books that people like the pastor press into her hands when they come to visit. I read the back of a few of them and checked the index and looked up the words I didn't know. I learned that grief is what is happening now. Grieving is what we are doing. It is the name for what happens on the insides of everyone left behind after someone dies. I don't understand why there are entire books about it. It doesn't seem that complicated to explain. It is just sad everywhere, going down and down forever. It is the feeling that nothing is ever going to be good again. When Dad read the comics to us, Charlie Brown was always saying "Good Grief," but I didn't know exactly what it meant. I don't think it means this, because there is nothing good about it.

Mostly, I wonder if I will ever be happy again. I don't think so. I think this heavy feeling will stay forever. I didn't know it was possible to feel this sad all the time. Some days feel worse than others. On the worst days, even the house feels sad. On the worst days, I can't find him anywhere, and everything just feels empty. Sometimes I want to ask Mom if she feels the same way, like her blood has turned to ketchup and is barely moving and she can hardly move. But I think I know the answer. I can hear her crying sometimes at night, and I know she still sleeps only on the left side of the bed.

My friends don't talk about it. We just go on like nothing has happened. Sometimes I forget and laugh, but then I remember again, and the heavy feeling comes back. I'm still not sure if it's for me or for my friends that we avoid the subject. I think they're afraid they will upset me. They are right. I'm afraid of crying in front of them. At the funeral, I was glad we were in the front row so they couldn't see my face. I think the church people plan it that way on purpose. They put the family in the front row to be helpful so you don't have to look at anyone. But still, I know some of my friends were there, because I saw them afterward when there was coffee hour. None of us knew what to say to each other. I stood in a group of my friends, all of us wearing stupid dresses, and we all tugged on hems and looked at our feet. Finally, someone started talking about a movie, and I silently let out a big breath of air. From there, they talked about the Girl Scout camp-out coming up in August and then about vacations everyone was going on. I had the strangest feeling that I wasn't in myself anymore. It felt like I was standing outside of the circle, watching myself stand there and pretending to listen, nodding at the right times and turning my face towards the person who was talking.

I think that there is a before and an after. Before, our family was one way, and now we are different. I feel different on the inside. I used to love being with my friends more than anything. Now, I like being alone much better. I make up stories for my dollhouse or build towns in the sandbox under the pear tree. My other favorite thing is building space stations from Legos. I sometimes design them out on paper first and color the design with my Crayolas. I make sure that the Lego people will have everything they need in the space station. It is like being safe in a bubble. They have a kitchen that is called a galley and bedrooms and science rooms and an airlock. My latest design even has a plant room so when they are orbiting in space, they won't miss green things growing. After I'm done, I put the Crayolas back into their special plastic case. I like to make sure all the crayons go in alphabetically by name so they don't get lost. If there is a space between mahogany and mulberry, then I know the midnight blue I used to color space has probably rolled under the rug. When all of the colors are in their place, it makes me feel calm. Reading also makes me feel calm. I can forget who I am, and the sad goes away for hours if I'm really into a book. I also design towns for the sandbox and build them. In my towns, everyone gets their own house just for them. The dollhouse family gets one, and G.I. Joes get another, and the He- Man figures get one, too. When they least expect it and everybody is doing their homework or going to work or feeding the cat, I fill a big white bucket with water from the hose, and a tidal wave dumps over everyone. It is a wild typhoon. Just like that. The G.I. Joes and dollhouse family and He-Mans action figures and all the other townspeople make it out just in time. They stand on the cinder block wall, surveying their flattened town.

"We are all OK," they say. "Everyone made it out. Nobody died."

They have a party in the rubble to celebrate their good fortune and start rebuilding. Everyone is happy. They will get new houses, as good or better than what they had before. I am making it all happen. I get to decide if anyone gets killed in the typhoon. But nobody ever does because everyone always gets saved in a special life raft that I made for them out of Styrofoam pieces and duct tape. They get to escape with all the moms and dads and live happily ever after.

⌒

"Turn off the TV!" Mom yells. "Everybody, up and out in five minutes. Last warning!"

Jack flops to the floor from the couch and then stands up. As he passes the TV, he flicks the knob, and the screen goes back to its dull gray color.

I sigh, stand, and nudge Carm with my foot.

"Get dressed," I say.

We trudge out to the barn, yawning, and we each take a rake. Mom is already kneeling in the flower bed by the side door in her floppy straw hat and gardening gloves, throwing handfuls of soggy leaves into the wheelbarrow.

"Get the black plastic from the barn, and start by the side door," she says.

I get the plastic and lay it out on the ground. Jack and Carm start raking piles of wet leaves into it to reveal the black dirt beneath. It smells like spring. It smells just like the days when we used to make rivers and dams in the driveway with the spring-melt water. I wish we were all playing with plastic buckets instead of raking.

"Hey, space cadet!" says Jack. A lump of wet leaves hits my shoulder. "This load is ready."

I grab the two corners of the tarp and drag the mess to the leaf pile in the orchard. We fall into a rhythm of trading off raking and pulling the tarp. We make it all the way around the house by lunch, and Mom calls us in for grilled cheese.

"How much more do we have to do?" I ask.

"We can stop," says Mom. "We did all the way around the house, and that's enough."

"What about the side gardens?" I ask.

She pauses, then says, "We have to let some of the gardens go wild, but we'll keep the main ones." Something in her voice makes Jack and Carm look up, and we all know what she means, but she doesn't say it.

We have to let them go because Dad isn't here to take care of them.

This is something that happens sometimes. One of us will be talking about Dad in a sideways way, and we all know it but nobody can say it. These missing words feel heavier than the ones that get spoken.

When I get off the bus and walk down the driveway, I see green shoots coming up out of some of the side gardens in between the piles of leaves. I put my backpack down to investigate and find daffodil stalks even in the gardens we didn't clear out. Within a week, the yard is full of yellow and white, plus the special hybrids that look like the color of egg yolks. They are the daffodils that Dad planted and kept adding to ever since I can remember. I'm surprised to see them growing up through the piles of soggy, unraked leaves. I thought maybe the gardens would stay underground and turn brown and wilt without him taking care of everything. It was a dumb thought, because I know how things grow. In science class I colored in diagrams that showed the stigma and pistil and stamen of the flowers and how they are designed to keep growing and making more flowers no matter what. But still, I am surprised when the daffodils come up and keep growing on their own.

This morning at breakfast, Mom said a prayer. It's been a year since Dad died. We all bowed our heads over our cereal. I knew it had been a year, but I wasn't going to say anything. I guess we all remember the date and will keep remembering every year no matter what.

We're at the cabin for the rest of the summer, and I'm glad for that. I am less sad here. Memories of Dad aren't everywhere like they are at home, since we only had two summers here with him. I go around the cabin and count the memories. There're only three. There are the felt dots he put on all the cabinet doors in the kitchen to make it quieter, his handwriting on a label for "bolts" on the tool table in the basement, and one plaid work shirt left in the closet. I checked and it doesn't even smell like him, like his drawers do at home. I sometimes sneak into Mom's room and put my nose into his shirts. Even though it's been a year, some of his clothes still have a little bit of his scent on them. I try not to do it more than once a day because it doesn't really make me feel better and it feels like it might be wrong, but mostly I can't help it. I know Mom is planning to clean out the bureau this fall, so I'll have to stop anyway. At home, I see him in everything. He's in the trees in our yard he pruned back every fall. He's in the flowers that come up in the spring. He's in the baskets of laundry that don't get folded and the bowl of cold cereal I have every morning because he's not there to make oatmeal. Every time Jack works in the yard and mows the lawn, I think how it's not Dad doing it.

Here at the cabin, it feels like taking a vacation from the sadness for a while. Gram likes to cook for us, and we have big meals and practice manners at the big table on the porch. I don't mind so much. She says, "Now, if you were having dinner with the queen, you would be sure to put your napkin on your lap." Or, "If you were dining with the queen, you would not reach across the table like that. You would say, 'Please pass.'"

Sometimes I do bad manners just so she'll say it, because it's funny. It's good having other grown-ups around, I think. Mom seems lighter here. She has Steve and Nancy from Michigan, who are friends that live on another lake. They make her laugh a lot. I like hearing it. I also like how Mom sits down more here. The phone hardly ever rings, and sometimes we just ignore it since it's never for us. It's usually one of Gram or Gramp's friends calling. There's nowhere to go in the evenings: no bell choir or committee meetings. Sometimes Mom spends entire hours just sitting on the porch with a book or watching us swim. I think Mom likes it here because she gets to be anonymous, which means that nobody knows us here, so we can go into town to the grocery store without getting stopped once.

Gramps makes us all sing "Amazing Grace" before meals. We only have to do the first verse, but sometimes he gets carried away and does more than one as a solo. Jack and me cover our mouths with our napkins and try not to laugh because his voice goes high and then low and sometimes cracks. If Mom sees us, she gives us a stern look, but once she cracked up too, and we all, even Gram and Gramps, ended up laughing instead of praying. I don't think God would mind. It feels so good to laugh, really laugh and for all of us to do it together.

Every few days Mom takes us into the library in town. I get a stack of young adult novels. I try not to read more than one Baby-Sitters Club or Sweet Valley High series books each time and instead choose the books with the silver and gold awards on their front. I do love the series books, but they are more like TV than reading. I can't really explain it, but although it's really fun, I feel empty after reading them, like after eating candy. It's the books with the award on the front that make me feel full and thoughtful afterward. They are usually sad books. It seems to take some degree of bad things happening to characters in books in order to make a good story. Even in books like Sweet Valley High, there is some problem that Elizabeth or Jessica has, and it has to be solved by end of the book; it's just that the problems are about boyfriends and school dances instead of saving a farm or an animal or going on a journey alone. I asked Mom about why the books that are considered really good are about the hard or sad things, or having to do something really challenging.

"It's life, sweetie. It's the hard and sad that make a good story, and it's the hard and sad that, in the end, contribute to a good life."

"I don't think so," I said. I went quiet and looked out the window of the van. We were crossing the dam in the center of town, almost home, and I could see the lake was rough and windy. Maybe I would go out for a sail later.

"You're thinking about Dad?" she asked quietly.

I wasn't actually, so I shook my head. But deep down, it *was* what I was thinking about. Her comment bothered me. There was no reason to have to have people die. There was just no purpose to it except sad and hard. It was an awful thing. There was no other way to look at it. We were stopped in the driveway, so I opened the door to get out.

"Wait," she said.

I sat back down, reluctantly.

"I know you think that losing Dad was terrible, and it was. And it still hurts and I still miss him and I know you do, too. What I meant about the sad and hard making a good life is that there are things that you've learned from losing Dad that will help you have a better life and be a better person. I already see that in you. You help out around the house more now and are nicer to your little brother, and you're really thoughtful in ways that you weren't before. I wish you didn't have to learn the lessons this way, but it's what you've gotten. It's what we've all gotten. One way to honor Dad is to keep choosing to live in a way that makes it happy and joyful even though there is plenty of sad and hard stuff."

I nodded but I wasn't sure I understood. I didn't understand being happy and sad at the same time. That life could be both, all at once.

"Happiness is a choice?" I asked.

"Happiness *is* a choice. In fact, do you know who always used to say exactly that?"

I shook my head.

"Your father said that."

⌣

In the fall, everything that is green seems dusty and worn out from five months of making leaves and absorbing sunlight and growing.

Every inch of space that can grow something has finished its growing and is turning brown and dried out. The air changes this time of year as soon as the nights start to cool down. And there's the sweet smell of ripe wild grapes. It makes me dizzy it smells so good. But as soon as the air goes crisp, the smell of grapes will leave as suddenly as it appeared. School will start, and I will turn another year older. I feel older now, but maybe because it's been over a year and a half since Dad died. It seems like a long time ago and just yesterday at the same time.

Mom is throwing a party for one hundred tonight. It's a dinner party before the organ concert at the church that is in memory of Dad. I watch Mom welcome people with hugs and direct the plates of food to the tables. I think Mom is the happiest when the house is full of people she's brought together for an event. She can smile, laugh, cry, and smile moment to moment, changing in an instant—and sometimes all at the same time. I think this is what people mean when they describe someone as "being in their element." Mom seems most herself here: shiny and bright in a way that is amplified. But I know tomorrow and the next day she'll need to be alone. Afterward, she always seems sort of sad. I guess I'm sort of like that too, where I feel kind of let down after something big is over. Maybe I got it from her, or maybe everyone feels that way. I don't know.

I'm not sure how I feel about this concert and party. I hope it won't be like another funeral. But looking at the faces around, I don't think it will be. Everyone seems happy. It seems like a celebration. Before dinner is served, Mom gets up and clinks a glass with a kitchen spoon and stands on the big rock slab at the edge of the driveway. Everyone gathers around, standing in the driveway, their feet crunching on the stones. I look around, and practically the entire town is here and everybody from the church. Mom's voice is loud above all the voices, and everyone quiets down. She's using her teacher voice.

"I wanted to have all of you here to say thank you. Your kindnesses have sustained our family over the last year and a half. You've delivered meals, mowed the lawn, fixed things, taken care of my kids, and done countless other things that have helped us through this difficult time. You have no idea what your support has meant. Through all of your actions, I can still feel David's love."

At this, her voice cracks, and I can tell she's trying hard not to cry. She swipes at her eyes and takes a deep breath. I will her not to cry. Not with all these people watching. I pinch my own hand because I am nervous, and I wonder if everyone is looking at me. Mom takes another deep breath, and her eyes are shining but she's not crying. She's smiling.

"So, thank you. I hope tonight is one of gratitude and celebration."

Then she calls up Pastor Ketchum to do a blessing on the meal, and everyone moves to the buffet tables and then to the chairs around the yard, eating with paper plates balanced on their knees.

Mom says she needs to sell Dad's landscape truck. On the Saturday morning that it's supposed to be picked up, I go out and sit in it one last time. It has been parked here at the end of the driveway for over a year. It smells the same, like gasoline and dirt, but it also has the stale air smell of something that hasn't been opened in a long, long time.

I remember driving around with him, playing with all the treasures he kept in the old silverware drawer divider. I thought they were treasures, but they were really just all the small parts for fixing lawn mowers that he didn't want rolling around in the back of the van. I'd hold an object in my hand, like a hose valve, and ask him all those dumb questions like it was a game. I wish I knew better. I wish I knew to ask him real questions then. I move over to the driver's side and sit with my hands on the wheel just to see what it feels like.

Later, after the man comes to pick up the truck, Mom comes into the TV room with a handful of fifty-dollar bills. She waves them in the air.

"We're rich! Let's go out to Friendly's tonight!" she says.

It bugs me when she jokes like that. We're not rich. Just last week she said she was going back to work as a teacher. When I asked her why, she said that it was time.

"Are you going back to work because we need money?" I asked.

"No, of course not! Don't worry about that!" she said. "I'm the parent, and that's my job."

But I do worry about it. In every family I know at least the Mom or the Dad goes to work.

⌒

Although I feel old, I don't feel old enough on the inside yet to be going to junior high. I especially don't feel old enough to go to school with kids in high school, but it's a regional school, so it's seventh through twelfth grades. It is going to be different than elementary school; that much I know. I've known all the kids in my class since we were in kindergarten. I know who wet their pants in first grade and who got an eraser stuck up her nose and who threw up on the class computer. It's kind of like we all grew up together. But we'll be thrown in with more than a hundred more kids from four other towns, so we might not even see each other that much anymore. We'll also have different classes for each subject instead of one teacher and have lockers, too. I'm pretty excited about that part. I already have plans of what I'm going to hang in my locker. Shelves for sure, a mirror, and pictures I'll cut out of magazines.

I've been to the high school lots of times for Jack's band concerts and awards nights. I like the way the hallways are lined with lockers: hundreds of them, one right after another. I also like the way a school feels at night, empty and waiting. I wonder if they'll let us skateboard down the hallway like I saw on *Saved by the Bell*. If I were to be a character on that show, I would choose Jessie Spano; she's really smart, but pretty and popular too. And she dates a boy named Slater who has dimples when he smiles. They're always with all their friends and do shenanigans, which I think is just a fantastic word. I know it's TV and it's not like that in real life, but still, that's how I think junior high might be on some level. I'll hang out with my friends and we'll do fun things and maybe I'll even have a boyfriend. And at the very least I know that I'll have my own locker.

Chapter Two

We're doing a unit now in Social Studies about the great world explorers. In my textbook it talks about how the explorers encountered the natives of each land when they anchored their sailing ships near the beaches. When the natives came out to meet them, the encounter is always described as either "hostile" or "friendly." Mr. Turcotte was talking about another great discovery and finding gold in South America, and I realized that I am like one of those explorers, but maybe not so great. I'm in the foreign land of Junior High surrounded by hostile natives. I sometimes see my friends from elementary school, but they're just a few "friendlies" in a big crowd. I feel like I'm part of a big city and don't know anyone. I spend the rest of the class period drawing pictures of me in my notebook wearing shiny metal armor with a huge sword, and the rest of kids in the class as natives wearing Gap jean loincloths, holding wooden spears and looking hostile. I am embarrassed when I think of how excited I was for junior high this past summer. It's nothing like I thought it would be.

I used to like getting up. My eyes would open, and I would jump out of bed when I was little. Now that I'm older, getting up for school is my least favorite part of my day. It's dark when my alarm buzzes. *No*, I think in my head when it goes off. *Night can't be over already. I'd give all the money I have for just an hour more, even ten minutes more.*

I allow myself to hit the snooze once, and then I have to get up. I have a checklist in my head that I go through every morning. I do everything in the same order so I don't forget anything, and each step is as efficient as possible so I get every moment of sleep that I can. I shower every night so I don't have to go out with a wet head. My hair ends up being really tangled in the morning, but it doesn't matter since I usually wear it back in a ponytail anyway. I get up, get dressed, brush teeth, brush hair, splash water on face, eat bowl of cereal, get lunch out of fridge, zip bag, zip coat. Done.

Sometimes I can be halfway to the bus stop before I realize that another day has started. I think that's a good thing. If I keep my brain moving slowly, I can keep the feeling of sleep on the bus until the gears start churning on the big hill up to the school. Even if my eyes are closed, I know we're getting close by the sound of the effort of the engine. I feel awake when my stomach flips as the bus turns into the big horseshoe driveway. I feel sick and sometimes put my cheek against the cold window. That seems to help. Then we're all pushing off the bus and through the front doors into a sea of people and the morning smells of hairspray and cologne, floor cleaner, and wet mittens, and stale lunch all together. I didn't think that it would be this loud all the time and this much chaos. It was dumb of me, I know, but I thought I'd meet lots of new friends and we would talk and laugh between classes at our lockers, and I'd walk to class, arm in arm with them. Instead there's lots of pushing and yelling and things like paperclips and rubber bands and tape balls that can hit your head if you're not watching. I'm a head taller than just about everyone, so my head sticks out above the crowd and seems to be a good target. I've been trying to walk with my knees bent low, and that seems to help.

It's third period Social Studies that is the worst. Mr. Turcotte, who is also the athletic director, teaches the class. But you can tell he'd rather be down in the athletic office than in a classroom. It's like being the athletic director is his main job, and being a teacher is just something else to do. His class is easy. I know I'm getting an A. All I need to do is memorize the notes and some maps. One of the annoying things is that he's always having us color maps. We have to bring our colored pencils to class every day. I can't see what coloring maps has to do with learning about the actual countries. I'm so annoyed that sometimes I hurry through the coloring because I think it's so dumb, and sometimes I don't get an A because my colors aren't perfectly shaded throughout the whole country.

The absolute worst thing about third period Social Studies is Ben Masony. He sits in the first row, five seats back. I'm on the other side of the room, but it does no good. I wait outside in the hall until right before the bell rings to minimize my time in the same room with him, but since Mr. Turcotte is always five minutes late, it's not a great strategy. I always end up in my seat with no teachers present. After the bell rings and there's no teacher, I can feel something in the classroom. It is like electric currents, and the voices get louder and louder. Ben is a short boy with thick, short hair and freckles. I don't think he's popular in the usual sense, and although he plays soccer, he's not a star. But he hangs out with the popular crowd from Barre and almost always has friends around him. For some reason, he hates me.

I have fantasies of meeting him alone in a hallway, pulling him into a janitors' closet or the girl's bathroom and punching him. I could do it, too. He's a foot shorter than I am. I try not to hate him. But I do. I know it's wrong, and I try to pray for him instead, like how in Sunday school we're supposed to love our enemies. But it's hard. I haven't cried in class yet when he lays into me, but I've come close. Sometimes his friends Carrie and Brittany join in.

They tap me on the shoulder and say, "Hey, Ben just asked you a question. Aren't you going to answer? He asked if you've had your cherry popped yet. I think you should answer him."

I say under my breath, "Scumbag." They say it on the cop shows to the criminals all the time. I think it's the worst thing you can say without actually swearing.

And then Carrie delivers the message, shouting across the room in front of the entire class.

"Ben! She just called you a scumbag!" She and Brittany laugh like it's the funniest thing that she's ever said.

Ben throws his arm over the back of his chair and says coolly, "I've been called worse. Is that as good as gay-lesbo can do?" For some reason he's decided to call me gay every chance he gets because my name is

Gay Ellen. It's not true and I'm not gay, but the truth is I've never been kissed, so I guess I don't really know for sure.

It goes on like that, and I try to ignore them until Mr. Turcotte finally makes it upstairs from the athletic office. He takes roll call every day even though he could just look to see which seats are empty. The boys who play sports yell out his nickname and say, "Here, Turc!" like they are all part of a secret club. I have to take deep breaths because I know when he gets to the Hs what will happen. He calls my name, and Ben whispers "muff lover" or "lessssbian" under his breath, drawing out the *s* sound long and quiet. Everyone laughs and Carrie pokes me in the back with the tip of her pen.

I don't know if Mr. Turcotte doesn't hear or just doesn't care. I watch the clock's minute hand crawl until the bell rings and wait until Ben and his group are gone before leaving. Each bell gets me closer to end of the year. I try not think about the fact that I'll have to hear thousands of bells until graduation comes in six years.

In the afternoons I watch TV until the cartoons run out, then do Legos or read until dinner. After dinner, I do the homework I have and watch more TV. If I can fill every minute with my brain either fully busy or fully shut off, it stops me from remembering that tomorrow I have to go back. I get to forget for a while that in the morning I will have to get on the bus that will take me to school for seven hours and twenty-three minutes.

One afternoon I am searching for a deck of cards in the chest of drawers underneath the TV. I find an old birthday gift of Jack's that Grandma Avi gave him. It is a VCR tape series called *Where There's a Will, There's an A*. The box has four tapes in it, and it says on the back that it includes all the techniques that a high school student needs to succeed in any subject. I open the box and read the pamphlet inside. It says that good students are made, not born, and that any student can succeed in school by learning how to study, thereby gaining self-esteem and respect from parents, teachers, and peers. There's a color photo of a group of multiethnic kids holding up books and rulers and calculators, smiling and cheering. The word "EXCELLENCE" is written in big letters.

It gets me thinking. I am already a good student, but maybe I could be not just good, but excellent. I could be the best. I'm not any good at sports and don't play an instrument and don't sing. I can draw all right, but I'm far from being really good—and there's no such thing as awards for reading the most books from the library or building amazing things out of Legos. Actually, I'd probably keep the Lego thing a secret even if there were awards for it. I'm sure Ben Masony would love to know about it so he could bring Legos to school and throw them at me in the hall.

I tell Carm we'll play cards later and unwrap the cellophane of the first tape and press play. The TV static clears, and the screen is filled by a man in a suit at a podium who introduces himself as Professor Olney. The lecture hall is filled with teenagers who are all really good-looking. He congratulates everyone on taking the step towards excellence and reminds them that the best students are made not born. There's a straight A student in each of us as long as we know how to study right, and he's going to teach us how.

The first thing he teaches is that we need to know how to take good notes. "These are your most important tools," he says, and holds up a stack of notebooks and a handful of pens. He then makes the teenagers in the audience raise their hands if they don't have a pen, and passes them out. The teenagers smile as they take them. In addition to being attractive, they all seem pretty happy to be there.

I press pause and go to the office to get one of the big yellow pads and two pencils, then pull the piano bench in front of the TV so I can sit under it and use it as a desk.

Over the next week, I work my way through the tapes. I take notes like Professor Olney teaches, press rewind, and listen to parts again. I divide my notebook into sections just like the tapes are divided into sections. There are sections on how to study for tests, test-taking strategies, how to organize your study area, and how to keep track of assignments and use a day planner. There are even relaxation techniques for "test-taking anxiety." My favorite parts are when Professor Olney talks about how your brain works and how to be efficient. It turns out your brain is like a machine, and you can make it work a certain way. You can train it to remember or let it forget. There's a system for everything from writing a term paper to organizing your desk. When I think about things in terms of rules and steps, it makes me feel calm inside.

Later in the week when I'm setting the table I say, "Mom, I need a workspace."

She stops chopping onions and looks at me.

"What?" she asks.

"A desk," I say. "I need a place to do my homework. You know, a workspace." I thought she'd know what it was. Professor Olney said it like it was an adult word.

"Um, OK. How about the table in the front hall?"

After dinner I run upstairs and move the small table into my room. I scour the house for supplies for it. I find scissors and get a handful of pens and pencils and put them all into a mug with a broken handle. In Dad's old office I find drafting rulers and a calculator. From the garage, I take a nut and bolt organizer and dump everything in it into a drawer. After cleaning it with paper towels, I fill all of the little plastic drawers with rubber bands, paper clips, scotch tape, pushpins, and erasers. I label each drawer with a piece of masking tape in my best writing. The last addition is my *Webster's* dictionary and thesaurus.

I am ready.

Just looking at the table set up with everything I need makes me feel determined to be the best. It will be like a game. The best grades equal the best scores. I can win at this.

I start doing everything I learned from the tapes. I spend two hours every afternoon studying, and three hours if there is a test. I add more of my own hints to my study technique notes from Professor Olney. I want more time to study, but I still want to watch more TV and read my books at night. I use a ruler to make a grid of my schedule and see where the time holes are. We have four minutes between each class. If I carry all my books with me, I won't have to go to my locker and I can get to class three minutes early. If I use all those three minutes to study, plus half of lunch and the bus ride, I can gain another ninety minutes a day of study time.

When my teachers hand tests and quizzes back, I make it a rule to slip it into my bag without looking at it. I review it when I get home. This prevents other kids from seeing my grade, so I won't be a target that day. When I get home, I get to feel happy for the grade, then I put them in my labeled folders. With a fat red marker, I circle anything I had to struggle to remember or got wrong so I can study it for the next test.

After the first month, I don't need Professor Olney's test-taking anxiety remedies anymore, although I still take deep breaths when the bell rings. Now I do it because I have test excitement. I wake up on test days and look forward to the period when the test is set in front of me with all of its blank answer boxes waiting for me. I love how the room goes absolutely quiet, and my only task is to fill in all of the answers one by one. Sometimes there is a bonus question, and it means I can get over one hundred points—more than perfect.

The best thing about all of the techniques is that doing them fills my head completely when I'm at school. It keeps me from thinking about what other kids are saying and doing. My brain goes inside instead of seeing and hearing what is happening around me.

I don't think about Dad as much as I used to. But sometimes I'll remember something, and it will feel like it's a wave crashing into me, and I might drown in the feelings leftover. It's happened twice at school, and both times I was in the library.

The first time, I was flipping through the pages of the big *Life Edition of Great People in History* book. In English Mrs. Chase had asked us to write a one-page essay about an important woman in history. I had already decided that I wanted to choose somebody from modern times so that I could include pictures. I had noticed that if I made copies of the pictures and then cut them out carefully with scissors and then glued them in my reports with typed captions I made on the word processor, my grade would be higher. Also, printing reports on the thick paper with a plastic binder sleeve instead of just staples helped, but I learned that one from Professor Olney.

There wasn't a lot on the modern women in the book, and I narrowed down the choices to Billie Jean King, Nancy Reagan, and Christa McAuliffe. Christa McAuliffe looked the most promising. I read the one-page biography of her life, sprinkled with pictures of her in her flight jumpsuit and standing in front of a classroom. I remembered the day the *Challenger* exploded. We were all supposed to watch it take off in a special assembly, but the janitor couldn't get a strong enough signal on the TV mounted to the cart, so we all were sent back to our classrooms.

We missed the launch entirely, and after school that day I handed the bus driver my note at Jessica Goodfield's house so I could get off at her stop. We were going to build forts in the hayloft. The hay bales up there were stacked to the ceiling in piles three stories high. It was warm and dark and smelled sweet and dusty. Light coming through the few windows made bright shafts that danced with dust. Sometimes, if the bales were stacked just right, you could slide down an entire side. When we got off the bus and climbed the steps to the front porch of her house, one of the farmhands told us that the *Challenger* had exploded that day. He heard it on the news.

We nodded solemnly, agreed it was a terrible thing, had a snack, and went to play. I hadn't thought about it in the last five years, but as I read about Christa McAuliffe's life, it came back to me. She was a teacher and a mother. The article said that at the time of the disaster her kids were nine and six. It never occurred to me that they would have been standing on the ground at Cape Canaveral, watching their mother be an astronaut, watching her wave at the TV cameras and step up to the elevator to take her to the shuttle. They would have been watching it all. I stumbled out of my seat and tried to keep my arms folded as I got the hall pass. I pinched myself on the inside of my arm. Don't feel. Don't feel. Don't think.

I made it to the girl's room and into a stall. The bathroom was empty for once. I put the seat down and sat in the stall, burying my face in the crook of my elbow and tried to muffle my sobs.

Why hadn't I ever thought of that before?

I had never considered what it was like for those kids to stand on the ground and have to watch their mother explode in the air. When I thought about it, I knew what they might have felt. And it was almost unbearable.

The other time it happened I was waiting in line to check out a book, and next to the front desk there was a display about American music. A songbook was open to "You Are My Sunshine," and I found out that it was written in 1939 and is one of the state songs of Louisiana. I didn't know it was a real song. I thought that Dad had made it up just for me. As it turns out, there are more verses to it about losing your love and hanging your head and crying. Dad only sang me the first one, the happy verse. But overall, it's a very sad song. I wonder if I'm going to keep learning about things I thought were one way but are actually another way entirely. The idea that what I know about the world is all wrong, along with the memory of Dad singing the happy part of that song, made me really sad. I didn't expect it, and I had to secretly pinch the skin on the back of my hand.

Right after the sadness passed, I looked around to see if anyone noticed. Nobody did. I think I can see sadness in most of the faces of kids at school. I can't explain it. It seems like all kids around me are sad. Even the ones who are talking and laughing and surrounded by friends have a sadness just under their faces. Even the ones who are angry and walk down the hall punching lockers are sad. I wish I knew. I wish I knew what other people were sad about or angry about. I think that's why I like books so much. Books tell you in words, exactly what is happening inside another person. You don't have to wonder or guess.

⌒

This winter seems especially cold, but it might just be because of waiting for the bus in the darkness of morning. I wear a hat and gloves, but always take off my hat as soon as we get to school so nobody sees me wearing it. It leaves my hair flat and clinging to everything because of the static. Usually I have time to get to the bathroom and put some water on it, but this morning the bus was late. I had only three minutes to get to my first class on the other side of the school and up one floor—no time to wet it down in the bathroom. I shove my winter coat into the locker and then feel something hit my head. I reach up and find something stuck to my head. The boys across the hall are laughing.

"Direct hit! You got tape balled!" They laugh hysterically.

I can feel a tightness in my throat, so decide to concentrate on not being late. I will not cry in front of them.

I feel the wad of masking tape stuck in my hair and give it a pull. It comes out but takes a clump of hair with it. I rub the sore spot on my scalp and make it look like I'm just adjusting my ponytail. I don't look at them, as if nothing happened. I pull out all the books I'll need until lunch and put the rest back in my locker. The less time I have to spend in the hallways the better.

As I'm putting my pre-algebra book back in the locker, my knuckle catches on the metal of the narrow door. It reopens the cut I got doing the same thing last week.

The first bell rings.

"Shit," I say under my breath.

Mary brings her head out of her locker next to mine, where she is applying a wide swath of lip gloss. I can smell the wacky watermelon.

"Shit? Did you say shit? Did Ms. Perfectly Perfect actually say a swear? I'm telling."

I put on my stone face and slam my locker shut.

"Shut up," I say. I can feel the tightness in my throat again.

"Shut the fuck up yourself. And by the way, your hair looks like it was electrocuted. Ever hear of hair gel?"

She laughs and walks away. I have to hurry by her. I have, at best, forty-five seconds to make it to class. I hear her yelling behind me.

"Run! Run! You're going to be late! Let me see you run, fatty-fat loser!"

I weigh the options of being taunted by her or being late to class. I choose the taunting and run.

I wish I could be suspended from school. It seems like a great thing. Three days to get a break and stay home, like your own private snow days. There're two kinds of suspension—in-house, which is less serious, and regular suspension, where you get the three days at home. For in-house, you just have to spend all day in a converted janitor's closet with a desk and white walls. You just sit there and do your work all day—you even eat your lunch in there. It's called the "rubber room" by all the kids and even some of the teachers. I think it's because it reminds people of an insane asylum type of room, with nothing on the walls and isolation. To me, it sounds wonderful. Teachers come and bring you your assignments, and you just get to work all day on your own in that quiet, white room. You don't have to go into the hallways at all or see any other kids. I wonder if the teachers have time to stop and chat when they bring the assignments. If I were in there, maybe they would stay and we could talk about *Julius Caesar* or plate tectonics. I'd do all my work and then spend the extra time reading books I brought from home or from the library. The only problem is that to get into the rubber room, you have to accumulate a lot of demerits. I read the student handbook and calculated what I would have to do to get into the rubber room. I would have to be caught smoking twice, or be late eight times, or have two unsanctioned absences, or show disrespect to a teacher three times (or any combination of those) to add up to eighteen demerits. I don't think I could pull those things off. It probably wouldn't be worth getting into trouble. And even the worst kids are always let out after a couple of days. Nobody gets to stay safe in there forever.

On Thursdays Mom still goes to bell choir, and we all stay home alone. We're supposed to clean up dinner and do our homework so we can watch *The Cosby Show* which comes on at eight o'clock. I don't like staying home alone without any adults. It makes me nervous. What if something happens or bad guys come or something catches on fire? I've gone over all this with Mom, and I know the steps of what to do. Lock the door, call the police number next to the phone, go to Sally's house, use the fire extinguisher. But still, it makes me nervous. I don't like the feeling of knowing that nobody is in charge except for us. For a few months, Mom had a woman from the church come and stay with us, but she says we're all old enough to be alone now. I worry sometimes that she's not going to come back. Or get in a car accident. It happens sometimes. I know because I see it on the news, and there were some teenagers in town who died because of car accidents. I wonder about what would happen to us, but I'm afraid to even ask. Sometimes it's better not to know things. I don't know if they have orphanages still.

Chapter Three

I'm working on my Latin homework and translating sentences about breaking camp and making camp and farmers fetching water from the *flumen*. If this is what the Romans actually talked about, the empire most likely fell from sheer boredom.

I put the textbook down and pick up the novel that I'd rather be reading. Mom bought it for me at the Tatnuck bookstore in Worcester, which is where we sometimes get to stop after my orthodontist appointments. Jack appears in my doorway.

"Hey, where's Mom?" he asks.

"She's at a meeting," I say.

"Again? Which one is tonight?"

"I dunno. Maybe school committee? Or church. Or PTO."

"Damn it," he says and kicks my door so it bangs against the wall.

"What'd you that for?"

"She was supposed to proofread my history paper tonight."

"Well, she's not going to be home until really late," I say.

"What about dinner?"

"She left out a can of ravioli," I say. "There's a note on the counter. Didn't you see it? I'm supposed to make celery and carrot sticks, and you're supposed to heat up the ravioli. We both have to load the dishwasher."

Jack sighs and leaves, then goes into his room and slams the door behind him, so I jump.

⌐——

A few times a year we have to go to the bell choir concerts. Once at Christmas and once in the spring. Mom says it is part of being a family to support what each of us does, which is why we go to Jack's band concerts and Carm's soccer games. I point out to her that my hobbies don't require anyone to watch, so why do I have to go watch theirs.

She looks at me with her stern face.

"It's what we do," she says.

At the Christmas concert, the choir stands in front of a long table, and Leon stands in front to direct. The table is covered with a foam pad and a thick, brown tablecloth to protect the bells. Everyone in the choir wears white shirts with little red bowties. It looks neat with the white gloves they have to wear when touching the bell, so they all look kind of like fancy butlers. Mom moves her wrist with a flair at the end of the song and holds her bell up high after she rings it, almost like she's won something. The look on her face seems to say that, too. I don't know why she likes it so much, but she does. She's good at it. You can tell who's been playing a long time by how many bells they have to manage. Mom has six and can hold two in her hand at once but only ring one at a time. Her hands move fast during songs, picking up one bell and ringing it before picking up another. Also, I like when they pluck the bells so they sound like rain plopping down instead of ringing.

Afterward there's a social hour, and Mom stays until the very end, talking to each and every person. All of the choir members bring baked goods, and Leon makes his famous meringues. There's punch and coffee. Mom always makes some cream puff things; they taste really fancy, but actually they just have Cool Whip and canned pineapple in the middle. I know because I helped make them. Jack and Carm and I wait and drink cup after cup of punch and get to finish off the meringues after every one leaves. That's the good part.

I know that the choir season is over when Mom brings the white gloves home to wash. After school, I come home and the table is covered with a pile of gleaming white gloves, drying flat on towels. I put on one and do the moonwalk on the way to the pantry to get a snack. Mom laughs. Sometimes I wonder if she's the only one left who likes me. She says I'm smart and funny and unique, but I don't know. I think she just says that because she's my mom.

I got invited to go caroling with the bell choir last year because one of the members was out sick. Seven of us piled into the minivan, and Leon took the front seat; Mom drove. We all held our bells carefully on our laps. Leon reminded us to only touch them with gloved hands. I was not tempted since it was below freezing and I knew the brass on the bells would be even colder than the air. The van's heaters were on full, but we never drove far enough for the engine to heat up sufficiently to make a difference. Eventually, Mom just gave up and left the van running between stops. We drove around the center of town going from house to house, assembling in the correct order on the front doorsteps. Leon rang the doorbell, and when the door opened, we started our carols. Usually it was "We Wish You a Merry Christmas" because it was short and the person didn't have to stand there with the door open, letting out the heat for too long. Leon pointed to each person, and as he pointed, we rang our bell once. People in the choir knew the songs somewhat, but without the music to read, Leon was the only one skilled enough to direct. We were short two people, and my mom took two bells in one hand. It was still a mystery to me how she could hold two together and ring one but not the other.

"It's all in the wrist," she said.

I didn't know the music at all and could barely handle one in each hand.

We were always invited in, and cookies were passed around, and tea and coffee offered and declined. Mom had warned me before we left: "Don't eat a cookie at every house, or you'll feel sick at the end!"

I never really like Christmas cookies except for gingerbread, which I adore, and decided to take a cookie only if gingerbread was one of the choices. Besides, it was hard to be hungry standing together in the small overheated living rooms that smelled like medicine and something else I could not name. It seemed to be the mark of old age, because it was there at every house. Mostly, our audience of one or two people settled into their armchair or sofa to listen, and some asked us to wait while they shut off the TV and turned on the tree lights for full effect. In the glow of blinking tree lights we played three or four songs at each house. "Jingle Bells" and "O Tannenbaum" were favorites, but we also did "Rudolph the Rednosed Reindeer," "Oh Come All Ye Faithful," "The Little Drummer Boy," "Deck the Halls," and a version of "White Christmas" that usually got mangled because of the complicated note combinations. We always ended with "Silent Night," and sometimes our small audience had tears in their eyes by the last note. Then we were off again, saying "Merry Christmas" as we descended the steps into the cold night. I listened closely as we settled into the van.

"She looks good; you know she turned ninety in September!"

"I heard he has to go in for a hip replacement next month."

"His kids live just an hour away, and would you believe they aren't coming to visit!"

"Did you have any of those buckeye balls? They were divine!"

Leon's voice came from the front seat, proper as ever. "Ladies, let's try and keep those note progressions clean, and be sure to let the note run its course before damping the bell." This, I was sure, was directed at me. A number of times I had let the bell touch my coat, and the sound had stopped abruptly instead of ringing through.

We went to all of the houses around the common, and I realized they were the exact same houses that I had delivered May baskets to in the years before. By the time we reached our house again, everyone had had enough cookies, but Mom put out the trays anyway. Everyone took off their boots and coats and settled into chairs in the living room. Mom offered the carton of eggnog all around along with a bottle from the liquor cabinet and let me have a sip. I almost spit it out.

"That's awful!" I said. "It totally ruins it."

I filled my tall Christmas tree cup with half milk, half nog, and ice, just the way I liked it. I found that as usual, in a roomful of adults, the best way to be let in was to become invisible. They eventually forgot you were there and stopped being careful about what they said. So, I sat in the corner of the living room and sipped my drink. I noticed Leon did the same in a roomful of chatty women. I wondered what it was like for him to be the only man and the leader of the choir. He had never married and lived with his mother until she died. I saw him every week because he was in the church basement setting up for choir practice whenever I was leaving the weekly Girl Scout meeting.

He was one of the adults I was allowed to call by his first name.

"Hello, Leon," I said, trying to be proper, like him, instead of saying just "hey" or "hi."

He said the same thing every week.

"Well, hello. How are you this evening?"

"Fine, thank you," I said. I imagined that we were characters in an L. M. Montgomery novel, talking like that, and sometimes he gave a little bow and I bowed back.

It's probably good that my corduroy pants don't fit anymore. Despite spending no time on fashion, even I can tell that wearing my old corduroys in pink and purple to school would be a bad idea. I tried to wear them, but they pinched at my thighs and around my waist, and I gave up and put them in the trash bag in the barn that goes to the Goodwill in Ware when it's full. I wish I was thin and small like the popular girls. Last month I tried to swing on the rope tied to the tree out front and had to let go after one swing. My arms can't hold me up. It's like parts of me don't work anymore. I know from doing sprints in gym that I'm not the fastest runner in my class anymore. I can't climb the rope at all, and I used to be able to go all the way to the top.

Mom says it is puberty and it is normal, but I hate it. Boys get bigger and stronger and faster. Girls get wider hips and boobs and start to have periods and "curves." That's just a nice way of saying that puberty means you get fat and weak. I know about this because Mom gave me a book to read called *What's Happening to My Body for Girls*. I read the whole thing. Mom said if I have any questions I can ask her, but for some of the things I don't think I can. I just don't understand why anyone would want to do the intercourse part. I can understand touching someone else and having him touch you in a way that is nice, but for him to stick his penis inside—just thinking about it makes me feel kind of sick. It's so gross. In the book it says eventually you grow up and that seems like a good thing to do, but I just can't imagine it.

In the hallways at school sometimes I see people making out. I walk by really slowly and try to watch to see how they do it, but it just looks like they are trying to take bites out of each other's faces. It happens more in the high school hallways that I have to pass through, but there are some couples even in my class that have been going out the whole year. I have noticed that having someone to go out with helps with your social status. It's like showing the world that someone wants you and likes you when you can walk down the hallway, holding hands and eating lunch together.

Nobody who is part of a couple gets picked on, I've noticed. I think that even if the boys who help out in the AV department started going out with the girls in band, they would all of a sudden be cooler. It's strange that they call it "going out," because people who go out actually don't go anywhere. It just means you hold hands in the hallway and maybe kiss. I think that if we lived in a place that was less in the middle of nowhere, it might be different. Maybe girls and boys would do things like go out for ice cream or go to the movies together if it didn't take over an hour for your parents to drive you there and back.

Mom says I'm not allowed to date until I'm sixteen. I don't have the heart to tell her she doesn't have to worry. I don't think she knows how unattractive I am. She says I'm a "beautiful young woman," but she's wrong. I could be a troll and she would still say that. I'm fat in the way that kind people say "big boned" and a full head taller than almost all the boys in my class. My nose is constantly in a state of breaking out, and I can't fit into any of the Gap jeans that the popular kids wear. Good thing I'm not wasting my time being thin or trying to be pretty or fashionable, because it's pretty much a lost cause.

I didn't think it would be like this. I thought that when I got older I'd have friends that were boys but I would still play football with them and have competitions with them and wrestle and put on skits. But it's not like that at all. All the boys who I was in Little League with don't talk to me anymore.

I remember when we had our first dance in sixth grade, before middle school started. It was fun. We decorated the gym with streamers and balloons and got to spend the afternoon dancing instead of doing math and reading. Amanda Thomson brought her boom box, and we played Debbie Gibson, and Aerosmith, and New Kids on the Block. At first nobody danced and just stood along the walls for a long time. Then Mrs. Brandon went out on the middle of the floor.

"I know everyone feels shy, but we're here to dance, so we need to get over our shyness! Tim, Matt, Nate, come out here."

The three boys reluctantly walked out on the floor.

"I want you each to choose a girl to dance with and go and ask her. Girls, if you don't want to dance, then all you have to do is say, 'No thank you,' and they will ask a different girl." She paused. "Actually, let's make this easier. Any girls who are willing to dance with these gentlemen, please raise your hands."

I could see relief on the boys' faces.

I raised my hand high. It felt like being picked for teams in gym class, and I was confident. I was one of the girls who always got picked first. I hoped this worked the same way. The boys were thinking the same thing, and I was picked.

I joined Tim on the dance floor and we jumped around to "Shout" and threw up our hands when they said "shout!" Then I danced with Matt and Nate and any other boy who wanted to. I even asked Scott since nobody had asked him. He has asthma, but he said he didn't want to.

Some of the girls were acting silly and giggling a lot, but I just liked dancing. I liked the way my pink Chuck Taylor high-tops moved fast and how I could spin in a circle on the balls of my feet. I danced so hard that I started to sweat, and my bangs stuck to my forehead. Afterward I either shook hands with the boy or high-fived him, depending on how good a friend he was. I thought that being with boys would be fun and easy like that, but I think it is a lot more complicated.

⟜⟋

In the spring Mom gets a letter saying I will be receiving something at the junior high awards night. For the event, I put on my Sunday slacks and blue blouse with the buttons up the front. Each department head comes to the podium and reads the award, then the name of the recipient. The recipient has to come to the stage, and everyone claps. My name gets called. Then again. And again. I can feel the eyes of all the parents, teachers, and kids in the audience on me. I make it a point to look at my feet. With every trip to the podium, all I want is for the stage to open up and swallow me so I can disappear.

I thought it would feel different. When I imagined this all year while I was working on *Where There's a Will There's an A*, I didn't think of the embarrassing walk to the podium in front of an auditorium full of people—most of whom either don't like me or don't know me. I thought this would be satisfying.

After my name gets called for the fourth time, the applause becomes more and more subdued and polite. My face burns, and I can hear some kids snickering as I pass their rows. I know it is only the presence of so many parents and teachers that is preventing things getting thrown at me. Two more trips to the stage. It is almost a full sweep. I even managed the girl's gym award. Finally, they move away from academics and on to music and band and other awards. I sit low in my seat with the stack of awards in my lap. It still feels like everyone is looking at me, and my face won't stop being hot.

Mom squeezes my arm. Later, as soon as we are out of earshot of everyone, she shrieks and pulls me into a hug that practically lifts me off my feet and tells me how proud she is. Did I know I was going to win all that? Why didn't I tell her I was doing so well? I wanted to surprise her and can tell she is proud.

But other than that, I just feel disappointment. I did exactly what I set out to do, but it didn't work out the way I thought it would. I thought it would change the way the other kids thought of me. I thought I'd show them how good I was and how smart. I thought that being the best at something would make them like me.

I want to go through each of the awards one by one and think about all of the work I put in to earn them, all the hours of studying. Instead, when I get home, I put the entire stack into a clean manila folder, label the tab with red pen as "Awards/Achievements," and put it into my desk drawer. It doesn't matter if I'm good at school. Unless I'm good at the right things, it doesn't count towards being liked.

I would trade in the whole folder of awards if it meant I could be liked. If it meant I could feel like I belonged and was popular and could walk the halls without being afraid. If it meant I could be part of the herd of kids sitting in the two back rows without their parents, giggling and passing around an issue of *Seventeen* and a box of Chiclets. When all is said and done, the awards are just words on paper.

I decide to go to the semiformal end-of-year dance. Almost everyone is going, and some people are even going with a date. I have a pink dress to wear with matching shoes. The shoes have a small heel that Mom talked me into, and I've been practicing walking in them. She said I could get a higher heel if I wanted, but I said no thanks, I don't need to be any taller.

"Are you ready?" Mom asks.

I nod and she fawns over me and makes me stand in front of the daffodils out front for pictures. She has pulled out the Cadillac and taken the top down, just like Dad used to do. Carm washed it earlier in the afternoon. Its gold sides glow in the evening light. It is beautiful, and at the same time I don't want people to see me arriving in it. At first I tried to talk Mom out of it and asked if she would just drive me in the minivan. But when she gets an idea in her head, especially about an event there is no stopping her.

She insisted and said, "It's a special occasion. Let's make it more special!"

I sit in front and keep my head tucked under the windshield so the wind doesn't mess up my hair. It is brushed and sprayed with hairspray and feels like hay.

Mom puts on the radio on the way there. It is a warm evening in late May, the kind of night when you can almost taste the coming summer. The wind blowing around us feels soft and smells like wet earth. I feel the familiar flip of my stomach as we get close to the school and have to remind myself that this is a dance. A fun thing, not a school day. Mom pulls the Cadillac up to the side of the school. I did at least get her to drop me off on the side instead of out front.

"Are you nervous?" she asks.

"A little," I say.

"Just stick with your friends. Don't be afraid to ask a boy to dance. In fact, try to challenge yourself to ask just one, OK? They are really shy at this age. Remember, you look great." She reaches into her purse. "Here, this can be a conversation starter if you need one." She hands me a box of Tic Tacs.

"What?" I ask.

"If you're not sure what to say, just offer someone a Tic Tac. Trust me."

"Um, OK." I put the Tic Tacs into my drawstring purse with embroidered flowers. It even matches my dress.

"I'll be back at nine-thirty, waiting right here. Have fun!"

I square my shoulders and smooth down my dress one more time, making sure the scalloped collar is lying flat on my chest. I look at myself in the little mirror in the visor. Before we left, Mom helped me put some rouge on my cheeks.

"Just a touch of color," she said. She tried to get me to wear mascara, but when the wand poked me in the eye, I said just the rouge was fine. I like how my dress matches my shoes and my purse and my hair is all sprayed up. It took hours to do. I can't believe some of the girls do up their hair every single day. This may be the best I've ever looked. I don't think I achieved "pretty," but I'm close.

Mom drives away, and I walk towards the entrance. When I round the corner of the school, I don't feel pretty anymore. Most of the girls are dressed in short black dresses with high heels. Some are wearing tight dresses in electric colors and with their boobs showing at the top. And everyone is wearing make-up. Lots of it. Their eyes are dark and shadowy, and their mouths are sculpted with gloss. A few, mostly my friends, are at least wearing floral print dresses. They are easy to find, and I am grateful.

There is an electric, restrained excitement in the air. Everyone is waiting for the gymnasium doors to open. Boys are standing in little clumps, adjusting and readjusting the level of their pants and repeatedly smoothing ties down across their stomachs. A parade of minivans is pulling up to the front of the building, pouring kids out like clown cars. The gym doors open, and we all rush inside.

The decorations committee did a pretty good job. It is an "Under the Sea" theme, so there are blue streamers and cut-outs of fish and mermaids all over the walls. The DJ welcomes everyone, reminds us to keep the dancing clean, and starts the music. It is tremendously loud. I can feel it vibrate inside my chest. Nobody is dancing. We are all pressing against the walls of the gym like the floor is made of toxic waste. I stand with my friends, and we shout sentences at each other and then take trips to the punch and cookie table. I look at the clock. It is not even eight-thirty yet, but it feels like I've been here for hours.

I turn to Chloe and yell, "This is ironic, isn't it? A dance but nobody is dancing."

"What!" she yells back.

I repeat myself two more times before she hears it. Eventually people start dancing, and we have something to watch. During the slow dances, the floor almost clears. I take mental notes on how you have to put your arms around the boy's neck, and then he rests his hands on either side of your waist. Then you sway back and forth with your legs kind of stiff and turn in a little circle. It doesn't look too difficult.

Later, my stomach drops when I see Ben and one of his friends walking by.

He yells, "Yo, lesbo, where's the tea party? Nice fuckin' dress." Despite the loud music I hear him perfectly.

At nine o'clock the dance is almost over, and I know I have to at least make an effort. I swallow the rest of the punch in my cup and walk across the floor. I smile at the tall boy with glasses who is in my math class and once borrowed a pencil from me, and I ask him to dance. His pants are a little bit too short, but he looks neater than he usually does in his button-up shirt. He does not look at me when I ask. Instead he glances around as if the answer might be on the walls and stammers back, "Um, no...no, thanks." He turns and walks away fast, and his dress loafers flip-flop on his heels. They must be too big for him.

I think that maybe if I just dance alone somebody will join me. I remember reading in a teen magazine that people gravitate towards people who are having fun. Well, I know how to have fun. I know all the words to Madonna's *Like a Prayer* album, can build tree forts better than anyone, speed-read, make entire cities out of Legos, bake Grandma's super-chocolate marshmallow brownies from memory, and have started at least seven secret clubs. If that's not fun, I don't know what is.

I walk onto the dance floor like I am just crossing it and then start to sway a little bit. I ignore the couples and groups and start dancing like I do in my bedroom with the music turned up loud: like I am on stage with ten thousand screaming fans yelling my name. I swing my hips, twirl around, and close my eyes. I let my arms do what they want, and they float up and around; it feels so good after not knowing what to do with them for the last two hours. I pretend like I'm the only one in the whole gym. When the song ends, I open my eyes. I expect throngs of boys and girls in a circle around me clapping like what happens at the prom in movies. Instead, there is nobody. I don't think anybody is even looking at me. I'm standing on the blue center court line, breathing hard and sweating slightly. The floor is gritty, and my shoes pinch my toes. Some streamers have broken loose from the rafters and are hanging in tattered lines. Ben is standing in a little group of boys near the exit door and is laughing as usual. Maybe at me. I can't tell.

I walk off the floor and spend the rest of the night waiting in the hallway or sitting in a bathroom stall. From inside I finally hear the DJ call last dance, and I hear people groan. The lights come on, and the teachers guarding the doors prop them open, and I'm the first one out. I can't wait to get out into the May night. I find Mom right where she said she would be in the side parking lot. I slide into the seat, and when I pull the door closed, it feels like I exhale the breath I've been holding all night. We pull out of the parking lot, beating the stream of cars waiting to get out.

"How was it? Did you have fun?" She looks so excited.

I consider lying to her, but instead I shake my head.

"Did you dance with anyone?"

I shake my head again. I feel like I might cry. I am disappointed. What's worse, maybe I am a disappointment.

"Well, you look lovely tonight, honey. Don't worry, there will be other dances that will be better. You know what? It's early. Let's go out for ice cream. Janine's is still open, I'm sure, on a Friday night like this."

We take the long way to Janine's and order, then sit in the car licking our cones, with the radio turned down low. The night has cooled, but the air is still soft.

Mom crunches down on her cone and then says in between bites, "It sometimes takes a while to grow into yourself. But I have no doubt it will happen for you. You're smart and beautiful and are talented in all sorts of ways. Like the ways you make cards for me and build things. And how you write stories and have such an imagination. And don't even get me started on academics." She winks at me.

"I know it doesn't feel like it now, but someday someone is going to see you for all that you are and love you for it. As much as I do." She smiles at me. I have the feeling that she can see an entire world that is different than the one I live in.

"Well, maybe nobody will love you quite as much as I do because I'm your mother, but close to it. I promise. The rest of it is all true." She pulls me to her in a one-armed car hug. "Let's go home."

Chapter Four

om and Gram are ironing on labels to all of my clothes, including all my socks and underwear. After each item has a label, I pack it into my big red duffel bag. Camp starts tomorrow, and although it's only fifteen minutes from the cabin, it is still over a thousand miles away from home in Massachusetts. I can't believe I'm spending three whole weeks of the summer away. It's a family tradition, though. Gram was one of the first girls ever to go to the camp in the 1940s and insists that it builds character. I think I'll probably hate it.

"Don't forget your address book," said Mom.

"Why?" I ask.

"You might need somewhere to write addresses of new friends."

I think this doubtful, but I pack my red address book, the one with the hieroglyphics on the front. I think it came from a trip to a museum store but can't be sure. I've collected all sorts of little books and folders for my desk at home and love organizing them and collecting information and coming up with systems for where to keep things. For my address book, I've decided to write everything in pencil because people might move and I'll have to change their addresses in the future. I've seen Mom's address book, the black one with "Addresses" written in gold lettering on the front. Addresses fill up every line and most of the margins. It is filled with index cards and Post-it notes and torn-off scraps of envelopes. There are little letter tabs, but they just give a general clue where you might find someone's address. The H section with all of the Huntresses has leaked into the I and J section and is threatening to overtake the Ks as well. You can tell who is transient by how many times their address has been crossed out and rewritten. It's like a history of migration, and when I see it, I think of the early people crossing the land bridge in North America and going south to populate the entire nation, before it was anything close to a nation. I can track my aunts and uncles way back to their college addresses, apartment to apartment, and then to a home where I know them to live today. I can't imagine ever moving. I don't understand how anyone does it. How can you ever leave your place, your home? I know that someday I'll probably go to college, but won't home always be home? Mom seems to think people might stay put, because she writes everything using BIC Rollerballs so everything is in ink. Pencil would be smarter, so that's how I start mine, by writing my own address under the H section.

We walk up the path that is lined with pine needles, the trees themselves towering high above so the whole place feels like it has a tree roof. We find my cabin on the map the registration table lady handed us. My counselor greets us outside, a woman just a little taller than me, with broad shoulders and blonde hair. She seems older than the rest of the counselors I've seen. Her nametag says "Charlie." For a minute I wonder if she grabbed the wrong nametag, but no, she introduces herself as Charlie. Mom talks to her in the way that Mom can talk to anyone, and we learn that Charlie has guided trips on the Colorado River, and she wanted to try working at a camp. Charlie leads us into the cabin, into a room with a twelve bunk beds and one single bed for her. All the beds are empty except Charlie's. We are the first ones here. Charlie says most of the girls in the cabin are coming up on the bus from Milwaukee or Chicago. I'm glad they're not here yet.

I put my duffel back on a bottom bunk in a corner against the wall. I like how the wall forms a little box that I will sleep in. I don't think I'll like being in a room with this many girls, and maybe my little cubby will seem more private. Mom helps me make the bed and pulls the sheets over the rubber mattress. When she's done, she helps me put my clothes into the little shelves at the foot of the bed.

"Well, I guess that's it," she says. She shakes Charlie's hand and says, "I know you'll take good care of them."

I follow Mom outside. I can feel the tears welling up in my throat, and I pinch my arm.

"I'm going to say good-bye to you here so you can stay and greet the other girls when they arrive," Mom says. She leans in and hugs me hard. "Just be yourself," she says into my ear. "You'll be fine."

I watch her disappear down the pine path. I go back inside and realize that everything, inside and outside here, smells like pine. I start reorganizing my cubby shelves and can't decide it if would be better to organize by activity type or by weather. I choose weather. I refold each of my long-sleeved shirts so the fold points out. Mom must be almost back home by now. Gram is probably making dinner. I'll bet they are grilling tonight. I stop to pinch my arm again, then let go and try to focus on the folding. I'm smoothing down a sweat shirt when Charlie startles me.

"This came for you," says Charlie. "It actually came yesterday."

She hands me a bright pink envelope. It has my name on the front, and it says "c/o Camp Manitowish," and I know the "c/o" means "in care of." I carefully tear off one end, and there's a card inside with a black-and-white photo of women in old-fashioned striped bathing suits.

Good luck on the swim test! And don't forget to smile at your cabinmates!

Love,

Your Fairy Godmother

Wow. It's from my godmother, Tammi. She must have mailed it from Vermont days ago, before I even got here. I wedge the card in between the boards above my bed. My first decoration.

I hear an explosion of laughter, and the cabin door swings open and slams against the wall. In an instant the room is full of duffel bags and canoe paddles and the sound of girls laughing. I retreat to my bunk in the corner. Moments later the door swings open again, and there's shrieking and hugging. A canoe paddle clatters to the floor. The pine walls amplify the sound of the high-pitched voices. When it seems like the room can't hold any more, an ear-splitting whistle cracks the air.

Charlie is standing in the center of the room, with her thumb and forefinger in her mouth.

"Girls, stop unpacking for a sec, and come outside so we can do introductions!"

In sobering silence everyone puts down the shirts or pillows they were holding and goes out in front of the cabin. Charlie makes us stand in a circle and introduce ourselves. She makes me speak up so everyone can hear. I'm the only one not from the Midwest. When we go back inside, I pretend to keep unpacking, and it gets loud again until Charlie says it's time to go to dinner.

I put on the sweatshirt I had carefully folded, and the girl in the bunk next to mine says, "I have that same sweatshirt! Champion, right?" She's taller than me, which is rare, and has hair so blonde it is almost white.

I nod. I almost didn't bring it because I didn't want it to get ruined, but now I'm so glad I did.

"I'm Sarah," she says. "Do you want to walk to dinner with me?"

I nod again. *Say something*, I think. *Don't just stand here.* "Where are you from?" I blurt out.

"Milwaukee," she says.

I don't know what to say next and wait a little too long before I say, "I'm from Massachusetts."

"I know," she says. "Don't they have camps out there?"

As we walk I explain how my grandmother was one of the first girl campers to come here in the 1940s and how it has been a tradition ever since. How we have a family summer cabin close by to here.

The final bell for dinner rings, and we all file in to our table. Charlie tries to get us all to talk as we pass around a pitcher of diluted Kool-Aid that everyone calls "B-dub."

"What's that?" I ask.

"It stands for BW," says Charlie. "Belly wash."

The food comes, and it's pretty good. Better than school food, but worse than Gram's cooking. After dinner there's a campfire and songs. We walk back to the cabin through the woods with our flashlights. I get into my bunk, and I was right about the pine walls being cozy. I wonder if I could hang towels up to enclose my bunk, and I'm sure I could, but I think that crosses the line of being weird. I'm trying not to do or say anything weird.

A bugle plays taps somewhere outside in the trees, and then we hear it repeated farther off, then a loon on the lake calls out. Sad sounds all in a row. I touch Tammi's card on the wall. Charlie calls, "Lights out." There's a scramble for everyone to get into bed and then whispering in the dark. I hear the crinkling of some paper above me and to my left, then something drops onto my bed. I feel for the object, and it's a Reese's Peanut Butter Cup. We're not allowed to have candy. I feel the foil edges and unwrap it quietly and let the chocolate soak into my tongue.

"Thanks," I whisper out into the dark.

Bells and bugles time our day, and I love how everything is divided up into sets of time. There's a specific time for sleeping and eating and swimming and resting and doing crafts. There's even a special language and words for things I've never heard before: revelry and bannock, portage and grub kit.

The highest compliment you can get is either, "You're awesome!" or "You're hilarious!" The girls are so much friendlier than at school. After the first few days, I stop being afraid and stop being careful. I wear my fishing hat to canoe practice, the one with the string and safety pin attached to my shirt so I don't lose it in the wind. I try and tuck it into my collar, but the girl I'm paddling with sees it anyway.

"That's a neat idea!" she says. "Will you make me one?"

I make her one during rest hour and then make three more for girls in my cabin.

Tammi's cards and letters come like clockwork. One every day. I'm the only one in the cabin who gets something every mail call, and soon my bunk walls are plastered with cards. Every few days she sends packages that have joke books and pens and other things I can share with my cabin mates.

During our canoe trip, I find I'm the only one who doesn't mind paddling all day, and I can carry the canoes on the portages farther than anyone except Charlie. Charlie teaches me how to swing a boat up over my head by myself.

The first chance I get to try it by myself, I'm standing knee deep in mud and pull the boat to my hip like Charlie showed me. Mud from the bottom smears my shorts and shirt all the way up, then I bump my hip out and roll the boat over my head. Swamp water splashes down my face and neck. I can feel the grit between my lips but can't wipe it away because my hands have to hold the gunnels. I spit and walk out of the mud, up the path the short distance to the adjoining lake, then heave the boat into the water. It makes a terrific splash. I turn back to shore to see the horrified faces of the other girls.

"What the heck happened?" asks Sarah.

"I made out with the Swamp Thing," I say and shrug. "He was totally into me."

This earns my first "hilarious" and "awesome."

The last day of camp, I try not to cry when they are calling the busses to leave from the front of the dining hall. I haven't been able to eat anything for breakfast knowing this moment is coming. It's over. The best three weeks of my life are over. When I went away to camp my little red book only had my own address in it. Leaving camp, I have dozens. The little red book feels like it has increased in weight over the summer now that it is full.

There was a moment just a few days ago when the second bell for dinner rang, and my cabin mates and I all headed down the hill to the dining hall. I had just changed my clothes into jeans and a favorite sweat shirt, since, as always, the nights became cool no matter how hot the days. We joked that the best camp days required at least four changes of clothes because that meant that you probably went swimming or boating twice and played capture the flag at least once. On our way to dinner, we were comparing how many times we had changed clothes that day.

Melissa won since she had technically gone to breakfast in part of her pajamas. She hopped on my back on the way to dinner, and I piggybacked her and spun around. The third bell rang, and we all shrieked and started running even though we could see the dining hall and would not be late. I wished I had a camera with me just at that moment. I wanted a picture to remember it. I was in the middle of a group of girls, and we were all clumped together and laughing. I was part of a tribe.

⌣

Back home, I spend hours in my room at my little desk that is really a hall table, writing to my camp friends. I try to make things funny, even the things that aren't so funny in real life. I get a lot of mileage out of what happens at school and describing my town. Since they're from the suburbs around Milwaukee and Chicago, just living on the East Coast is something special. I tell them about cows and manure spreaders and haylofts and even the bus being late because it gets caught behind a tractor, and it seems to bring them no end of amusement, especially if I tell it just right. It is in the telling and retelling that things begin to seem interesting. If I write things out, those things seem less ordinary, less sad, less small. These are the girls that laughed at my jokes, praised me for my strength, shared their secrets, and loved me for wearing unmatched socks and a fishing hat. They even gave me a nickname since they decided saying Gay Ellen was too long. I think of Gayle as the better version of myself and decide it is the name I will use from now on.

Every day or two, I put the letters I write into a pocket in my jacket and ride my bike to the post office to mail them. I slide them through the little slot that says "Mail" underneath the barred window, the one where Ruth worked until just a few years ago. I get our mail out of Box 117 and comb through it. Usually, there is a letter for me. I always wait until I get home to open it. Within them there're similar stories to what I write: everyday things of field hockey practice and swim tryouts and upcoming tests and papers, crushes and family dramas. I hang on every word. I love knowing they are out there in the world reading my words and they will write back, and that is enough.

School feels different. It might be because I'm in ninth grade now, and I get to be clumped more with the smart kids who are nicer. In addition to honors courses, I get to take Advanced Art with Mrs. Adams, who might be the coolest teacher at the school.

The best part about being in the class is that during lunch we're allowed to hang out in the art room instead of in the cafeteria. I'm never going in there again. We can bring our lunches to the art room and just sit quietly, but usually I end up talking with the group that meets there. Everyone who comes is either artsy or plays in the school band. They say I'm the only one who is actually a nerd and maybe even a geek, but they say it like it is a compliment, so I don't mind.

There's a boy named Mike who sits at my table who has dark eyes and black hair. He's the first boy since sixth grade who might be my friend. I'm not sure. We talk and laugh a lot while we're working and sometimes share a paint tray. I've noticed that the other boys are really mean to him and call him faggot and shove him against the lockers in the hallways without a teacher seeing. It may be because he wears button-down shirts that are sometimes ironed, or it may be because he is short. Or it may be just because kids decide something about you and that's it. I still see Ben Masony sometimes, but we don't have any classes together, so he's easier to avoid.

Besides, he doesn't matter so much to me anymore, because I have camp friends. I know there's a place where I'm not a loser. I may not wear the right jeans or do my hair in the right way with the hairspray poof of bangs, but I know how to do things, important things. I can start a fire with one match and lift a canoe by myself and know how to paddle in a headwind. Sometimes I wish I could video myself doing all these things and make everyone in this stupid school watch it, but it probably wouldn't matter. They'd still be the same douches, which is an awesome word I learned at camp. It's also a feminine hygiene product, so it's funny, too. The difference is that now I know it's not me that's weird and wrong.

"You ready?" Jack asks.

I nod and hand him his lunch in a paper bag. It's the same lunch I make for myself every day to save time: a turkey sandwich with lettuce and one slice of American cheese, a granola bar, and a fruit punch juice box. When Jack drives me, I make him one, too, as a trade-off.

I open the garage door, and he backs the car out, then I close it and get into the front seat next to him. He drives fast, and eventually we get stuck behind a bus. I feel cool walking in the side entrance near the gym instead of the front entrance with all the bus kids who are wide-eyed and jostling each other. The juniors and seniors seem so relaxed getting out of their cars, calling to each other across the parking lot. It's like the school is theirs, which I guess, in a way, it is.

When I see Jack in the halls sometimes during the day, he lifts his chin at me but doesn't stop to say hi. I don't blame him. I wouldn't say "hi" to me either. Just being associated with someone like me can reduce your popularity. He has a lot more friends than me. I think he might even be popular because he's tall and has never had to get braces and he's good at sports. I don't think he has a girlfriend, but there are girls that sit at his table at lunch, and sometimes I see him in the halls talking to them. I wonder what people think when they know we're related. They probably think I'm adopted, from looking at us. But on the inside, I know we are more the same than anyone else.

The brown car top box that Dad made needs repainting. Mom, Jack and I lift it onto the roof of the van, and Jack ties it down with rope. It takes all three of us pushing hard, and Mom and I have to stand on scraps of wood to reach high enough.

I can't wait to get to the cabin. Sometimes during the school year I go into the garage and get the Rand McNally map out of the van to find Manitowish Waters. It's on the Wisconsin page, up in the top part of the state that is covered with hundreds of blue dots of lakes. I don't know why, but just seeing it on the map makes me feel better, like it's a reminder that it is still there waiting for me.

Now that we're older, we do the trip in two and a half days instead of four. I still like to sit and look out the window when we drive. I think the best time to think is when you've just left somewhere and are going somewhere else. It's an in-between time with only highway and trees to look at.

When we take a break at a truck stop, Mom gets us milkshakes. Afterward, she yawns, turns to Jack, and says, "I'm going to lay down in the back seat. Can you drive for a while? It's a straight shot on Eighty, but wake me up when we get close to Toledo."

"I get shotgun!" I say.

We pile back in, and Jack turns onto the highway.

"Can I pick the music?" I ask.

Jack nods and I switch on the dial on the radio. Every twenty miles I have to find a new station when we drive out of range. Carm is playing his Sega video game in the back seat. It makes me carsick to use it, but Carm seems to be able to play it until the batteries die, and he has to ask Mom for three dollars to buy more at the gas stations.

After a while, Jack hooks his thumbs under the steering wheel and leans his head back into the headrest, just like Dad used to do. I wonder if movements like that are genetic or if it's something that he picked up from watching Dad. I think I'm going to drive like that when I'm older, just to see what it feels like.

Jack's profile against the afternoon light from the car window looks like Dad's. He'll go off to college next year. It will be so strange to not see him every day. I think of the cold mornings in the middle of winter, getting up for school in the dark, alone and having to wait for the bus. I shiver.

"You cold?" he asks, reaching for the air conditioner dials.

"No, fine," I say.

"So, there's going to be boys at this party, right?" Mom asks.

"A few," I answer. "Mostly girls though."

"I want you to be…" she pauses. I can tell she is searching for a word. "Careful." She continues, "Sometimes boys can get…" She pauses again, thinking. "Pushy. In a way that is uncomfortable. Physically, I mean. Just be careful about being alone with anyone, any boy, you don't know very well. Especially when you go to college and haven't grown up with them."

I almost want to laugh. She doesn't realize that date rape in some form or another has been covered ad nauseam in most of the teen TV shows I watch, complete with the public service announcement at the end with a hotline number to call if you or someone you know has a problem. It is also funny because it would be a relief to have a boy try to take advantage of me. Nobody has ever expressed any interest in me at all in that way, unless you counted thrown projectiles and tape balls. I read in a teen magazine that sometimes negative attention from boys means they like you, but I am smart enough to know that the kind of attention I get is much too mean to indicate anything resembling romantic interest. The magazine also suggested that boys think about sex an average of twice a minute. I myself think about it a few times each hour, and even that is distracting. I wonder what sex is like, and I think often about kissing a boy, maybe even with tongues, and having him say I am beautiful.

From the driver's seat, Mom looks at me sideways t in an anxious way. I can't believe she is actually serious and concerned about this. It will never happen, but I am embarrassed to tell her how undesirable I actually am.

"Mom, I really don't think there's anything to worry about in that department. And even if there was, the truth is that I'm as big or bigger than most boys in my class. Really, I'm as tall as most of them, and after training for track and canoeing every summer, I'm as strong as them too, I think."

It strikes me that maybe this is why the most popular boys choose the most petite girls and the ones that don't play any sports. Maybe their desirability comes from weakness and the ability to be overpowered and taken advantage of. I hope not. If so, I am doomed.

Mom looks like she has never considered the size issue. I am a full head taller than her and broader in the shoulders and hips. We had never gotten to the point where we could share clothes. I seemed to have skipped over her size entirely in my growth spurt. I am the one who she asks to get things from high shelves in the pantry and open stuck jars and carry things in from the car. My strength is something I am proud of, even if I'm not proud of the body it comes in. I have trouble finding clothes that fit right and hate the way I look in a mirror. My thick thighs and waist seem to defy any logic when it comes to pants sizing. The fabric of most girl's shirts pinches at my arms and shoulders. Clothes shopping always leaves me with a vague feeling that I don't fit in anything, so I avoid it. I end up wearing the same things over and over and just have my clothes on a five-day school rotation in my closet, left to right, so I don't wear the same things too often.

I sigh. "I'll be fine, Mom. Really. This isn't a big deal."

We've been sitting in the driveway of Sharon's house for too long. We can hear the music faintly from inside. I can see kids through the picture window in the living room, holding red plastic cups. There are bowls of pretzels and chips on the table, and Sharon's mom is pouring Coke from one of those enormous three-liter bottles that you can get in the value section at Costco.

I open the car door to go, and Mom asks, "Wait, there's not going to be any drinking at this party, is there? We haven't had the alcohol talk yet."

Exasperated, I draw her name into two syllables, "Mo-om."

She puts her hands up in surrender.

"OK, OK. Go. Have fun. Be safe. I'll be back to get you at ten."

I ring the doorbell and give Mom a little wave from the stoop. I know she'll wait until I am inside to pull all the way out of the driveway. Here I am, almost sixteen, and this is my first party of high school and my first ever co-ed party. Inside, I have a feeling that we'll politely drink soda, have cake, and maybe watch a movie until it is time to go home. I stand in the dim porch light and have the strangest feeling that I am missing an entire other teenage life that is happening in an alternate dimension, just like the ones the crew on *Star Trek: The Next Generation* are always falling into. In that alternate reality, I would be driven to parties by an older friend in a beat-up station wagon with fuzzy dice hanging from the mirror, blaring loud, angry music from the cassette player. We'd be wearing black concert T-shirts, maybe from the same band that was blaring out of the speakers. The party would be in a dimly lit basement, and we'd play spin the bottle games that ended in groping in closets and steal alcohol from the liquor cabinet. I'd be pretty and petite, with a clear complexion and perfect outfits. I'd have a boy there I had a crush on, and we'd sneak off together and share a beer, then he'd kiss me gently and tell me that he liked me.

"You're so pretty," he would say. "So pretty I can hardly keep my hands off you."

I'd smile coyly, and then we'd get interrupted by the sound of something breaking or someone yelling that the police were there to break up the party. He'd take my hand, and we'd run off into the darkness.

Sharon's mom opens the door, and the stoop is flooded by squinting-bright light from inside. "Hi, sweetie! C'mon in. We're having cupcakes!"

Mom is sitting at the dining room table, and it is covered in so many stacks of paper that I can hardly see the wood underneath.

"What are you doing?" I ask.

"Paying bills," she says. "I shouldn't have let them go on this long. I was just so busy."

I stand next to her as she opens an envelope, frowns, then scribbles a check and stuffs it and the piece of paper back into an envelope.

"Lick and seal this, please," she says, handing it to me. I do, and then put the envelope on a stack with others.

"Is it OK to have this many bills?" I ask.

"We're fine, sweetie! Why don't you go start making a salad for dinner? I'll be there in a minute."

I leave but stop in the doorway and watch as she jabs numbers into the adding machine and then looks at the white tape curling out of it, and the line between her eyes is deep and creased.

Jack is sitting at the kitchen table still in his orange vest, eating a bowl of Cheerios. His cheeks are red and chapped.

"Did you get anything?" I ask.

"Naw. Nothing was moving today. We got a shot at a pheasant though."

"Oh," I say. "Um, Mom said to ask you to take me driving. Will you? She said you'd be better than her at it."

Jack looks up from his bowl. "She hasn't taken you driving yet? Didn't you get your permit, like, months ago?"

"Yeah, but I've only driven the minivan, and she wants me to learn stick."

"Oh, yeah," says Jack. "That's probably a good idea." He drinks the rest of the milk from his bowl and wipes his mouth on his sleeve. "There's that space in front of the town hall that's paved. You want to go there?"

"Sure," I say.

We walk outside, and when we're in the barn, he hands me the keys to his Volkswagen Rabbit. It's a convertible that used to belong to my aunt, and there's just a touch of rust around the wheel wells.

I hesitate taking the keys from him. "But I've never backed out."

"You gotta start somewhere," he says.

I take the keys, and I pull the driver's seat forward so I can reach the pedals and do the five-point safety check that my driver's ed manual said to do every time. Three mirrors, seatbelt, foot on brake, start car. I put my hands on the steering wheel at nine and three.

"Do you know about the clutch?" he asks.

"Sort of," I say.

He explains the clutch and the brake and the gas using his hands to demonstrate pushing on each one while you let off on another. It seems complicated.

I stall twice in the driveway but make it up Sessions Road, then stall again at the top of the hill when I have to stop.

"Clutch," Jack says. "You gotta remember: clutch whenever you brake."

The half mile to town is easy, and I even get the car into third gear when we pass the ball field. I bring it to a stop in front of the town hall and remember the clutch before it stalls.

"Let's just practice some easy starts," Jack says.

I jiggle the stick into first gear.

"Try again; you're in third," he says. He covers my hand with his and moves it to the left and up in one smooth motion. "OK, easy on the gas," he says, "and easy off the clutch."

I press on the gas, but too hard, and the car leaps forward. I stomp my foot on the brake. We're both thrown forward into our seatbelts. The engine sputters.

"Clutch," says Jack.

I sense the impending stall and stomp again, this time on the gas. We're thrown backward, and my head whacks into the headrest.

"Clutch," says Jack. "Clutch and brake."

I reach for the clutch but miss it and press the brake and gas at the same time. The car leaps forward again. I stomp down on a different pedal that I hope is the clutch. When I look up, there's a telephone pole in front of us. I yank the wheel, and the tires squeal.

"Clutch and break, not gas," Jack says. His arms are braced against the dashboard, his fingers splayed out to hold on, but his voice hasn't changed. "Foot off the gas," he says.

I try to look at my feet. The feet I see don't seem to be mine and are mashing at pedals without my consent.

"Help!" I yell, "What do I do?"

In one quick motion, Jack reaches down and yanks the parking brake between us. We're thrown against the seatbelts one more time, then the car stalls and goes quiet. I take my hands off the wheel and press them to my face. I can feel my lip trembling beneath my palm, or maybe it's just my hands that are shaking; I don't know.

"Sssorry," I choke out.

Jack sighs. "You don't have to cry about it," he says. "It's just driving. You'll get it…eventually."

"I think I've had enough for today," I say, wiping my eyes with the crook of my elbow.

I unhook my seatbelt and move to open the door.

"Wait," says Jack. "You need to drive home."

"No, I'm done," I say. "I can't do it." My voice is whinier than I mean it to be.

"You can't just give up," he says.

"I'm not. I just don't want to drive anymore today, OK?" I say. I keep my hand on the door handle.

"You need to drive home," he says, in the same way he was saying "clutch" earlier when we were slamming against the seatbelts.

"You drive home," I say. "Please?"

"Don't be such a wuss," he says.

I sigh and let go of the door handle and wipe my eyes again. He's right. I'm being a total wuss.

"I might crash us," I say.

"You'll do fine," he says. "Put your seatbelt on."

Chapter Five

We paddle into the cove next to the dock, and I let the canoe float in the lily pads. Mom had asked me to take her out for a short paddle. I'm leaving in the morning for a trip to Canada. I've spent all of the summers during high school at my beloved summer camp and had been invited to come back for one of the extended trips. Mom cried when I first told her I wanted to go. I'd be gone for almost two months, and we'd be paddling over four hundred miles in remote areas of northern Saskatchewan. We'd have no way to communicate, and she was scared, I think, that something would happen to me. But that's what I love: the remote wilderness and the clarity of purpose of the trips. I love the solitude and relying just on our minds to think smart and our bodies to move us.

"I need to do this, Mom," I implored. "It's kind of a dream trip. I'll be safe, I promise. I've been working up the skills to do this my whole life. Please?"

She wiped her eyes. "Of course you can go. I know you're strong and capable," she said. "I'm just crying because I'm just going to miss you, that's all."

I squeezed her shoulder.

"I'll miss you, too. And I'll come back intact, I promise."

We had that conversation six months ago, and I can't believe the day to leave is finally here. We float in the lily pads, and I tell her I will wear my life jacket at all times and try to call her at one of the last outpost pay phones before we set off. The day is hot, and dragonflies buzz around our heads. Mom bends over the side of the canoe to inspect one that has landed on a nearby lily pad. She asks me to maneuver the boat closer. I have seen her do this sort of inspection before.

"Mom, why do you have such a thing for dragonflies?" I ask.

"Well, they're really symbolic," she says.

She counts off three fingers. "They're a symbol of transformation, adaptability, and grace. And what's more," she continues, "they are some of the fastest flying insects in the world and most maneuverable in the air. They get where they need to be and do what they need to do."

Her voice takes on a tone as if she is standing at the front of a classroom. It is her teacher voice I tease her about.

"Then there's the transformation. They're beautiful but they're not born with it. Did you know," she says, getting on a roll, "that they spend most of their time as larvae on the bottom of a pond? They struggle up from the muck, and then they transform and develop the vibrant colors. It takes time."

Her voice becomes softer, and she looks off across the lake.

"I've always liked that idea: that they are always transforming and changing to show their colors."

"That is very metaphoric," I say.

She turns around and looks at me like she doesn't recognize me.

"What?" I ask.

"Nothing. It's just that I forget sometimes how much you've grown up. It surprises me."

⸺◦⸻

The morning announcement crackles over the school's PA system during homeroom the first week of my senior year.

"The Farmer's Cooperative Exchange is still looking to hire a high school student. If you're over sixteen and have reliable transportation, please visit the guidance office for more information."

I am over sixteen. I have a car. I could use money to support that car and college. It is close to home, and I'll bet they pay at least minimum wage, which is a full two dollars higher than what I make baby-sitting. I want that job. I need to get there first. During morning study hall, I get signed out right away and go to the guidance office.

"Hi, Mrs. Murray. I'm here for information about that job at the co-op."

She looks at me with sad eyes. "Sweetie, I'm so sorry. They're look-ing for a boy. It's a job in the warehouse."

"Oh," I say.

I go back to study hall and sink down to do my Physics homework, but instead I end up making angry doodles with my mechanical pencil until I break the lead. This is so unfair. I want a job. This is just like el-ementary school again: the secretary asking to have boys come help her move chairs in the cafeteria. I stew. I'll bet I can do whatever they need and more. I'm still taller than a lot of boys, even the seniors. I can carry an eighty-pound canoe on my shoulders for two miles. By the time study hall is over, I've made my decision. I'll apply anyway.

I stop by on my way home from school and ask to speak to Bob, the president of the co-op. He comes out to meet me and shakes my hand.

"I hear you're here about the job."

I have often baby-sat for his three kids. Well, at least he knows I'm reliable, I think.

"Come with me, and I'll tell you about what we're looking for." *So far, so good*, I think.

He leads me into the back of the store through the door into a cav-ernous building.

"Well, this is the warehouse," he says.

I have only been in here a few times; usually when we come to the co-op we're buying gardening supplies or birdseed. There are thousands of white bags stacked in neat rows stretching from one end of the build-ing to the other. The lighting is dim, and it smells like dust, grain, and dry dog food.

"Nobody else came about the job. We were looking for a boy, but you're the only one who has applied. We've never had a female work in here, but it doesn't matter to me. Can you drive a stick shift?" he asks.

"Yeah, my car is a manual."

"Good," he says. "I don't want anyone who can't shift to ruin the transmission on the forklift. Can you lift that?" He points to one of the grain bags closest to us.

I lift it easily and nod.

He nods back.

"You're hired. Come every day after school and Saturdays. School comes first; that's what I tell all the kids."

I want to tell him that will not be a problem, but he keeps going.

"People will come out and give you their receipt; your job is to get them what they need and load it into their cars. Wheelbarrows and hand trucks are in the corner over there. Keep the product organized and clean out here. If you have any questions, talk to Jason or Russell. Closing time is at five. We open at eight on Saturdays."

He sticks his hand out. I shake it. I want to whoop and jump in the air. I have a real job.

"Come see Pat in the office before you leave today to get your paperwork and an employee shirt."

I soon discover that baby-sitting is much easier in some ways, but warehouse work is far more interesting. The bags of grain are fifty pounds each. Birdseed and dog food are forty. I can carry two in front of me, or up to eight on a hand truck. I tried to replicate how Russell carries them, two on a shoulder, but they ended up just sliding down my arms. I found I could balance them on my hips though, so I do that. If I don't bend my knees a lot my back hurts when I lie in bed at night, so I start bending my knees all the time. It is easier to use the forklift to drive a pallet of product over to the customer's vehicle if they are getting more than twenty bags. I remember to use gloves when handling the eighty-pound bags of Portland Mix concrete so the leaking lime doesn't burn my hands. Some of the men don't feel comfortable with me carrying their bags, so I ask them to please carry a portion of the order and hand them the lightest bag. It seems to work. Once a customer asked me to sit with her baby in the car while she ran into the store. I said I would and made faces until I got a smile out of the toddler. After she left I wondered if she would have asked one of the guys to do the same. I decided I didn't mind being asked.

Once, after loading a big order of chicken feed for an older man who walked with a cane and drove a brand new truck, he said, "That's some nice efficient work," and tried to give me a five-dollar tip. I thanked him but said we couldn't accept tips. But it felt as good as if I had been able to take the money.

Between customers, I neaten the rows of bags and sweep the floor of the warehouse. I move bags around so similar products go together. It wasn't very logical the way they were set up. I spend an afternoon organizing the pet food area by brand color and weight to make them easier to find. It is like when I organized my ninety-four box of crayons as a kid. I didn't know work could be fun.

"Looking good out here," Bob says. "Looks like the weighing area could use some help."

I tackle the row where the open bags of hay seeds and potato starters are stored. It really needs to be swept every three days for all the spills. Every month a semi truck arrives and pulls up to one of the outer loading dock. It is, filled to the top with hay bales. We take turns walking into the dark dusty tunnel of the semi and taking out one bale at a time. Each weighs more than a grain bag but less than cement. The baler twine digs into my hands, but nobody else is using gloves, and I don't want to run and get mine. For a day afterward, my hands sting and my snot is black from the dust. The next time the truck comes, I am ready with gloves and a handkerchief to cover my nose and mouth.

In the winter the building is under constant construction. They are building a new post-and-beam addition to the back of the store for the growing popularity of weekend gardening supplies, birdseed, and Carhartt clothing. They are trying to cater to the local homeowners instead of the farming community, which is shrinking every year. I help with the construction when they're short, cutting rebar away from the concrete foundation. Afterward, I have trouble lifting my arms. Later, I spend a rainy week in December in the basement, painting the clapboards that will be put on as siding when the building gets finished. It coincides with preparing for my English final, where we have to memorize one of Shakespeare's soliloquies. I choose Hamlet's because it's the one that always gets quoted in movies, but only the first line. I want to know the whole thing and understand what people mean when they say "that is the question." After a I read it a few times, I figure out that Hamlet is asking why people keep on living if life is so hard. He thinks it's because people are afraid of dying. He may be right, but also I think that people want to stay alive to get the good parts of life, too.

I spear my printed copy through a nail on one of beams so I can refer to it while I paint, and I fall into a rhythm.

Dip the paintbrush.

To be, or not to be, that is the question.

Four long strokes back and forth.

Whether 'tis nobler in the mind to suffer the slings and arrows of outrageous fortune.

Four more strokes on other end, and one long one stroke to finish it off.

Or to take Arms against a Sea of troubles,

Move board to the sawhorse. Get a new board. Dip the brush.

And by opposing end them: to die, to sleep...

I get stuck once during the exam and draw a complete blank. I can't remember the next line. I start to panic, then close my eyes and think of red. I think of full buckets of New England Barn Red Benjamin Moore paint. And the rest of the monologue comes easily. I reproduce it perfectly, including punctuation.

Mrs. H's trembling voice comes out of the speaker in the corner of the wall. Her voice always seems to tremble when she uses the school PA system.

"Would the following students please come down to the office?"

She reads off a list of ten names. I hear mine.

Mine? What could I have done?

I look around at the handful of people in my class gathering their things. It must be something good. Everyone who is leaving is in the

National Honor Society. In the hallway we ask each other what it is about. Nobody knows.

When we gather in the office, Mr. Maga straightens his tie and says that he called us all down because they have tabulated the class rankings, and we are the top ten. Mrs. H hands us all an index card with our GPA and class ranking.

This is it.

The moment I have been waiting for for four years. I thought it happened like a surprise on Senior Awards night, but then I realize we need these numbers for college applications. I have no time to prepare. Mrs. H calls my name and hands me an index card. Handwritten on the back in neat printing, it reads:

5th, GPA 3.959

I didn't even make the top three.

I am crushed.

Above the din, Mr. Maga raises his voice. "Your attention please! Attention! You'll notice that none of you have the number one spot. The honor of the valedictorian will go to Laura Graham this year because she is in the accelerated program at a local college, and accelerated classes are weighted higher than what we offer here. Congratulations to all of you for all of your hard work at Quabbin Regional. I hope these standings will make a big difference on your college applications. Again, nice work!"

He dismisses us.

By lunch everyone knows everyone else's numbers, even mine. I have no reason to keep it a secret. My friends congratulate me and say how great it is. My art room friends make me laugh by saying it is good I didn't make the top three because at least now I can pretend I'm somewhat cool. There is some outrage about Laura getting the valedictorian spot and murmuring of a petition that would circulate tomorrow. She left our school sophomore year to go the special program at Worcester Polytech but technically was still part of our class here.

When I get home, I find Mom on the porch. I hand her my index card, now folded into tiny squares and frayed at the edges from so much opening and closing. She jumps up.

"This is fantastic! I'm so proud of you!"

Only then do I cry.

"What's wrong? What's the matter, hon?"

I had never told her that I had wanted to be the best. To be valedictorian. I never told her or told anyone that was what I had been working towards every year since seventh grade and knew it might be possible. All those stupid awards. I told her now.

"I failed! I wanted to be the best at something and I *failed*!"

"Oh, honey. This is so small. I know it feels big right now, but being valedictorian of your high school, especially a little one like Quabbin, isn't a huge deal. Trust me, in ten years, it won't matter. You didn't fail. You have done great—more than great. I'm so proud of you for these grades. *Fifth* in the class. That's spectacular!"

I am still crying and will myself to stop. She sits me down on the deck steps and sits next to me, putting her arm around me.

"You did your best. You worked hard. I've always told you that your best is most important—not how other people do in comparison to you."

"But I could have done more! I could have studied instead of doing track and field. Or taken more credit-bearing classes instead of Art. I could have joined that stupid program at WPI!" I am angry as well as sad now and don't know why.

She looks at me for a moment as if considering what to say.

"Are you listening to me? This is important!" she says.

I nod.

"Academics are just one part of who you are. Developing one area of your life with the goal of a single achievement, anytime in your life, probably isn't going to make you happy. Remember what Dad said: 'Happiness is a choice.' He chose to do a lot of things that made him happy—working with plants even though Grandma wanted him to be an architect and not a landscape architect, baking bread, cooking, being with you kids. Happiness is not a simple formula or a single achievement—it's lots of things rolled up together to make a life. Do you understand?"

I do. I am still upset but feel a little better. I had made choices to do other things besides just school, and they were choices that had made me happy.

"One more thing," Mom says. "I am proud of who you are much more than what you do in the world. Remember that, OK?"

In February we need to stock the new addition to get it ready for the grand opening at the Farmers' Co-op. All of the shelving needs to be put together and stocked from the boxes that are arriving daily. Bob says we can work as much as we want since school isn't in session for the week. I work six of the seven days. With almost all the employees there, including the part-timers, we get everything ready with a half day to spare. When Friday comes, I get the biggest check that I have ever seen in my name.

"Wow," I say when Pat hands it to me. I can't help myself. It is $292. Pat looks up.

"Oh, you got some overtime. That's time and a half. Plus Bob gave everyone a twenty-five-dollar bonus for getting it done on time."

"Wow," I say again. "Thanks."

"You earned it," she says and turns back to her typewriter.

It is so satisfying to work a real job, and I love watching the money grow in my bank account. If I get a scholarship, I might even have a cushion of money starting out in the fall. I'm still not great at driving the forklift, but I do all right. Russell and I spend a lot of time talking as we work. He is so different from the boys at school. He graduated five years earlier and has an easiness and a confidence about him. He knows how to do just about everything, including how to fix the warehouse doors when they stick or replace wheels on the hand trucks or even adjust the hydraulics on the forklift. When things are broken, he always shares what he knows without making me feel dumb. His favorite thing in the entire world is his brand new Ford F-250 pickup in cherry red that he bought last fall. Every few weeks I stand at the warehouse's open doors and gaze out.

"Hey, Russell!" I yell. "That sure is a beautiful truck in the parking lot. Do you know who owns it?"

He always smiles. It's our thing.

It is five below zero in the warehouse. I am wearing two pairs of long johns and all of the layers I can fit under my employee sweat shirt and still get it over my head. It is a little hard to move my arms. I brought two lunches today knowing I'll be starving all day from the cold. On Saturdays like this, Russell and I have to keep moving and take turns watching for customers while the other one warms up in the store. Hardly anyone is shopping today, and the sky is threatening snow.

I am warming my hands on the forklift motor when Bob comes out.

"I have some inventory if you guys want to get out of the cold. It's a slow day." We take off layers and leave them gratefully in a heap in the back room. Bob gives us a thick stack of printout pages. Our job is to go aisle by aisle and mark how many of each item we have on the shelves. Russell takes the printout and overturns a black feed bucket to sit on. He poises the pencil he keeps behind his ear above the pages.

"Tell me what we got."

"Eight metal pails, four large feed buckets, plastic, six small feed buckets, also plastic."

"Got it."

"Four of these things." I hold up a long metal screw with a metal housing around it and hooks on either end.

"That's a turnbuckle."

"One electric calf dehorner, two one-inch manual dehorners."

I hold them up. "Does it hurt them when you cut off their horns?" I ask.

"Yeah, they don't like it very much, but it's quick. You gotta do it or else they gore each other. How many seven-eighth-inch ones we got?"

"One," I say.

We continue down the aisle slowly, and the hours pass. We get up twice to run to the warehouse and load bags for people. In the late afternoon, I look up and see a familiar car in the parking lot. At the same time, I hear his voice next to me. It is Mike.

"Hey, whatcha doing?" I jump and I can feel my heart thumping away. I hope he can't hear it.

"Inventory." I try to sound casual. "How about you?"

I bring a hand up to check my ponytail.

"Nothing. I was just driving by. We needed some ice melter pellets," Mike says.

I remember we aren't alone. Russell looks at me from his bucket and raises his eyebrows. My face is turning red.

"What's that in your hand?" Mike asks.

I whip the cattle bander I am holding behind my back. "Nothing, just some tools. For cows. Nothing really."

"It's a castrating tool," Russell says. "You know, for cutting their balls off."

I try to kill Russell with my eyes while at the same time trying to will myself to be invisible.

"Oh," says Mike. "Ouch. Well, I should be going."

"See you in art!" I call after him. I watch him walk out the door. Through the window, I see him carefully place the bag of pellets on the back seat and check his mirrors before spinning cold gravel with the tires as he pulls out onto the road.

I turn back. Russell is looking at me from his bucket.

"You're awful," I say.

"You like him," he says.

"No! I don't!"

"You like him."

"He's just a friend!"

"Whatever," says Russell. "He drives a totally gay car. Real men drive trucks, you know."

"Well, not everybody can be as manly as you," I say, turning back to the shelves. "So, yeah, how many of those castrator banders are we supposed to have?"

⟶

The warehouse holds the cold even though it is spring outside. I wear my employee T-shirt for the first time since the fall and am finding things to do outside. I eat my lunch out back facing the river, leaning against the building. At closing time when we lock the warehouse doors, Russell pulls two fishing poles out of his truck.

"You wanna go see if there's anything in the river?"

We walk and slide down the bank in the back of the building. The river is high from the spring rain and muddy with runoff. The ground is wet and smells like dead fish. Water seeps in the cracks in my boots. Russell hands me a pole and a new bobber. I am so grateful I know how to attach it correctly from fishing with Jack and I don't have to ask. We dig in the mud with our hands until I find a worm and Russell finds a centipede, hook them to our poles, and toss the lines into the current.

We each find a rock to sit on that is out of the mud. Our feet are inches from the water. I look at Russell from the corner of my eye. He has a dark shadow on his face of beard growth. I wonder what it would feel like to touch, if it would be prickly or soft—how long it takes him to grow it.

No, I tell myself. It's not like that and never will be. I wonder what it would be like to kiss him. The more I try to fend off the thoughts, the more they come.

What would life be like with a boyfriend who is really a man? I think about driving around in his truck with him and going to his apartment where there are no adults. We'd be the adults. Maybe we'd drink wine. It would be so casual because he is old enough to buy it. There would be no sneaking it out of liquor cabinets or waiting nervously in the parking lot of the convenience store.

"Whoa, I think you have a bite!"

I pull up on the line and reel in.

"Darn. I had something." The hook is empty. I root in the mud again and find another worm, cast it into the water, then rinse my hand in the river.

"Are you doing anything tonight?" I ask.

"Yeah," he says leaning back. "I've got a date."

Please say it's with me, I think. *Please be like the movies and say it's with me.*

"It's a girl I met in Ware about a week ago. Friend of a friend, you know," he says.

Stupid thoughts. Of course it's not me.

"What are you doing?" I ask.

"Probably going to go to Janine's, then maybe a walk up at the reservation. You ever been there? It's pretty cool."

I nod. I had gone on hikes there with my family. I'll bet they will probably make out in the little hut over the pond. She probably will be wearing makeup. And she definitely will not be wearing a sweaty shirt and muddy boots.

"You?" he asks.

I am going to go home, eat dinner with Mom and Carm and most likely spend the rest of the night watching TV or reading and getting my Sunday school lesson ready for the next day. I couldn't be more lame.

"I dunno. Maybe go out with some friends."

What am I saying? I never go out.

I correct myself. "No, maybe just stay home and watch TV. I'm kind of lame that way."

"That's not lame. It's what I do most nights," he says. "Hey, are you gonna keep working this summer?"

"For a month after graduation," I say. "Then I'm going to Wisconsin with my family."

"That's cool."

We sit in silence for a while. I realize that I will only see him for a few months more. Graduation is in June. After that, I'll go to college. The thought makes me strangely sad. I'll miss these moments with Russell. I'll miss him a lot.

"Do you think you'll find another job?" I ask.

"Yeah, they're hiring over at Chase Precast. I might apply there. The pay is better, but work is harder."

We watch the river for a few minutes, then he asks, "You going to prom?"

"Well, the senior dinner dance," I say. "Maybe."

"Same diff." He waves his hand. "You going with that guy Mike with the gay car?"

I smile. "Yeah, I hope so."

"Well, make sure he treats you good. Brings you flowers and all that shit."

I want to tell him "Thanks." I want to thank him for teaching me about what makes a truck good and how to change the propane on the forklift and use a hand truck. I want to tell him that I love the way he can throw three bags of feed over his shoulder and make it look like nothing and work without gloves in the coldest weather. I want to tell him he is one of the smartest people I know. I want to go and sit on his rock with him and rest my head on his shoulder and say I'm sorry there are five years and a lifetime separating us. Otherwise maybe we could have been something other than just pals. I want, more than anything, to tell him how great I think he is and thank him for being my friend.

Instead I just look at him from my own rock. He is watching his bobber doing little circles in an eddy of the river.

"I will," I say.

We don't speak any more but sit and watch our lines until the sky turns red and the air turns cold enough that our rocks feel warm. Neither of us catches anything, but I don't think we have any bait left on our hooks and don't get up to check.

"Beth called and was wondering if you want to go to an art show with her," says Mom.

"Who's Beth?" I ask.

"She's your godmother's niece."

"Why?" I ask.

"Just because. She visited when she was a girl, and you were one or two, and she hasn't been back since. She lives outside of Boston now and is going to see an art show in Northampton for fun. I have to work, so she wants to go with you."

"How old is she?" I ask.

"She's about a decade older than you. Twenty-six or twenty-seven, I think," says Mom.

"But I don't even know her," I say.

"Well, she knows all about you," Mom says. "Tammi says she's seen all your letters you've written from camp."

"Mom, that was years ago," I say.

"Well, I think you should go. She's a fine young woman according to Tammi, and it was nice of her to invite you."

⟋

I'm waiting in the kitchen when the Honda Civic pulls into the driveway and stops under the lilac bush. It's on the opposite side of where everyone usually parks. I go out to greet her as she's stepping out of the car. She's tall with brown hair that feathers around her face. She's heavyset and pretty with bright blue eyes.

"Hi," I say. I don't know if we should hug or shake hands. I decide on a handshake.

"Hi!" she says and takes my outstretched hand.

"Do you want to come in?"

"No, that's OK. I'm ready to go if you are," she says.

We drive to Northampton, and mostly we talk about college. She went to college in Boston and decided to stay afterward instead of going back to Michigan. I tell her about my acceptance to Hartwick College in New York and how I'm glad I won't be too far away from home.

"Has anyone pointed out that you're going to Hartwick College and you live in Hardwick?" she asks.

"No," I say, "But it will likely get confusing."

She parks and we walk to a restaurant with wood panels and road signs up on the walls. After we order, she tells me about visiting her aunt years ago and meeting me and how I had an adorable tuft of red hair that stuck straight up from my mostly bald head.

"Well, I've been pretty busy since then," I say and take a long sip of my soda. "I've gained a hundred and fifty pounds and grown four feet and also learned to talk. And I've gotten a better stylist."

Beth squints at me, then she throws her head back and laughs. It's a delightful hold-nothing-back musical explosion of laughing. The people at the neighboring tables look, but it's catching, so I laugh too.

⟋

"How about this one?"

Mom holds up a dark green gown, fitted from the neckline down in satin with lace sleeves. It looks out of place on the rack with all of the washed-out pastel dresses, with ruffles exploding from the hangers, competing for rack space. If this were Sesame Street, it is clear that this is the dress that doesn't belong.

I take it into the dressing room and slip it over my head. This is futile. The senior dinner dance is just three weeks away. We have been to a dozen stores already since March when after an awkward discussion in the art room, Mike and I had come to the conclusion that we would go together. Definitely not a date, just as friends. He will borrow his Dad's Bonneville to drive us there. We split the cost of the couples ticket during homeroom in March. I am glad to be going. It doesn't seem right to get through all of high school without doing this. But I still don't have a dress.

I walk out of the dressing room, and the folds of fabric make swishing sounds. My Mom is smiling at me in peculiar way, her eyes shiny. I look at myself in the three-way mirror. I can see my front and two sides all at the same time. It is weird. I have never seen myself from the side before. The dress hugs my waist in a way that makes it look thin and curvy. The breast area has some padding in it, and my chest looks like I am older, twenty at least. I turn around, wide-eyed. It is me, but it isn't me in the mirror. The person in the mirror smiles back. I take a few steps and think about what it would be like to dance in the dress.

I hear the sales clerk say to my mom in a low voice that I'm not meant to hear, "You can tell it's the right one when they walk taller."

I look at the price tag. It is expensive. Really expensive. More than a leather jacket, which is the most expensive piece of clothing I know you can buy.

"We'll take it," Mom says.

Mike shows up three weeks later on the appointed Saturday night with a bouquet of purple irises.

"Roses didn't seem right," he says." I agree and put them in our best vase in the center kitchen table, moving Carm's homework to the sideboard.

Mom makes a fuss of pictures in front of the fireplace. She makes Carm stand in for a couple of them. He runs out to the barn and gets a pitchfork and a rusty shovel and says, "Ha! Stand there and hold these like that picture of those two farmers."

We do it and laugh, and after that I feel some of the butterflies in my stomach relax. We dance to the slow songs and fast songs I have heard on the Top 40 station they play on the school bus. I like the way my dress flares out when I twirl to "Love Shack" and "Pour Some Sugar on Me." Mike is shorter than me, so it takes two slow songs until we figure out the best way to put our arms, mine around his shoulders and his holding my waist. I go to the bathroom twice to check my French braid in the mirror and poke in loose strands of the baby's breath. We stay all the way until the end when they play "Stairway to Heaven," and the staff is removing the last of the cake plates from the round tables. We drive home in silence.

Mike moves the Bonneville carefully around the twisting country roads. I make a joke about it being a good thing he is the designated driver since I had too many Pepsis to operate a motor vehicle safely. My house is quiet with just the shed lights on. On the kitchen table, there is a veritable buffet of snacks in the ceramic bowls we use for company. There are pretzels, chips, nuts, foil-wrapped chocolates, and cups with a stack of sodas next to it, plus a note in looping script that says, *Hope your evening was great! xo, Mom.*

I am suddenly starving. Mom seems to know what I need before I do. Mike takes a soda and a handful of chips. I go for the nuts and chocolate and fill up a cup with pretzels. The chicken dinner at the country club had been hours ago, and I hardly ate, the feeling of butterflies in my stomach never quite leaving.

"I think I'm going to change," I say. "I'll be right back."

I slip out of the dress and hang it carefully on my closet door. I put on the denim shirt, the one I love with the pocket on one side and the green-tinted jeans I wore yesterday. Without the dress, I feel ordinary again. I stop in the bathroom and check my hair. Some of the strands of the braid are coming loose at the bottom, and I tug at a piece of baby's breath that is about to fall out. My hair feels stiff and plastic from all the hairspray. The braids feel like ropes of hair disappearing under other ropes. I pat it one more time and smile at myself in the mirror. Tonight I had really looked good.

I take one last look and then go downstairs. Mike is sitting on the orange sofa that is actually a single bed with large cushions on it. On the wide bed he is sitting cross-legged just like I do so that your legs don't stretch out in front. He hasn't loosened his tie or taken off his jacket, but it is like him, to remain intact and put together.

He glances up.

"That's a change," he says.

"Yeah. Hey, can you help me take out my braid? There's like a million bobby pins in it, and I can't see them to get them out."

"Sure." He pushes to the edge of the couch and swings his legs down.

"Why don't you come sit here?" he says, pointing to the floor in front of him.

I sit, hugging my knees to my chest.

I feel his hand on my head and a tug as he removes a sprig of baby's breath.

"Your hair is wicked stiff. Did you use gel or something?"

His question makes me feel warm inside. It is the first time a boy has asked me about something where I have the opportunity to be the kind of girl who knows that sort of thing. Like in the lunchroom when one of the guys asks, "How do get your hair to like, be all poofy in the front like that? It's so cool." And then the girl gets to laugh and toss her head and say, "That's my little secret. You can't know because you're a guy." And then he will try to playfully mash her bangs and she will shriek, and the lunch monitor will give them a mean look from her perch on the stool near the door. I feel a flood of joy knowing that after graduation I'll leave lunch monitors and hall monitors and all manner of monitors forever. But even without the monitor, I know I can never be that girl, even if I try. I decide I don't want to.

"It's hairspray," I say. "And a lot of it. The stylist did the French braid and then put in the flowers and then sprayed the whole thing about five times."

"Mmm," he says.

I feel him pull out the elastic at the bottom and start to work his way up. He pulls each stiff rope of hair gently and works it between his fingers so it softens and at the same time searches for the bobby pins. When he finds one, he holds the hair with one hand and slowly pulls it out, smoothing out the strands as he goes. The pile of pins next to my hip grows. A boy has never touched my hair before. A boy has never touched me anywhere before. I have always been curious as to where people look when they touch each other; I am certain that for me, I would not know where to put my eyes. But this is all right, with him behind me and my back resting against his knees. It is more than all right actually. I love the feeling of his fingers brushing my neck, my scalp, and the backs of my ears. I wish I had longer hair, ten feet of hair, a braid that circled into the next room so that he could keep undoing it forever.

He stops and runs his fingers through my hair one last time, checking for any missed bobby pins.

"Thank you." I don't know what else to say so I add, "You did that very well."

He stands and stretches and swigs the last of his soda.

"I should go. It's late."

It is late. It is past two, and I have to be up in five hours for my Sunday shift at the warehouse. But it doesn't matter. I want him to stay. I want him to put his hands back on my head and gently run his fingers through it again and again. I wonder if we have crossed a line with this act. I wonder if, on Monday at school, we will be more than friends.

I walk him to the door, and we stand facing each other. He takes one step towards me, and I know he is going to kiss me. He takes my cheeks in both his hands and pulls my face to his. Instantly, his tongue is in my mouth. I am not expecting it, and feeling something inside my mouth freezes me. I can't move. He thrusts his tongue in and out, deep into my mouth. I think I am going to gag. I feel a scratch on my lip, and it takes a second to understand that it is the stubble on his upper lip. Then it is over. I want to wipe my mouth, but my arms seem frozen in place.

My manners push out the words, "Thank you for the evening," and the syllables come out thick because I have to say the words around where his tongue was just in my mouth. I am seventeen and have finally been kissed, but I thought it would be different. I thought it would feel soft and tender like when his warm hands were running through my hair. I thought that kissing was a declaration of connection, but maybe it is just lips and teeth and tongues touching.

"Well, I'll see you on Monday," he says quickly, and I know that we will not be anything more than friends on Monday. I close the door behind him and then from my bedroom window, I watch the Bonneville's taillights go up and over Sessions Road.

⟨⟶

Carm, Mom, and I visit Beth for the Fourth of July at her little apartment in Manchester-by-the-Sea. The name is something out of a storybook, and Beth herself seems like someone I read about in a magazine. She has her own apartment and a career where she goes to work every day in pressed suits. Her apartment is tiny with white walls, bright colors, and mirrors. The coffee table is a tarnished copper disc, and her bed has six puffy pillows. She drives us around Boston, shifting as smoothly as a race car driver, darting between traffic while talking nonstop about her work, dating, politics, cooking, and growing up in Michigan. We walk on the beach after the crowds have left, then walk into town to have dinner. There are no tables left, so the four of us sit in the bar area, and Mom and Beth order wine. Beth asks for a glass for me and pours an inch. She raises an eyebrow in a question at Mom, who nods in approval. I sip it slowly, barely touching it to my lips so it lasts all the way through dinner.

We watch the fireworks exploding over the water, then go back to Beth's apartment. She insists on giving up her bed so Mom will be more comfortable. Mom had minor surgery the week before and is still slightly sore. Carm takes his sleeping bag to the couch, and I help Beth put up a small tent on her back deck, where we'll sleep.

We settle in.

"My family really likes you," I say. "I can't believe we've only known you a few months. It seems longer than that."

"It's mutual," she replies.

We talk and giggle late into the night. I think this is what having an older sister might be like. I would have wished for one sooner had I known it was as good as having brothers. As the night wears on, the words get more space in between them. We hear fireworks in the distance, the quiet pop of bottle rockets launched in the neighborhood.

After a long silence when we are dozing and looking up at the stars through the mesh tent screen, Beth says, "If things don't work out with your mom, if something happened to her, I'd be there for you. I mean, if you ever need me, I'd come to stay with you guys."

I am suddenly very awake.

"Beth, don't say that," I say, louder than I mean to. "First of all, Mom is fine. She's healthy. The surgery was no big deal. The doctor says she's fine. And second, you just can't say something like that. You barely know us. Granted, we adore you, but you can't promise to drop your life and come and live with us. No way. You can't mean something like that." I am angry but not sure why. The air in the tent is hot and close.

The peepers outside fill some of the silence, then Beth says, "I'm sorry. You're right. You're Mom is going to be fine. I guess I just want you to know that you've got people."

"Thanks," I say.

The peepers fill the silence again, and I'm glad when Beth says brightly, "Hey, you know, tomorrow let's get your mom and Carm up and walk down to the beach. There's a great breakfast place right down the street. They have amazing pancakes."

"I do love a good pancake," I say, happy to have the subject changed.

More bottle rockets pop in the distance. A car alarm a few streets over starts wailing, then stops. Then it is silent except for the peepers, and we sleep.

⌒

I look up at the birches, their leaves dancing in the breeze. It is one of those days with just enough wind to keep the mosquitoes away. The paperback I just finished is lying on the ground next to me under the hammock, *Zen and the Art of Motorcycle Maintenance*. I've given up the young adult section at the library and have been moving into the adult fiction and philosophy sections for the last few years. The librarian no longer tries to steer me into something "more suitable"; in fact she doesn't even look at the titles I check out. I consider it one of the biggest signs that I'm not a child anymore, although on the inside I don't feel much different.

My family has gone to the grocery store in town and will be back within the hour. I think it's one of the only times I've been here all alone, and I love the feeling of it. I decide this is, by far, my favorite place in the world, this little spot of shade under the birches next to the cabin in northern Wisconsin. High school is over. If I turn to the side, I can see off across the lake, and some of the leaves of the maples along the edges are already starting to yellow. I'm off to college in a month and have gotten almost a full scholarship. It is not my top choice of a school, but it's all right. Mom claims it will provide me with an excellent education. Jack was away for the summer working but has come with us here. I think we are the best version of our family when we are here. It is something about all being together with just each other and only each other for company.

We have toast and cereal in the morning together and then swim in the lake and take boat rides. Jack goes fishing. Carm gets out board games. Mom and I read on the porch. At night we play cards and eat hamburgers from the grill and buy sweet corn out of the back of the pickup truck in LaPorte's parking lot.

This feeling of everything being good and right came so softly I hardly noticed it. I thought that after Dad died I'd never feel this way again. But now, I can think of him and it's not so sad. It is OK. I wonder sometimes how we'd all be different if he had lived. It's hard to imagine life any other way than it is now with just the four of us.

"Wake up, honey." Mom is sitting on the edge of my bed. She has an old flannel shirt over her nightgown.

"You've got to come see the moon. Come for a paddle with me."

"What? It's the middle of the night." I groan.

I want to go back to sleep. I hate being woken up. She insists.

I sigh and can tell she's got an idea and there's no arguing. I pull on a pair of shorts and tuck my nightshirt into it. We walk barefoot down the dock. It is bright out. The moonlight casts long shadows behind us and makes everything look bluish and white. I have never seen anything like it. It is so bright and I can see everything, but it is completely different from daylight.

"Wow," I whisper.

"I know," Mom whispers back.

We quietly slide the old aluminum Grumman into the water.

"You take the stern," she says. "You're the expert."

We fall into rhythm, and the old paddle feels good in my hands. The Grumman doesn't move as well as fiberglass boats, but it floats fine and has a nice keel to keep it going straight. It is perfectly still and quiet. Only the smallest of ripples break up the wide swath of light cast by the moon. We lapse into silence and paddle. The moon is enormous: a perfect circle above the eastern tree line of the lake.

From it a path of light shines on the water, stretching from the shore all the way to our dock. We paddle into the light. When we are at the center of the lake, Mom stops and sets the paddle across her knees. She turns around and smiles at me from the bow. She is backlit by the enormous moon. The light reflects off the water and onto her face.

It strikes me all at once. I haven't ever really seen it before. My mother is beautiful. Really beautiful. People tell me I look like her all the time. So maybe there is hope for me yet. We float for a long time. Conversation would have broken the spell. After a while, Mom picks up her paddle and wordlessly I swing the bow around and we paddle home.

We stow the boat and the paddles and she takes my hand as we walk back to the house. We stop at the front porch.

"Are you coming in?" I ask.

"No," she says. "I'm going to sit here for a while." She pulls one of the towels drying on the porch railing and drapes it around her shoulders and settles into a beach chair.

I move to go back inside then say, "Thanks, Mom. That was amazing."

"Sweet dreams, honey," she says.

I go back to bed and fall asleep immediately. In the morning I have to think to remember if the moonlit paddle was a dream. It seemed like a dream. All of the edges of the images in my mind are blurry and filled with light. Then I see on the bedside table, a piece of paper with neat lines in Mom's looping script.

The poem describes how the moonlight is the sun's reflection rather than being the source of its own light. I read it four times, and at first I think it is about God—how we reflect God's light back into the world, but when I read it two more times, I think it could also be about us, about Mom and me. Her the sun. Me the moon.

I find Mom in the kitchen at the stove and hug her from behind and rest my chin on her shoulder. I have to stoop a little to do so. I squeeze her around the middle once.

"I liked your poem, Mom. Thank you."

Chapter Six

*C*hloe comes over to help me pack the night before I leave for college. We play Madonna loud and dance in my room. I can't believe how much stuff I'll need. It's more than what I packed for a month away in the Canadian wilderness. There are two duffel bags, milk crates full of books, a huge comforter, pillows, and sheets divided into three trash bags. I even needed to pack a few dishes that I never thought of until Mom pointed out I might actually want to eat outside the dining hall at some point.

We pack the minivan in the morning, and I walk around the house one last time, going from room to room, picking things up and putting them down again. I try to take mental pictures of everything to seal it into my mind. Each moment seems significant. I don't even have a plan for when I will be back again. Definitely by Thanksgiving, I think. It seems like years away. I want to do everything for one last time, and that's how I think of it. For the last time I'm standing on the porch, looking out across the field. For the last time I'm running my hand across stagecoach rock. For the last time, I'm in my room, looking at the top of Sessions Road. For the last time, I'm hugging Carm, now almost as tall as I am. With Jack away at college over the last two years, Carm and I have become close. I make his lunch sometimes in the morning and drive him to school. He doesn't complain when I play the mix tapes my camp friends have sent me. He makes me laugh so hard sometimes that I can't breathe. I'll miss that.

I spend a lot of time standing at the northeast corner of the house, resting my palm on the gray clapboards. I swear I can feel the house breathing and pulsing with all the life that has happened and is happening inside it. It is the only home I've ever known. I know I'm being overly sentimental and all this saying good-bye is probably going to make us late, but I can't help it. Every moment, every last moment, seems so significant. Mom seems to notice what I'm doing.

"Take your time," she says. "I'm going to have a cup of tea in the kitchen. Come and get me when you're ready to go."

Finally, I look at my watch and decide it's time. We need to get going. I have the terrible feeling that I'm forgetting something as we're going down the driveway, and then that feeling gives way to tears when we crest the top of Sessions Road and I can't see the house anymore. Past the cemetery, past Butler's and the ball fields and the churches and the common. I don't understand the love I feel for all these buildings and patches of grass. Mom pats my knee across the console of the minivan.

"You'll be back before you know it," she says. "Everyone has to leave home at some point."

The bottom of my stomach drops out when we take the exit off the highway for Hartwick College. A banner proclaims, "Welcome Students." We unpack in my dorm room that seems impossibly small and then follow the day's schedule of welcome meetings. Late that afternoon we say good-bye in the parking lot. Mom's eyes are moist, but I'm grateful that she doesn't cry. I hold on to her tight, but I can't say anything for fear it will come out as a sob. I tell myself I'm being ridiculous with all this sadness, and I force a tight smile. I stand and watch the minivan until it's out of sight.

I follow a group of students, and we're herded through registration for freshman orientation camp. We're put into our groups for the week, and we throw a tennis ball around a circle while repeating each other's names. They say there will be lots of these name games over the coming week. Everyone looks guarded and is trying hard to smile a lot. I feel like my cheeks are made of plastic, I'm trying so hard to appear open and friendly. I think about Mom, and I'm surprised when I realize she must be home by now, making dinner. I can't stop staring at the guy across the circle from me with curly hair that flops into two of the most perfect eyes I've ever seen.

Soon, we pile into a van and drive to a campground where we'll spend the next week. The tents and tall pines feel familiar and help me relax. Just like camp, I think.

I find a note in my bag as I'm unpacking and getting my sleeping bag out of my duffel bag. Mom's writing fills the lines of folded notebook paper. I wonder when she wrote this and hid it in my bag. Was it just yesterday? Or weeks ago? In the note she tells me to just be myself, reminds me that it's the beginning of a great journey, to make the most of my time here, study hard, and that she's proud of me. I'm overwhelmed with a wave of homesickness and bite my lip.

I sense someone standing in front of me. It's the guy who was across the name circle from me, the one with the beautiful eyes.

"Hey," I say.

"Hey, there's room at our picnic table. You want to come eat with me?"

Grateful, I join him. His name is Jonathan, and he is my first friend.

Over the course of the week, I make a handful of more friends, but Jonathan is the best one. I've never met anyone so worldly and sophisticated. He's been to Spain and Mexico and lived in Italy with his family. He tells me that he is gay. I am kind of disappointed, but it also makes him seem exotic and more wonderful somehow. Later that semester when I turn eighteen, he throws a surprise party for me and helps me smoke my first cigarette.

"You really should try it at least once in your life, and now you're no longer a minor!"

We mix vodka with Kool-Aid and tap our plastic cups together. He disappears into the small closet and bursts out fifteen minutes later, hair curled, dressed in drag in a sequined red dress, wearing fake eyelashes, twirling a cake from the Hannaford's grocery just down the road from campus.

He shuts the stereo off and starts singing a breathy version of "Happy Birthday, Mr. President," making his eyes tilted and lazy. We all cheer and hoot. He ends the song by pressing his sock-created cleavage into me. I guess he's supposed to be Marilyn Monroe and I'm the president, and I suppose it is my birthday, but I'm a girl and he's a guy and the whole thing is so weird and wonderful. He holds the last note long and winks at me before disappearing into the closet to change back into jeans. We oblige with endless jokes about him coming out of the closet.

After the party, he washes his face and puts on a baseball hat to walk me back to my dorm and holds my hand.

"Tonight was sponsored by your mom, you know," he says. "She called me two weeks ago and said she wanted to make sure you had a good birthday and sent me a check in the mail. So, the cake and vodka and stuff are actually from her."

I imagine her talking to the college switchboard operator and tracking down Jonathan's number and address.

"She asked you to get vodka?" I ask, incredulous.

"No, of course not! She wanted you to have a good time, but she didn't say how. That was all me!"

"Well, I will tell her you succeeded, but in my retelling, the vodka will become just punch, I think…Although she'd get a kick out of you in a dress."

I squeeze his hand.

"Thank you. That was…"—I remember him in the make-up and tight dress that actually looked pretty good on him—"unlike any other birthday I have ever had."

Through mutual friends I meet a quiet guy who is in my chemistry class. His name is Joe. He always knows the answers and sometimes asks questions in class that are so complex that I don't even understand them, never mind the answers. We meet and talk for hours about books and high school, our hometowns and families. Time moves at a different pace with him, and sometimes four hours pass before I realize we've been talking for half the night. In the early morning, he walks me back to my dorm and in darkness takes my hand. He makes jokes about us studying chemistry and having chemistry together.

Soon our conversations lead to kissing on his beanbag chair with the small hole and the Styrofoam beads coming out of it. It's gentle at first, but soon we both open our mouths, and I try sticking my tongue in his mouth, just a little. It actually feels nice. It doesn't feel at all like it was with Mike, his tongue hard and pushing. This is softer, and I like being this close to Joe. I can smell his spicy aftershave and the roughness of his cheeks. He gets a dark shadow if he goes just one day without shaving, and I run my fingers across the growth.

Soon, he moves his hand down to my breast, then pulls his face from my lips to ask, "Is this all right?"

"Yes," I say and go back to kissing him.

We meet every few nights and kiss and talk for hours just like that. Our mouths on each others' mouths and necks, and his hand sometimes on my chest or under my shirt. He gives me my first hickey, and I admire it in the mirror the next morning for a long time. I can't decide whether to wear a T-shirt to show it off or a turtleneck to cover it up. I finally decide on the turtleneck. My secret.

The next time I see him, I kiss him hard on the neck, sucking and biting until I leave a mark.

"We're even," I say.

"Not even close," he says and pins me down as I squeal.

I can't believe the good fortune of him having a single room so we can do this. A week later we are making out, and I stop him. I'd felt something pressing into me but am not sure.

"I have to ask you something….do…do you…um…have an erection right now?"

His face immediately turns a deep red. He looks away and nods.

"No, no don't be embarrassed!" I say. "I've never made that happen with someone…to someone," I falter. I don't know how to say it. "I thought you had to do more to make it happen. We're just being together and kissing, and you have one. It means you're turned on, right?"

He looks me back, full in the face, smiles sheepishly, and nods.

"Wow," I say, "I didn't think I could do that to someone…with someone."

"Yes, you have. Trust me. I'm a guy and you have," he says.

"How do you know?"

"You have no idea what it's like. We think about it, about sex I mean, almost all the time. Some guy has looked at you at some point and thought sex and gotten an erection. It is for sure. Especially because you're really pretty. Or beautiful. I don't know which word I like to describe you. You're both."

I love it when he talks this way. I will never get tired of hearing it. And even better, I can tell that he means it. Nobody, I am sure, has ever looked at me the way he does. He sees me thinking and takes my face in his hands and says it again.

"You're both...pretty and beautiful."

I'm not sure what to say back.

"Well, if this was 1850, I'd swoon right now," I say. "But since it's not, I'll do what *Cosmopolitan* would advise and kiss you back."

We kiss some more, and then I look at the clock and tell him I have to go to an Outing Club meeting. We're trying to get approval to get a canoeing trip to the Everglades for spring break next semester. He sighs.

"If you must," he says.

I pull on my sweater. "Thank you."

"For what?" he asks.

"For wanting me. For saying I'm beautiful."

"You are. I'll keep saying it until you see it, too." I know without a doubt that he will.

I leave his room buoyant and catch sight of myself in the glass of the door as I'm stepping out of the dorm, into the cold night air. My face is flushed, and my eyes stare back, bright and clear. *What if he's right?*

My worst fear is coming true, and I'm failing Calculus after the first exam. I tested out of the basic math requirements, but the college-level course is too much. Math has always been my worst subject, and I have to pass it because it's a requirement for premed.

Joe is also taking the same course, except with a different professor. He hardly ever studies. He is part of the reason I'm not doing well. There've been many nights that I can't pull myself away from him or other friends to go study. I always wondered in high school why other students couldn't just sit down and do their work, but I understand it now.

"How about you let me tutor you?" Joe asks. "I love math."

"Of course you do. You're more of a nerd than I am." I'm scared. If my GPA drops, I lose my scholarship, I will go home in shame and end up enrolling at the community college that will take anyone. If I'm lucky, I might land a job in a secretarial pool somewhere—if they still even have secretarial pools.

"No, really. It will be fun. We can study together."

And so it begins. He sits next to me at my little desk, looking over my shoulder as I do my homework. He watches me do the same problem three times, getting it wrong each time. The one difference between high school and college is that you can always get the answers out of the answer key. The important part is knowing how to get there. I wish I didn't have to know how it should come out so I could just get it wrong and move on.

"I'm stuck," I whine. "This doesn't make any sense at all. What is the point?" I throw my pencil down.

"Relax." He puts his hands on my shoulders and kneads for a few minutes, then sits next to me. Our legs touch. I can smell his aftershave.

"What do you know about constants?"

"Well, they don't change their value no matter what the variables in the equation do."

"Yes, and what do you know about them in relation to derivatives?

"Um…The derivative of any constant is always zero. So that's zero, right?"

"Correct." He kisses my neck. "And what is the next step?" he whispers into my earlobe.

"Apply the product rule?" I ask.

He pulls back.

"Almost. Think it through. You can do this."

I stare at the page. He runs one finger along my spine at my neck.

"Oh, no, the quotient rule! I need the quotient rule here!" I say.

I scribble furiously, and, miraculously, my answer matches the key. I circle and underline it. He pulls me to him and kisses me deeply. I start to unbutton his shirt. He puts his hands over mine to stop them.

"Nope, you have nineteen more problems to do, and then you have to read ahead so you're ready for lecture tomorrow."

"Come on! Let's fool around. I can finish later." I really don't want to keep doing math at this point.

"No way. I'm your tutor, and you have to finish before we leave these chairs. Come on. You can do this. If you fail out, we won't have any of this."

I can see his point. I relent and turn back to the book.

He comes back in close to me and points to the next problem. "This one is a bit different than the last one. Notice how the constants are grouped on the other side of the equation."

I can see and start scribbling. It makes sense, and the equation clicks into place. My God, the elegance when the numbers come together like this.

"Good, good," he says and runs his tongue around my ear.

I shiver, from that and from having my answer come out again to match the key. Both are exhilarating, but in completely different ways.

I wake up early on Thanksgiving morning, and it is still dark. I hear dishes clattering in the kitchen. I consider going back to sleep; I am still exhausted from exams, and the prospect of sleeping late on a cold November morning in my own warm bed is just about the best thing I can imagine. But I feel like getting up. It is my favorite holiday. I can always nap later after turkey.

I pull on sweatpants and thick socks and go downstairs to the kitchen. Mom is chopping celery.

I shuffle over to the counter and pour myself a cup of coffee, then rummage in the fridge for milk and maple syrup to make it palatable.

"You drink coffee now?" Mom asks.

"Yeah. Sometimes." The truth is that I have only had it a handful of times and don't really enjoy it, but the benefits of caffeine are worth its bitterness. These moments are happening more and more where instead of telling me what to do or giving advice, she just acknowledges something. It is thrilling to be treated like an adult in this way. But part of me wants her to knit her eyebrows together, tell me it will stunt my growth, and to please have a glass of milk instead. Things have changed. It feels strange to visit home. It feels like I'm a guest here, and then I will leave and return, leave and return, for the next four years. When I arrived home last week, everything seemed so special. I ran my hands over the bedspread in my room, looked at the childhood treasures collected over the years on the little shelves next to the bed. Seashells and colored rocks. Three ceramic mice. A stretching cat made out of glass. A lopsided vase made out of coils of clay, painted with a splatter of yellow glaze. A macramé star woven during camp arts and crafts and all the shelves of books. It still feels like I'm visiting the room of someone I used to know, an old friend who will be back any day. But I think that girl is gone.

I take a long sip of the coffee, add some more syrup, and eye my mother over the steaming cup.

"I thought I wouldn't see you for hours," she says.

"What are you doing?" I ask.

"Getting the turkey ready. It needs to be in by five if we're going to eat at two."

The caffeine starts to kick in. I love the feeling.

"How can I help?"

I get put to work chopping garlic. Soon, the kitchen is full of the smell of celery and onion cooking in a pan with butter. In the biggest wooden bowl in the house, I toss the two bags of stuffing together along with sausage and onions and celery. The hard bread crumbs turn moist and soft. Mom and I sneak little tastes of it, right out of the bowl. Mom talks out loud while she does everything. I ask questions about amounts and cooking times. I have never taken an interest in this part of the meal before; I have never been up early enough to see what happened in the darkness in kitchens around the country on Thanksgiving morning.

By the time the sky is turning pink, Mom is holding the oven door open, and I am sliding the dressed turkey into the oven.

"Now what?" I ask.

"Well, usually I go back to bed."

"Sounds good to me."

I crawl back under the covers, and it is still warm. I fall immediately back to sleep, and my next conscious sensations are the smell of roasting turkey and bright sun streaming in my windows. Mom and I meet for more coffee and toast and continue the cooking. I watch carefully how everything is prepared. I'm not sure why it's interesting to me other than it is the first time I see all the work that goes into the day. Carm helps peel potatoes and squash and polishes the silver. Jack gets home from hunting, happy to have gotten two pheasants. Jack's godparents and their daughters arrive from New Hampshire, and the day proceeds in the same way it has for as long as I can remember. I listen to Jack's godmother talk as she cooks. Her thick accent is like a continuous song and makes me wish I had more Norwegian blood in me than just a few drops.

Just as the November tin-gray sky darkens, there's a flurry of activity as Mom tries to get all the hot food to the table at once, and every burner on the stove has pots on it. Jack and his godfather carve the turkey, and we gather together. Mom says a blessing and then we sing, first in Norwegian, then in English.

For health and strength and daily bread we praise thy name, oh Lord.

There is one moment when the last note hangs in the air, and I have the feeling that everything I could possibly want or need, I have.

The Saturday after Thanksgiving, one of my new friends from college flies out with her dad from Boston in a little Cessna and lands at the airstrip in the next town over. Mom comes with me but declines the invite to go up. Instead, she stands at the side of the grass airstrip and waves wildly when we take off. I watch her become smaller and smaller in her turquoise down coat and white hat as we gain altitude. Through the microphone headset, I direct the pilot over the town common, and he buzzes low, then follows 32A to my house. We make two big loops, buzzing low, and Carm runs out into the yard to wave. The pilot tips his wings, and the world tilts. Everything goes flat. The fields and woods join together in enormous spans of unbroken green. Up high, the town looks like the town of my childhood. It is made of small country roads and white houses surrounded by wildness. I know there's a bigger world beyond its boundaries, but from up here, it seems like all there is.

The pilot banks west, and within minutes we are flying over the Quabbin Reservoir. It was built in the 1930s to provide water for Boston and five towns, and all the inhabitants had their land taken by eminent domain. Their houses were dismantled or moved, the cemeteries dug up, and everything was wiped out and flooded. It took five years to fill and 4.5 billion gallons of water.

Now, I can see stone walls moving through the young forests and disappearing into the water. From the air you can see their outlines in the shallows, and then they just disappear into the dark water. It sends a shiver up my spine to see it. A ghost town where thousands of lives were uprooted.

When I was little, Mom started a program in the elementary school to help get kids interested in local history and ecology. Each class would adopt an animal to study over the course of the year: white-tailed deer, beaver, fish, frogs, bald eagles. The study culminated with a field trip to the reservoir in the spring. One of the best years was going out with a famous tracker who would pick animal droppings off the ground with his bare hands and break open the poop pellets with a pocket knife to show what they ate. For nine-year-olds it was equally horrifying and fascinating.

I ask the pilot to head south and go by the big dam that holds back all that water. Again he buzzes low, and I point towards the visitor's building. It was near there, next to the water, that Dad proposed to Mom in 1968—before he was my dad and she was my mom. He packed a picnic, and they sat near the water, watching the waves in the sunlight. He produced a ring, and she said, "yes." As I know the story, they solidified the engagement by going to Sears to buy an iron. They were not living together at the time, but Mom had been ironing Dad's shirts and charging him a dime each, so the iron was their first purchase for their new life together.

After they were married, they moved to a little trailer in Gilbertville before they bought the Sessions Road home. It was astoundingly ugly and shabby, and over the years we watched it disintegrate and eventually fall into the Ware River and get washed away. When we drove by it, I would exclaim, "There, Mom! You used to live *there?*"

"It used to look better when we lived there. Well, a little better." Then she got a dreamy look in her eyes. "We were so happy there. It was our first home."

They were a thousand miles from their nearest family members, deciding to settle in this tiny town in the middle of nowhere. Two Midwesterners displaced to New England, but it suited them, and they made it their home and rooted down deep.

We get into my Volkswagen, and his big duffel bag barely fits in the back seat. There's no hope of it fitting in the tiny trunk. It's snowing hard now, and the flakes are enormous. I take it slow, and still the tires slide a few times down the hill into town. At the bus station, which is actually just a small office and an old dirt parking lot behind Main Street, people are standing in the snow with bags next to them. Almost everyone seems to be a college student waiting to go home for break. The bus isn't here yet. Joe already has his ticket; I drove him down last week so he could buy it early. I park on the edge of the lot and turn the heater up full blast.

I feel like crying.

We exchanged Christmas presents last night after our last exams were over. He gave me a book of paintings, but the best part was the inscription he wrote, taking up the full two blank pages at the front. He wrote out in detail all the things he loves about me in his uneven and slanted printing. The aftershave and the scarf I bought for him seem pale in comparison.

He leans across the car seat awkwardly to put his arm around me. We can barely see the outlines of the people standing in the parking lot through the big flakes falling steadily outside the windows.

He tucks a stray hair behind my ear.

"Are you OK?"

I nod. I'm afraid if I open my mouth I'll start crying.

"It's only four weeks," he says.

I nod again. It sounds like forever. This is so dumb. I don't know why I'm being such a girl right now.

"I'll call you," he says. "You have my number at home, right?"

I nod again. He wrote it down for me in an open notebook on my desk and again in tiny numbers at the bottom of the inscription in his gift.

One tear slides down my cheek. I hate myself for being so weak, for crying at the idea of not seeing him. He wipes it away with his glove.

"Don't start," he says quietly. "If you start crying, I might start, too, and I have to get on that bus with all those people."

That does it for me, and the floodgates open. He admits it so readily, his declarations of emotion and love. I haven't been able yet to say that I love him, even though he's said it many times. I've never felt this way about anybody, so I don't know what to call it. It is not love like I know it, the thing I feel for my family or my friends. This is something more and different, and I don't know how to name it. To call it love seems like lying. It is different.

We get out of the car and he hugs me hard and we kiss once more. There's a crowd of people queuing up to board. I realize it's the first time I've ever kissed him in public. I don't even like to hold hands with him when we're out. Public displays of affection make me uncomfortable.

"It's private," I explained to him, the first time I evaded one of his kisses on campus. "I don't want anyone to see something that's just for the two of us."

But now, with the impending separation, I kiss him without restraint. He holds me tight while people load suitcases around us and the snow falls, making all sounds muffled so it feels like we're alone.

He hugs me to him one more time and puts his mouth to my ear to whisper.

"The best thing about college so far is you. I'll miss you."

Suddenly I'm certain in a way I haven't been before.

"I love you!" I say.

He smiles wide and nods definitely, nonchalantly, as if he's agreeing with me, and climbs the bus steps.

"I know," he says. "Bye."

I stand there for a long time, watching the red taillights of the bus as it slides out of the parking lot, leaving deep tracks in the snow.

⟨——⟩

I drive home the next morning after the snow stops and has been cleared from the highways. I unpack in my childhood room, and it feels so strange to know it is a temporary homecoming. The fridge is packed with food. I can tell Mom has gone out and bought all my favorites and Jack's too. He got home three days before I did. The food extends out into the fridge in the shed. After eating in the dining hall, it's a marvel to have meals at odd hours, to cook in a kitchen instead of eating everything premade.

At least once a day, Mom says, "I just love having all my children under one roof!"

Soon, we can tell when she's about to say it and groan when it comes. She just laughs. "Well, I do! I miss you kids!"

I spend nights visiting friends who are also home for break. Allison is still in high school and updates us on people and teachers we know. She's gotten into art school as early decision and can't wait to go. It's been a hard year for her with all of us gone now, leaving her behind in that jungle. I divide my time between being at home, decorating the house and baking and cooking with Mom, and going out with friends. It is strange not to ask permission anymore when I go.

"Just tell me when you'll be home so I know when to expect you, or call if you're spending the night."

But I can't imagine wasting a night on a couch at a friend's when I can be at home in my own sunny bedroom and wake up to the smell of coffee and waffles. Jack, Carm, and I still gather for an hour in the morning and watch cartoons or *The Price Is Right* like it's a snow day. I didn't realize how much I missed them until we're together. Effortlessly, we fall into the same rhythm of exchanged jabs and laughter, private jokes and nicknames, our own sibling language developed over three childhoods' worth of years. They feel more like friends than brothers now. I can't tell if it's me who has changed or them. Or both.

I share my anxiety with Mom about maintaining the scholarship and about not being able to keep my grades high enough.

"First off," she says, "just do your absolute best, and don't worry about it. Secondly, if you should lose it while doing your best, don't worry. We'll make it work, and you won't have to leave school. We have some savings for you, and there's always loans. Just do your best."

I'm relieved when my fall semester grades come in the mail. I've met the GPA requirement for the scholarship, but just barely. Mom puts them on the fridge. Turns out chemistry, my chosen major, is actually my worst subject. I chose biochemistry/premed because it would be challenging, but I'm surprised at how hard it actually is. I'm leagues behind the other students and struggled through General Chemistry. Calculus is my highest grade. I get an A. When Mom sees the grades, she says they must have some great teachers at the college in order to make my worst subject my best. I blush uncontrollably.

Christmas Eve the four of us go to church as always. I wear the forest-green blazer Mom gave me for my birthday, and a long skirt. She teases me about the days when we had enormous fights over making me wear anything but pants. As usual, the church is packed with people. The ushers have put up folding chairs at the end of each aisle to accommodate the overflow. I only recognize half of the people; the rest come only to tonight's service and Easter. At the entrance we each take one candle with a paper ring attached from a big basket, and we find seats while waving and smiling at people we know. The service is shortened, and the sermon is an abbreviated version of the Christmas story. It is one of my favorites, right behind the Good Samaritan and Jonah and the Whale. I never get tired of hearing of Mary and Joseph traveling to the inn that has no room for them. The visit from the angel, a guiding star, and the wise men bearing gifts. Between segments of the story, the organ starts up and we sing. Charlotte pounds the keys to be heard above the voices, and the church walls seem to shake with the noise. When we sing "halleluiah" and "gloria," I like how each syllable is drawn out individually across the page in the hymnal. Carm fidgets with his candle and shaves wax off with his fingernail. By the end of the service, it resembles a chunky looking snake, and I smile at the pile of wax shavings at his feet.

Carm.

A year ago I would have been annoyed at this, but being away for so long I can't help but feel a swell of love for him. I have missed all of this: our neighbors and church friends, the little town common, my house, and especially these three people next to me whom I love beyond measure.

After the story of Christ's birth and all the hymns, the ushers walk to the front and light their candles from the two big ones in the middle of the evergreen wreath on the altar. They walk slowly down each side, lighting the candles held out for them at the end of each aisle. Pastor Alice, who replaced Pastor Ketchum, reminds us again from the pulpit to tip the unlit candle, not the lit one. The points of light spread, and when the ushers reach the back, they click the light switches off, and a hush falls over the church. We stand for a few minutes in silence and darkness with just the sound of faint rustling and breathing. Even the babies in the crowd seem to sense the reverence of the moment and are quiet.

Then, Charlotte starts up the first stanza of "Silent Night," and the congregation joins in.

Silent Night, Holy Night. All is calm, all is bright.
Round yon Virgin Mother and Child, Holy Infant so tender and mild.

After the first verse, I stop singing so I can just listen and look out at the faces of all the people, glowing and reverent in the candlelight. There is my mother, next to me, her eyes shining in the soft light. She sees me looking at her and squeezes my arm. I know exactly what she is thinking: "All my children here, home, in the same pew, together for Christmas. This is so great."

The song ends, and we stand in the glowing darkness for one moment more, then the ushers flip on the lights. The church hums with murmuring voices and the sound of breath being exhaled to blow out the candles. The smell of smoky wax fills the air. The moment is over.

It takes an hour to finally leave church because of all of the people to greet. When we get home we settle into the living room and each pick one gift to open. We drink tea and eggnog and eat the gingerbread I made yesterday. Mom turns the tree's lights to constant instead of blinking, which is the way she likes it. There is a fire in the woodstove, and its door is open so you can see the flames.

Soon, we go to bed and unlike the Christmases of childhood, I have no trouble falling asleep. In a half-sleep I hear rustling paper downstairs as Mom puts out the rest of the gifts, which will be signed in her hand-writing as "From Santa." We are too old, but still.

Christmas morning we all sleep late and joke about the time just a few years ago when new toys were worth getting up for at dawn. Mom makes cinnamon rolls and oysters and bacon. We lounge in our pajamas and open presents most of the day, taking our time, going one at a time, working our way through the pile under the tree. She has her continual cup of tea going, and I tease her about going senile every time I find it in the microwave, forgotten after a reheat. She's gone all out with the presents. There's a pile of brand new camping gear from L.L.Bean for me. New clothes. A small stereo for my dorm room. It feels like too much. All this abundance and comfort in one place all at once.

In three weeks it will be time to leave and go back to school, where there will be friends and Joe and classes and my own life, separate from all this. And then I will come home to this, again and again. In three days we will all fly to Oklahoma to visit Mom's sister and her family for New Year's. It will be more of the same there. Mom and Alice will embrace in the airport, embarrassing us all by their sobbing for joy at seeing each other again. The rest of us will hug each other hard and comment on how big the little cousins are getting. There will be big family meals around the tables, more gift exchanging and laughter. Being away made me see how precious it all is—how lucky I am to have a life like this. I think of the night before, of the faces in the candlelight and the quiet.

All is calm, all is bright.

Part III

Chapter One

We wait in the Family Room. It actually has a little plastic nameplate outside the door with "Family Room" written in white letters. It is quiet in here, and instead of being in a hallway like the other waiting rooms in the hospital, it has a door and deep armchairs. We are the only people here.

Hours later a nurse comes in. "Your mom is out of surgery. She's going up to intensive care now. The surgeon will be in to see you in a just a moment."

The day after Christmas, Mom wasn't feeling well. She attributed it to all the rich food and excitement. She still wasn't better three days later, and we canceled the trip to Oklahoma and she went to see the doctor. They ran some tests and found a blockage in her intestine that they were going to do a routine surgery to remove. She was supposed to be out three hours ago, and now Jack, Carm, and I are in the Family Room, still waiting.

The door opens, and a man appears in blue scrubs and says he is the surgeon. He starts speaking and then remembers he is still wearing his mask. He pulls it off, then pauses.

"It's cancer," he says.

My breath leaves my body. All motion and sound stop. He gives details of what he did and how he did his best to get it all and that's why it took so long, but I can't hear anything. I look down at the floor. There is a spot of blood on his left sneaker, bold red against the white leather. I feel dizzy. He leaves. The nurse comes back.

"Do you want to see your mom? Just a minute, though, OK?"

She leads us down the hallway and into a dimly lit, cool room. There are other patients there, and the nurse pulls the curtain around us. It is a flimsy piece of fabric around our family.

"I'll be back in two minutes," she says.

Mom is in a high bed with railings on each side. Tubes and wires are everywhere. She looks impossibly small in the bed, and an oxygen mask rests crooked on her face. We each reach in between the wires and tubes to find a part of her to hold on to. As soon as we are all positioned, the nurse is back.

"She needs to rest. She'll be awake in a few hours."

The nurse leads us back to the Family Room. Carm starts crying. I wish he wouldn't, because I don't know how much longer I can hold it in. Already I am pinching my upper arm as I hard as I can while I try to stave the hysteria I can feel rising out of my belly and chest.

"It's OK," I say. "It's OK. She looks like that because she just got out of surgery. Everyone who gets out of surgery looks like that." I'm not sure this is true, but it sounds convincing. I don't know if I am saying it more for him or me.

The kind nurse comes back in. I think of her as kind because she is the only other person here, and she looks calm.

"It was hard to see your mom like that, huh? Here, drink this." She hands Carm a paper cup of orange juice.

Carm's hands shake, and some of the juice spills over the sides. I help him hold the cup to his lips. Then I take a sip and hand it to Jack to finish. It is watery and tart. I forgot I could taste things. I don't know if she meant it for all of us, but we share it anyway. She asks if we want more, and we all shake our heads. Jack even mumbles a "No, thank you." She tells us to come out to the nursing station if we need anything, and she'll come get us when Mom is awake. I want to ask her to stay with us, just sit here and be someone calm, and maybe then I can hold in this feeling that my chest is going to burst open. But instead I watch her white clogs with the thick heels leave the room.

After she's gone, Carm leans into me, and I put my arms around him. Maybe I can hold it together if I'm doing it for him. Maybe. Over his shoulder I look at Jack, and our eyes lock. His eyes mirror the fear in mine.

How can this be happening? What are we going to do?

An hour later the nurse comes back and tells us to go home and come back in the morning. Mom is stable and doing well. On the long drive from Worcester, I try not to think about how empty the house is going to be with just the three of us in it. Jack pulls the car onto Sessions Road, and there are lights on in the house. The sight of Beth's blue Honda Civic in the driveway makes me inordinately happy.

I had forgotten. I had forgotten about the promise she made on her deck behind her little apartment. I had forgotten about the Fourth of July fireworks popping in the distance and her saying that if things didn't turn out well she would come. I thought they were the kinds of words that people say late at night that just fill the space but carry no weight. But she's here, cutting up a plate of apples and putting them on the table in front of us. She's here, asking for details. She's here, saying she can stay two days and asking how she can help.

Mom comes home from the hospital a week later and Beth comes to live with us part-time. Jack and I return to college to finish our semesters. In March, after a grueling chemotherapy and radiation schedule, Mom is feeling better and decides to throw a party for Jack's twenty-first birthday. She goes through her black address book and invites everyone. Relatives fly in from around the country. As a surprise she decides to buy Jack what he's always dreamed of, a brand new Ranger fishing boat, and presents it game-show style using the garage doors. When he chooses door number three and sees his boat, everyone cheers, and Mom cries. During the height of the planning, we tease her that she's nuts from the tumors in her head and the massive amounts of Demerol she's taking. But we all know the truth that she'd do something like this anyway, even without tumors and drugs.

In April, she insists that we all go to Disney World for winter break. She's feeling great, and we take turns pushing her in the wheelchair. We bypass all the lines for Thunder Mountain, and Carm runs the wheelchair up the ramps, making hairpin turns. Mom shrieks with laughter and says we could forget the ride, this is good enough. On the ride she throws her arms in the air and laughs. When the cart comes to a stop, her eyes are shining and she's breathless.

"Again!" she says. The attendant says she has to go through the line again. Mom takes off her hat to show her bald head and nods to the waiting wheelchair.

"Again," she repeats, fixing him in her gaze. The attendant shrugs and pulls the lever.

⟵⟶

I come home when I can. Beth comes and goes as needed during the week and is there every weekend. Friends come daily to help Mom get to her appointments, drive Carm home from soccer practice and band. When I'm home, I try to overdo it, making up for the time I'm not there, then realize that they're just fine without my help. There are people always available when I'm not there.

Mom pats my cheek. "We're fine, sweetie. Live your life at college. I love when you're home, but really, we're doing fine."

I sleep late, then clean things unnecessarily, reorganize the pantry and make Carm elaborate lunches for school when I'm there on weekdays. One weekend a church deacon drops off an enormous bouquet after a late spring snowstorm. He says, "It's from the vestibule from the funeral this morning. Thought you all might like it."

When he leaves, Mom stares stone-faced at it and mindlessly pokes at the stems with her finger. "I'm not fucking dead yet," she says.

I am horrified. Partly at the fact that this is the first time I've heard her use that word and partly at the word "yet."

In a flash she's outside tearing the bouquet to pieces and sticking the stems into the snow bank lining the walkway. She comes back in with the empty basket, and we admire her work from the window. I can't decide whether to keep being horrified or laugh at the dozens of flowers sticking up from the white peaks of snow.

"That's better," Mom says with a sigh.

These uncharacteristic outbursts have become more frequent. Maybe it's the Demerol or the residue of the tumor that was pressing somewhere in her brain. Maybe she's just plain angry and can't keep it in anymore.

"It looks nice, Mom," I say, my voice completely flat. "Really. Nice."

She gives me a smile where she shows all her teeth, and we collapse into laughter.

Mom has another surgery in June. I am so glad to be home from college for her hospital stay, and at the same time I wish I was still in my dorm, far away from all this. I take my favorite books to the hospital and read while she sleeps, or we watch daytime shows on the TV mounted on a big metal arm in the corner of the room. Usually there is a constant stream of visitors, but today it is quiet. It's a relief to be done with my freshman year and to be able to go back to reading what I want. I page through one of my favorites about canoeing. The prose reads like poetry. I keep turning to a certain passage that has soothing rhythm which talks about pine and granite, paddle and water, aster and primrose, tansy and yarrow, clover and pearly everlasting. I read for a while, the sounds of the wildflowers and the familiar words are calming. I lean forward in the chair and put my head down on the bed near Mom's hip. I am tired and confused at my own exhaustion. I do nothing during the day that requires any brain power or any physical strength besides driving to the hospital. I just don't understand it. How can a body feel this worn out for not having done anything? It is a tired deeper than anything I have ever felt. It is the kind of tired that can't be fixed by sleep or food or coffee, no matter how many cups I try to choke down.

Mom puts her hand on my head, and it's warm through my hair. She always has warm hands. I want to cry badly but can't. It doesn't seem like the right time when anybody could walk into the room: a nurse with some clipboard or a visitor or an orderly. More and more this is happening. The tears seem to get stuck inside me somewhere between my throat and chest. It is a hard, black ball wound tighter and more stuck, and then everything goes flat and I feel nothing. Mom strokes my head and I fall asleep, one hand still on the book about blue water and wildflowers.

Mom insists we go to Wisconsin as a family for a few weeks. She can't walk for long distances, and we take the wheelchair with us. I push her in it, and Jack and Carm carry the luggage through the endless terminals. Mom pays the under-twenty-five driver surcharge so Jack can drive the rental car. It is surprising when we walk in the cabin door to the smell of pine wood and mothballs, and I feel the same surge of summer excitement. Maybe the two weeks here will be good.

I get Mom settled in the downstairs back bedroom since she can't do the stairs. For some reason this undoes me, and I pretend to have to go upstairs to look for something. I go to the loft she and I usually shared and stare out at the water for a long time. I lie for hours in the hammock and look up at my favorite birches. It is hard to imagine that it was only a year ago when I was in this same spot thinking about college, about how everything was working out, how I had put all the sadness behind me. A year ago, I had the sweet anticipation of not knowing what was going to happen, but I knew it was going to be good. The certainty and courage of that girl seems like another person entirely. Me, this body, is afraid all the time now.

I take the rickety three-speed into town to deliver and pick up the mail. I pedal fast there and lean the bike against the post office's brick wall. Sometimes I get an ice cream at the Soda Grill and then put the mail into the basket of the bike and pedal home slowly, holding the cone with one hand. At the cabin, I take my letter to my room and open it in private. Joe is working full time as a dishwasher at a resort, but he manages to send something every day. Even if it is just a page ripped out of his notebook with "I love you" scrawled big across the page, he always sends something. I read his letter fast once, then twice more, slowly. Then, I put one of his mix tapes into the cassette player and spend an hour sitting in one of the deck chairs overlooking the lake, writing back to him.

I haven't been a serious letter writer in years. The habit dwindled to a few exchanges a year when my camp friends and I grew up. But now, I find myself again living in a world where the process of writing things out in letters keeps me tethered in a world that feels like it is disintegrating. Our time here is quiet and uneventful, but I seem to be able to fill up pages and pages to Joe. I write about helping Mom to bed each night. I write about how I'm not very good at it, taking trip after trip from bedroom to bathroom to kitchen, getting what she needs. I can never seem to remember to have everything in the same place: medication, book, fuzzy socks, water, reading glasses. Then, it's just the two of us, and we have conversations about life and love. In my letters I write about how she said that loving my dad had the feeling that the entire world could fall apart around them and they might not even notice, or care. I write about the way the lake looks in the morning, full of sparkle and sunlight, and how the loons call to each other late into the night. I write about getting Mom down to the dock, just once, to see the water-ski show. We walked very slowly down the hill, she holding my arm, Carm behind us, pushing the wheelchair. After a short time, she was ready to go in, and it took both of us to push the chair up the bumpy path to the house. She was too weak to make the climb back up. I write about how I make foul-smelling Essiac healing tea every morning and half a piece of dry toast. She hardly eats anything but comes to the table with the three of us every evening and pushes food around her plate. Carm gets us in stitches at night with his wicked imitations, or we get each other going remembering funny events of years past. But just under the surface, there is a somberness that we don't speak of. We all know this is most likely our last summer with her.

I ache for Joe, for someone I can be a wreck with. After writing to him, I take the canoe out on the lake and pull into the shallows on the north side where Jack fishes for bass. There are just a few houses on this side, and I put the paddle down and lie down on the bottom of the Grumman. The aluminum is hot, and it almost burns the back of my legs. I put one arm behind my head and look up at the sky, just floating. From this angle, all I can see is the open sky straight above. All around me, the sides of the boat hold me in, its sturdy metal rivets running up the seams. It calms me down, lying in the boat like this when it feels like I am about to come undone. All of the feelings inside are a tangled mess of springs ready to uncoil if I don't check them constantly. If I let them, they will uncoil and consume me. I need to keep them where they are. If I let them out, there will be no turning back, and I'll be consumed by sadness and anger and other emotions so large and complicated I don't know their names.

Beth meets us at the airport. She moved in permanently while we were away and put all the stuff from her apartment in storage in the upstairs of our barn. It is strange to have someone who we've really only known a year becoming part of our family. I don't think any of the relatives understand it. I've heard Mom on the phone trying to explain it. But it seems right. We joke sometimes that we're adopting her. But really, she's adopting us. Or maybe we're adopting each other. I don't know.

The old office with its paisley green wallpaper and dirty carpet is replaced by cream-white painted trim and gauze curtains and a double bed with a handmade bedspread. There're six pillows on the bed and ornate mirrors on the walls, just like in her old apartment, so it looks like something from the pages of a Pottery Barn catalog. We compliment her on it, marveling at the transformation. She seems pleased.

"I was so nervous I'd do something you all would hate. It took me almost the full two weeks to find the trim color. I'm not sure it's right."

"No," we assure her. "No, this is just right."

"Mom, I'm thinking of not going back to school in a few weeks. It seems to make more sense for me to take a semester off."

Jack had already planned to do this and was taking some classes at the local university instead of going back to Boston. I couldn't imagine going back to New York—to dorm rooms and midterms, having to talk to people—in the midst of all of this. It was hard getting the energy to keep myself clothed and fed every day.

She almost yells her reply.

"No way! You are not going to put your life on hold for me. You're going back to school. You can come home on weekends. End of discussion." She waves her hand dismissively. It is unlike her to talk like this, so loud and direct. I wonder if it is the medications.

"There's nothing here for you. Beth has Carm covered, and Jack's here, too. Go, go live your life."

I want to scream. *I can't! I can't go back to school when my life here is falling apart.* But the truth is even deeper than that. She is so central to my life that I cannot imagine my world without her. I cannot imagine living a life that does not include her.

She must see the hurt on my face.

"Honey, come here." She pats the side of the bed. I sit down.

"I love that you want to stay here and help. But what would be the most help to me right now, what would bring me the most happiness, is if I knew you were back at that college, studying and being with friends and doing what you love."

"But I love *you.*"

"I know you do. And I love you. Which is why you can't stay here. I'm not going to be here forever. I don't know how much time I have. And when I'm gone, you'll need to have something other than what's here to sustain you. Trust me on this one. I'm your mother and I know. College is the right place for you to be now. I'll call you when I need you. I promise."

She has said it. This is the first time we've talked about the future without her in such certain terms.

"You're going to be fine," she adds. "My job, my mission in my life, was to raise you kids and be your mother. I've done that, and you'll be fine."

My eyes well and overflow. I shake my head. *How can she say that? Not fine. Not fine at all.* She reaches up and touches my cheek, then guides my head to her shoulder. She holds me there and kisses the top of my head and smoothes down my hair. I want to rest in her certainty like I'm resting on her shoulder.

I drive away a week later, the Volkswagen packed full. I cry all the way to the Mass Pike and even pull the car over in Ware, clutching the steering wheel in indecision, wondering if I should turn around. I have no idea what is right. I keep going by telling myself this is what she was asking of me. And I will do whatever she asks.

I come home every weekend. On my second weekend home, Mom stands at the bottom of the stairs, holding on to her oxygen tank. She has been getting weaker.

"I don't know if I can do this," she says. "Get your brother."

Without a word Jack comes and gently picks her up and goes up slowly, one step at a time. She looks like a child in his arms, impossibly small, holding on around his neck, her knees draped over his other arm. I ache for Jack for having to feel the smallness of her against him like that, for having to carry her in the same way she carried him as a little boy.

At the top of the stairs in the hallway, he pauses, and she says, "I can make it from here."

"No, I'll take you the full way," he says.

We follow them into the bedroom. A somber procession. Jack carrying Mom. Me carrying the oxygen tank. Beth trailing with a tray of medication and a glass of water. Carm behind her, instinctively knowing it is a time to stick together.

Within days the hospital bed comes for a downstairs room, and the nightly ritual ends. The nurses show up not long after that.

Months earlier Mom had been insistent that hospice would be there when it was time. Twenty-four hours of someone else besides us taking care of her failing body. I remember her determined expression that day around the kitchen table when we were planning.

"Care about me, not for me. That's the way it needs to be."

I make an appointment with the Dean's office that week, and she is able to see me. I introduce myself, and when she asks what I need, I say, "I have a family situation, and I need to leave school for a while."

"How long do you think you'll be gone?" she asks. I am grateful that she doesn't ask why.

"Two weeks. Maybe three."

"Please talk to all your professors about making up the work; I'll also have the secretary send a formal memo to all of them, notifying them you'll be gone."

"Thank you," I say. I am grateful for her perfunctory manner. "I have another question—I'm here on the Abraham Kellogg scholarship. If it becomes necessary for me to take the semester off, can I do that and still keep the scholarship?"

"I'll have to check. Wait here."

She leaves and returns a few minutes later.

"I'm sorry. I checked and the terms of the scholarship are very clear. You have to finish all twelve semesters sequentially. There are no circumstances in which you can take time off."

I stand up. It doesn't matter very much to me at the moment.

"Thank you. Thank you for looking that up."

We shake hands again, and as I am leaving, I hear her voice behind me.

"Good luck with your situation." *Luck won't even begin to cover it*, I think.

Joe watches me pack. I'm randomly shoving things into my big duffel bag. He helps me strip the sheets off the bed. I wonder if I should take my quilt with me or not.

"Do you know when you'll be back?" he asks.

I know it's not fair, but I'm angry at him and my voice has an edge.

"Joe, I don't even know if I'll be back. At all."

I sink down onto the bare mattress, and he sits across from me in the desk chair.

"Listen, things are going to get bad here. They are going to get bad with me. I am going to become more of a wreck than I am now. I think it's time for us to split up. I have nothing to give you. I won't even be here, for Chrissake. I'm a horrible girlfriend now, and it's only going to get worse. You could do better—should do better. Be a normal person, and don't get sucked into all this."

"Stop. Just stop." He holds up a hand. "You can't get rid of me. Call me whatever you want: boyfriend, friend, ex. I don't care. I'm still going to be in your life to help you no matter what you say." To emphasize the point, he stands and zips the duffel and hefts it over his shoulder. "Let's take a load out to the car."

I pick up my other two bags and follow his back out the door, down the stairwell. I don't have the energy to argue. I'll be away. It doesn't matter. We take one more trip so I can get more books and my backpack. I remember right after we started going out I once put my hands on his shoulders when we were leaving class and he was in front of me.

"God, I love when you do that," he had said. "I don't know why, but I just love it."

"It's because it is all massive amounts of public affection you get," I said. "I warned you I'd be terrible at this girlfriend stuff."

He had smiled and said, "You're not that bad."

Now, I manage to free one hand so I can press on one of his shoulders going down the stairs. He doesn't try to kiss me in the parking lot, just busies himself getting the bags loaded. He tries to give me a long hug, but I push him away and get in the car. He stands in the parking lot, getting smaller, and he's still standing there when I turn onto the street.

It's my favorite part of the drive. Heading away from Oneonta, Route 88 rises and falls dramatically about halfway to Albany. I'm driving east, so the sun is setting behind me. The leaves are turning, not yet peaked, but just starting. I adjust my mirrors so I can glance at the colors exploding in the sky behind me as I drive. I've managed not to think too much or feel, and I concentrate instead on the feel of the steering wheel in my hands and steady click of the odometer. The gap in the roof of the Volkswagen is whistling again, so I reach into the duffel bag behind the seat and stuff a sock into the hole to muffle it and turn up the radio.

A flock of geese, hundreds of them, appear and then fly over headed southwest into the colored sky. In that moment I realize how incredibly, startlingly beautiful it all is. The surprise of it lets the thought break through that I've been trying to keep away.

This is the last time I will take this road with her still living. This is the before part. Everything following right now will be the after part.

I pull the car over to the side of the highway. My hands are shaking, then pounding the steering wheel. I'm glad I'm in the car alone on a mostly empty highway. I put my face in my hands but don't even try to stifle the sobs. It is a long time before I can drive again.

Chapter Two

M om is sitting at the kitchen table with a legal pad and folders in front of her. She's wearing her turquoise fleece hat over her bald head, and it is lopsided over one ear. Everything she wears now looks two sizes too big. She hasn't been out of bed in two days, so this, her getting up and putting on a lopsided hat, is an event. Jack, Carm, Beth, and I sit around the table, looking at her expectantly. She reaches up and adjusts the oxygen tube fitted to her nose, then reaches down to the tank and turns up the flow.

"OK," she says, her voice breathy as she presses both her hands into the stack of papers in front of her. "We need to do this."

She pulls out page after page, points to it, and says what it is. There's life insurance. Account numbers. Health insurance forms. Bank statements. Birth certificates.

"My health insurance has covered everything," she says. "But there will be some hospice bills. The life insurance and savings will be enough to get you through a few years."

She holds up a tiny manila envelope with the number "15" written in bold numerals. "Here's the key to the safety deposit box at Country Bank, the one across from Big Y, not the one on Main Street. In it, you'll find the deed to the house. Borrow against it if you need to."

She opens the thickest folder at the bottom of the stack.

"This is my new will." She turns her head to look directly at Jack and pushes the papers towards him. "You're twenty-one now, so you can be executor and legal guardian for Carm."

Her head turns to the other side. "Carm, you want this, right? You want to stay here and live with Beth like we talked about?"

Carm nods quickly.

"Here's a form from the high school that will give Beth the ability to sign parental consent forms, too."

Mom hands the pen to Beth first, who signs, then hands the pen across the table to Jack. I read upside-down the form in front of him that has Carm's name and birth date at the top. Jack swallows and the muscle at his jaw squares. He uncaps the pen and signs on the two lines. When he puts the cap back on the pen, I feel a pang and I can't tell if it's because I want to sign to be Carm's guardian too, or if it's because I want someone at the table to sign to be mine.

"Good," Mom says. "That's that." She slides two yellow legal sheets across the table to nobody in particular. They are covered with scribbled writing.

"These are notes for my service," she says. "At the reception I don't want any food. Just angel food cake, maybe with some fruit..." Her voice trails off.

"I think I need to lie down now."

⟨────⟩

People stop by. They say they are coming just to check in, but I know they are coming to say good-bye. There are people from the church, bell choir, teachers and colleagues, Dad's old friends, neighbors, and people Mom served with on dozens of committees. At first there is a constant stream of people and then just a trickle. I'm grateful for the quiet. At least one visitor comes each night and brings dinner. Some come inside, others just leave a basket on the milk box next to the shed door. People put flowers and stones and colorful cloth napkins in the basket or box along with dinner. Our neighbor, Doug, leaves fresh cuttings of flowers from his garden on the doorstep some mornings, a pile of color on the gray stones. I marvel at their efforts at bringing beauty to us.

Sometimes one of us sits with the visitors, but usually we just get them settled, straighten her sheets, and then leave the room.

One of her close friends, Pam, drops by, and Mom becomes lucid briefly. When it is time to go Mom, becomes agitated.

"Don't go! Don't go!" She clutches Pam's arm. "If you go I'll die. I'll swear I'll die."

I hear the yelling and come in. Pam sits on the bed and rests a hand on her head.

"Gwen, it's all right. I have to go to work now."

Mom is screaming now. "Don't you dare go! Don't you leave me!"

I follow Pam outside to apologize and then realize I don't know what to say.

"She's on a lot of medication," I say. "Thank you so much for coming."

The polite words roll out of my mouth on their own accord, an easy standby of what to say when there are no words.

The scene repeats itself the next day with Mom's friend, Liz.

This time, I go outside to get some air. I have heard that expression many times and seen it acted out in movies by people who had just had some sort of shock or revelation. But I have never actually had the experience of needing air. I understand what it means now. It means that the room closes in, and it feels like there is no oxygen left. I have to get to a place without walls or people. I bolt from the room and go out to the back porch and sit on the stone steps overlooking the field. I gulp in big breaths.

Liz comes out and sits down next to me. She puts a hand on my shoulder. I expect her to say something, but she just sits, her warm hand on my back, both of us gazing ahead. The pool looks like hell. The surface is completely covered in leaves, and the water looks green. Huge tufts of weeds grow up between the patio bricks. I am embarrassed that we aren't taking care of it.

How can we? How can we keep taking care of this big house where something always is broken or breaking? How can we keep going as a family? How can this be happening again? I thought that tragedy was doled out to people in equal portions. If not, it should be.

Liz squeezes my shoulder and stands up. I had forgotten she was there. The feeling of her hand brings me back, and I am startled to realize the colors are turning and the air is clear and dry, still warm with a hint of summer. The wild grapes are beginning to ripen and, although they are barely noticeable, in the air here. They are sweet in the front of the house. Still, none of it seems good or right. I can't appreciate any of it because it is so incongruous with the terror I feel inside. It can't decide what scares me more—what is happening in the house behind me right now or what will happen afterward and in the years ahead.

I go back in the room, and Mom is conscious and agitated. She twists the sheets and works at the thin cotton blanket in her hands, and her eyes dart around the room. She's saying random words but not making any sense. She seems to be talking to someone.

"Mom, who are you talking to?" I ask, smoothing her blankets.

"My mother. My mother is here. Can you see her?"

"No, I can't. She's not here, Mom."

"Well, she's here. Over there in that corner. She's here."

I look again in the corner near the china cabinet.

"She says it's time to come home. Is it time? Is it time now?"

Her brown eyes are wild with fear, and the worry lines are deep. I put my hand on her head. It feels like Carm's head when he had that buzz cut years ago, short and prickly. I hate when the drugs or the tumor or whatever it is in her take over like this.

"It's OK. Shhh."

I use my thumb to smooth the worry lines between her eyes. They used to appear when she was paying bills or thinking about something really hard. Now, she is afraid, and here are the lines again. I'm afraid too, afraid at her agitation and her being out of her mind. I'm afraid that she's seeing visions of my dead grandmother. I'm afraid all the time now, and it's hard to calm someone when you're afraid yourself. I push the feeling down and concentrate on smoothing the worry lines on her forehead.

"You're OK. Rest now."

I sit up on the bed so I can get my arm around her and ease her back on the pillows.

"I'll sit with you…and Grandma," I pause, not sure how to continue. "She can sit here too. We'll stay with you."

I'm not sure if this is the right thing to do, to lie to her when she's in this state. But the truth is I will say anything and do anything not to see her afraid. So I say it and sit next to her and try to smooth the lines on her forehead.

I turn my head. I didn't know the human body could produce something that color. The liquid Mom is gagging into the basin looks like charcoal water.

"See! See!" she says, pointing at it with her thin hand. "That's the cancer coming out me. God is healing me."

It isn't. I had asked the nurse the last time this happened, and she said, no, it was just stomach bile. But Mom's eyes are so innocent, and I want to believe her so badly. Again, I have to remind myself that it is the morphine or maybe the tumor in her brain pressing on something. I open my mouth to correct her.

No, I want to say. *It's not God, and you're not getting better. It's worse.* All day I've been angry and just barely holding it in.

Her eyes stop me from speaking. They are so hopeful and earnest. At this moment she looks how I imagine she looked like she did as a five-year-old girl.

"OK, Mom," I say, putting one hand on her head. The short hairs prickle my palm, and I rub her head. It seems to calm her.

"Lie back for me." I press her shoulder with my other hand, and she eases back onto the pillows. Then, I press the button on the morphine pump at her waist. It beeps once. Her face relaxes. I stroke her forehead.

When she is asleep, I dump the contents of the basin into the toilet in the downstairs bathroom and flush twice. I watch the black charcoal water swirl down and feel sick myself. God is not healing her, but she still believes right down to her core. I cannot understand her unwavering faith. All of the evidence points to the opposite—that God abandoned her and us nine months ago when this all started.

I rinse the basin, then sit on the edge of the tub and fold my hands to pray.

"God, I don't know why I'm saying this, and I don't know if you even exist. But now is your chance. You're letting someone who believes in you fully and completely go through something terrible. Help her, please. If you do, I'll believe in you. I'll do anything you want. Anything. Amen."

It isn't eloquent, but it is the best I can do. Praying this year has become increasingly difficult to the point that I rarely do it anymore. It seems so useless. I think of the irony of sitting here, praying to God, in the same place I used to talk to Mimi, my imaginary friend who lived behind the paisley shower curtain. I hope there is a difference between talking to an imaginary friend and God, but maybe there's none at all.

It is another spectacular fall day. I have been forcing a focused calm for the past few days, just keeping the anger out of reach. It is the brilliance of the morning that puts me over the edge into rage. The world keeps going, and my mother is dying. I want everyone to stop and acknowledge that fact with me.

Weep and rage with me. Stop your stupid little lives, and realize that in a rented hospital bed in the room where my family has celebrated Christmases, Thanksgivings, and birthday parties, the person I love the most is in pain and is dying. How dare the sun shine and the wind blow when this is happening?

I make it through breakfast. I make it through a load of laundry and a rerun of *Three's Company*. And then I find myself in the barn with a piece of metal pipe in my hands. It feels good, cold and steely. Holding it in one hand, I tap one of the center posts, a sturdy six-by-six. Then I wrap both hands around the pipe and hit the post again. I feel the crack of the metal against wood in my hands. It feels good. I start swinging it like a bat. I hit the post, and my tears start to come. Again and again I hit it until small dents start to form in the corners of the post. I think about God.

Either God is all powerful and lets this happen. Or, he can't do shit and is useless to help. Both scenarios leave me baffled and angry.

I don't need him. Don't want him. Miracles. Bullshit. Maybe miracles happened in Biblical times, or maybe it is just a bunch of stories the fucking disciples made up to spread the blasphemy of some fucking eternal being that actually gives two shits. I can't believe what lies I have believed in.

I strike the post, rhythmically at first, then with more force.

What kind of God leaves someone so good, so loyal and faithful, to puke stomach bile into a little plastic basin and still declare that she is in the process of being healed by him? I don't know who I am more angry at: that fucking thing I call God or my mother for believing in all that bullshit. Clearly prayer isn't working. Clearly her life-long faith isn't working. Clearly we all had been abandoned years ago, but just never knew it until now. We have already done this. We have already paid enough. Death came to us already in this same form and took my father. Not by a quick heart attack or accident or aneurism, but cancer. Fuck God.

With each hit, the pipe stings my hands. I don't care. I hate that beam. I hate the world. I want to wreck something. It needs sound.

"Fuck. Shit. Goddamn it. Fucking beam!" I yell.

Over and over I swing at the beam. I take little dents of wood out of the corners of it. It stands there, solid and unmoving. Its solidness shoots back into my hands. I swing harder and faster. My hands are on fire. I can't stop it. Snot and tears are streaming down my face, and my words turn into one long scream of profanity.

"Fuck-shit-fuck-goddamnit-to-hell-cancer-fucking-cancer-it's-fucking-not-fair."

Fucking not fair.

That is it. Again. It is not fucking fair.

I crumple to the floor, spent, and drop the pipe on the concrete. It clatters and rolls into a corner.

My hands are cold and bruised from gripping the pipe. I stretch my legs out in front of me and run a sleeve over my hot face. I have nothing left. I can't even cry anymore. After a long time, I get up. Even though nobody saw me, I feel embarrassed. What was that? Who was that? I don't lose my shit like that. Ever.

My legs feel weak when I stand to examine the beam. It is pocked and dented but otherwise fine. I leave the pipe where it is and go back into the house to splash water on my face and change my shirt.

Two days later, a heavy boxing bag is hanging from the beam, attached by a thick chain. Next to it is the old Louisville slugger wooden bat, the one we each used going through Little League.

I go into the kitchen, and Beth is chopping peppers.

"Beth, did you buy that boxing bag?"

"Yeah, Jack helped me hang it. It's pretty heavy. I thought it would work better than destroying the garage." She doesn't look up from the peppers. I wonder if she had heard me out there a few days ago and saw the dents in the post. I feel a wave of embarrassment.

"Don't worry," she says. "We could probably all use it. Could you pass me that platter?"

I make up errands to get out of the house. I go to Big Y and buy two cans of cat food even though there are two dozen cans in the pantry at home. I decide it is good to see people continuing like everything is normal: running errands, buying carts of groceries, dealing with screaming children. We are in a state of suspension where there is no going backward and going forward seems unimaginable. Time is standing still for me. Going out into the world reminds me that it is going on for others and maybe, someday, it will go on for me, too. I go and get the mail and drive around the common over and over until I'm certain there are no cars I recognize parked outside before I go in. I don't want to answer the question about how Mom is doing. If I were honest instead of polite, I would say, "She is scared, in pain, peaceful when the morphine is high enough." Or maybe just, "She's dying."

Mom's sister, Alice, comes from Oklahoma to be with us, and I give her my room. At night, I sleep in Jack's room, back in the bunk bed although now that we're older I've been relegated to the top bunk.

The ladder hurts my bare feet when I climb. Most nights I just take off my shoes and sleep in my clothes. Getting in pajamas and brushing my teeth seems to take too much energy. With a rueful smile one night, I remember that Dad would be disappointed that I'm not completing my "bathroom jobs." None of us can bear the thought of using Mom's room, so it sits empty.

Mom is conscious less and less of the time. Her cheeks are sunken back into her face. If she was not my mother, she would scare me. But I can still see her deep inside that face, behind the sharp angles of bone and skin, beyond the bald head. It's a face I know almost as well as my own. The phone doesn't ring, and sometimes I walk by and realize that someone has taken it off the hook. I don't bother to put it back. I have no words for anyone.

I'm glad Mom insisted that there be a nurse here around the clock, and now I see how smart that is. It feels like there is someone in the house who knows what to do—who is in charge, at least of the health-related parts. Sometimes I ask the nurse if she'll go and have a short walk or a cup of tea. She seems glad to. I sit next to Mom and talk in a low voice. The words I am saying are only meant for her. I lay my head down on the bed and remember back in the spring when I did that and she stroked my head. It seems like lifetimes ago.

Kathy, the hospice nurse who was here when Dad was sick, comes a few times a week now. She doesn't make us sandwiches anymore, but just having her in the house makes all of us feel better.

I try to keep remembering Kathy's words. "It's important that you say the things you think you need to. This is your time to say good-bye. Use it. She needs to hear the things you need to say as much as you need to say them even though she's not conscious."

Finally, after a few days and piles of words, I run out. No matter how much I talk, I realize there will be volumes left unsaid. I am preparing for a lifetime of the unsaid. I start ending our one-sided talks with the words that almost stop my heart the first time I say them, only managing a whisper.

"You can go, Mom."

I am awakened by Jack standing at the foot of the bunk bed, gently pushing my ankle from side to side. It's still dark out. I forget where I am and feel like I might have been asleep for days, but I squint at the glowing clock numbers and realize it's only been a few hours.

"It's time. Come downstairs. The nurse says it's time."

Time for what, I almost ask, still asleep and disoriented. But then I see his face, level with mine in the dull light from the hall.

It is time. If I had asked, I doubt he would have been able to say it. I could not have said it myself.

She's going. She's dying. Now.

I climb out of the bunk, and the ladder pinches my feet and me awake. It feels like floating. Everyone is already there. Beth and Alice, Jack and Carm, and one seat left for me.

Her breathing is labored. I take her hand. We all find a hand or arm or foot to touch.. It reminds me of that day in the hospital after Christmas when she first got out of surgery: all of us standing around her, trying to find something to hold on to. That seems like years and lifetimes ago. I am not sure what I expected, but it is not this. It all seems so quiet. In moments my world will flip on its axis. This will be the time that will mark the before and after. A few more breaths, irregular and choppy. And then she goes still.

"She's gone," Alice says quietly.

It is not loud or terrible as I thought. It is colorless and quiet and brief.

At that moment I feel something open and release. For an instant everything inside me goes still. It's as if the structure of the walls of the house have gone transparent. They become completely permeable. I feel the trees outside and the fall air and the land stretching out for miles. I feel the night sky as if there is no roof. It doesn't make any sense, but I feel the full expanse of the blackness and stars above and around me.

Then it is over.

The house becomes solid again. I feel the walls and the roof and the room close in around us and hold us. Then the stillness inside is replaced by an endless emptiness.

I wander around the house and think how strange for all of us to be up so late and to have the pastor in our house. I wonder if this is a normal day for her—to be with a family in the darkest hour in the middle of the night. Maybe it's not strange at all, and she doesn't feel anything anymore after doing this for years.

"You want to go out to the barn?" Carm asks.

Jack and I nod, and we follow him. He switches on the lights as we walk and turns on the overhead hanging above the Ping-Pong table. He picks up a ball and starts bouncing it on the table. Jack goes to the other end of the table, and soon they are batting the ball back and forth, not really playing, just bouncing it across the net over and over. I sit down on an overturned bucket and watch.

When Carm is getting a ball that rolled under the Cadillac, Jack hands the paddle to me, and I switch in. We keep doing this, the three of us, switching in and out of the game, silently handing off our paddle and moving to the overturned bucket when we've had enough.

It's still dark, but it seems like we've been outside for hours when Carm puts down his paddle and says, "I'm tired."

We move slowly back to the house through the shed, and Jack turns off the lights behind us. Beth meets us at the door.

"They are going to be here soon. The nurse called them," she says.

And by "them" I know she means the men who come in middle of the night in a hearse to do this sort of thing. I do not want to be here when they come. I do not want to see her carried out. We follow Carm upstairs to his room, and he gets into bed with his clothes on and pulls the comforter to his chin. I want to do something tender for him, to smooth the hair back on his face or kiss his forehead. But he's fifteen, and I'm afraid that something like that will crack open whatever it is that is holding me together. Instead I squeeze his shoulder, turn off the light, and slide down to the floor where Jack is sitting, our backs against the bed.

We sit in the darkness and listen to Carm breathe.

Minutes or hours pass then I hear the crunch of car tires on gravel and see a swath of headlights in the driveway. Carm turns over in his sleep. I hear low voices, the sound of furniture moving, then the side storm door squeaks open. A car door opens and shuts. A motor starts, and the street is illuminated again by the swath of headlights. Moments later I see the black hearse crest the hill into the circle of streetlamp light, and then it slides out of view.

Everything in the house goes silent.

I look over at Jack.

Even in the darkness I can see a hollowness in his face. It is the same look I see on the faces of refugees on TV, and I think my own face must look like that, too.

"Jack?" I whisper.

"Yeah," he whispers back.

"Are we gonna be OK?"

He doesn't turn his head, and I'm not sure he heard me. But then slowly, he nods twice, staring straight ahead.

I move my leg two inches so our knees touch, but just barely.

At some point before dawn, we stand and I pull the covers to Carm's shoulder. He's grinding his teeth. Jack and I fall into our beds, and I wonder if I will have trouble sleeping, but before the thought is through my mind, I fall into a dark and dreamless hole. When I open my eyes, there's sun streaming through the skylight. I can't remember where I am. I forget I am in the top bunk in Jack's room and why I am here. And then I remember.

I climb out of the bunk bed, still in my clothes from the day before. Two days before? It doesn't matter, and I don't care. I go to the room with the hospital bed and check, and the bed is made, the sheets flat and white. It still smells like medicine and antiseptic, but it is empty.

All of us wander around the house. We avoid each other's eyes. We put food in front of ourselves that someone has brought. My brain says it is delicious and homemade, but I can't seem to taste it. I don't feel hungry, but I don't feel full either. I eat until everything on the plate is gone and decide that is enough. We sit together and stare at the TV but don't really watch it. We take turns taking phone calls from relatives and friends that leave us so wrecked that eventually Beth yanks the phone cords out of the wall. The silence is good but makes us more restless. By early afternoon we all end up in the barn. The September sun hurts my eyes. It is so bright. The barn is dark and cool. We start putting things away—putting things in order.

This is a task we can do. Sweep the floor. Throw trash away. Put the hammers and screwdrivers and random nuts and bolts in their places. Organize the workbench. Put the baseball gloves and Wiffle bat on the yellow shelves and the rakes into their wooden holders on the barn wall.

It takes most of the rest of the day, especially at the speed we are all moving. I pick up a single screwdriver, walk it over to the workbench, and then stand there for a few minutes staring out the window, holding it, wondering what to do next with it. Eventually I remember that I am here to put it away, and I place it in the correct drawer and wander off to pick up something else. Jack and Carm move at similar speeds.

But we do it. It gets us through the day. We have a task. We are together. We are taking care of our home. As darkness falls, we look over our work. It looks good. I wonder what we should do next. I wish there was another barn to clean tomorrow. And another one after that. Standing in the darkness in the driveway, looking in at the yellow light bathing the clean and organized space, it seems like doing this over and over again is the best way to keep going.

I know that today is our brief reprieve and calm before the storm. Soon, there will be a flood of relatives and friends coming in. A memorial service. A burial. There will be a face to put on; that is how I think of it—a face. The face shows strength. The face shows that I am fine, we are fine, everything is fine. I don't know how to fall apart even if I wanted to. But I do know what to do when things are hard or sad and that is to be "strong" and to be "good." We made a plan as a family, and we are going to try to see it through, no matter what. Carm will stay with Beth. Jack and I will go back to college. I'll come home frequently. We'll get Carm through high school and keep the house as long as we can take care of it. Any degree of falling apart will jeopardize our plans, and at the moment, they are the only plans we have. This is the roadmap I have to keep going.

In the afternoon, Carm's friend, Dan and his mom come over. Their minivan creeps slowly up the driveway, and I feel anxious for having to see people outside the family. I don't know how I will be. They hug us all, put the food they brought in the kitchen, and then help us with the garage for a while before leaving. Dan and Carm are always funny together, and Dan makes Carm laugh a few times, makes us all laugh, and the thought crosses my mind that I might laugh for real at some point in the future.

I am amazed at how little all of my work in school and all my studying prepared me for this. I thought school was supposed to prepare you for life. That was a lie by my teachers and a miscalculation by me. Now, I find out school has prepared me for nothing of the stuff life is made of. All those years of math and science. The hard classes. All useless. Maybe if I had taken Psychology my senior year instead of AP Physics I'd be better prepared. The Psychology teacher, Mr. Webster, wore his pants too high, cinched tight by a woven belt. He had rheumy eyes and arranged all the chairs in his classroom in a circle instead of neat rows. The walls were covered with inspirational posters. There was a picture of two giraffes nuzzling, with bold typeface underneath saying, "Everybody needs a friend." And a kitten hanging from a tree branch with the words "UH-OH! Time to ask for help." There was even an old plaid couch in the corner with a yellowing computer printout proclaiming it to be the Comfort Corner.

I had felt nothing but contempt and maybe a little bit of pity for the students who chose to take a blow-off class like that. Psychology wasn't weighted as heavily as the AP courses, so they were ruining their GPA with every minute they spent in the Comfort Corner. I had thought those are the kids who will never get anywhere. Those are the kids I'll see working at the Cumberland Farms minimart before our tenth reunion for sure. Now, I wish I could join them and lie on that couch for weeks and let the comfort, as the sign promised, seep in through that plaid fabric into my skin, into my bones, and into my broken parts.

Maybe if I had sat in that circle of chairs with Mr. Webster among those posters and taken two semesters of Psychology instead of learning how to calculate velocity and absolute gravity, I'd be all right now. Or least not so completely and irrevocably broken. If I just knew the formula of what to do next, I'd know how to fix this.

Chapter Three

I wonder if they named it the rib cage because it is designed to hold in our hearts, to cage up the wild and terrible residue of living. If it wasn't in captivity it might overtake us, so a cage of bones is there to contain it all. I think I am too young to have a heart attack, but that's what it feels like. My chest aches and presses against itself as we file into the church. I keep my head down. As soon as I enter the vestibule, I can feel the closeness of a crowd of people and look up and stop short. Carm almost runs into my back; I can hear him stumble behind me. The church is full of people. Both of the choir seats on the sides are full, as well as the balcony. I can't see the walls because people are standing along each aisle two deep, and the ushers have thrown open the double doors of the vestibule, where a crowd is standing. I can see outside, just a slice of sky above all the heads, and realize there are some people standing on the lawn as well.

I sit in the front pew again, the same place where I had sat eight years earlier. But this time, it is different. I do not cry. I haven't cried in two days. It is as if all of the tears I had were used up over the last nine months. I have nothing left. I can feel it deep in my belly right below my rib cage. It is a black pressurized lump that I can't let out. I will let it out in small pieces, over time. But the whole thing is much too big to release. I can feel its pressure, and I know I can't even let out a piece of it or I won't be able to stop it. I cannot fall apart. I will not fall apart. My brothers need me to be stable. I need me to be stable. We have life to carry on. That was the final directive Mom gave me, and I will do it.

The entire town is here. People have flown in from across the country, driven from my college, Jack's college, Carm's high school, Beth's friends and all of our relatives. I knew there would be a crowd here, but I was not expecting this. They are here for Mom, I think. All these people loved her, but she is gone, so they are not really here for her. My next thought opens a space that releases some of the pressure in my chest. They are here for us.

They are here for us.

Her bell choir plays. It is a song I've heard them do before, and I know it's one of Mom's favorites. I don't know the name. They've left her spot open at the table, and there's a bouquet of flowers there instead of the music stand. I think of her bedroom at home and how none of us have touched it or wanted to use it even with all the relatives in town needing spaces. Her space is too big. We just can't fill it yet or maybe not ever.

We've arranged ourselves by age in the pew automatically, and Beth sits on the other side of Carm. The program is printed on thick paper, just the way Mom wanted it. I turn the program over and over in my hands and wonder why I can't feel anything. It's as if I'm watching someone else sitting here in this dress, in this pew. I don't know where the rest of me is. The part that knows how to feel, has gone. People speak and then I stand and hold a hymnal and then sit down again. More people speak. Suddenly everyone is standing again, and Jack nudges me, so I stand and follow him out into the aisle. I guess the service is over. Maybe the part of me that keeps track of time is gone, too.

In the hallway outside the vestibule, Jack says, "We should line up with the relatives."

"Oh, right. Sure. I just need…" I try to decide what I need. I need to get as far away from here as possible. I need to go out into the woods, miles from any people, and completely lose my shit. I need to not feel numb. No, I need to feel numb as long as possible because I don't know if I can survive feeling.

"Um, I need to use the bathroom," I say. "Be back in sec."

There is nowhere to go; there are crowds in front of me and crowds in back. I remember the children's room at the end of the hall and duck between people to get there. It feels like all eyes are on me. I pass the bathroom and open the children's room door. The nursery is smaller than I remember; it seems to get smaller every time I come in here. I close the door behind me and sink down into one of the miniscule wooden chairs, my knees up at my chin. I smooth my skirt down. It's too hot for long sleeves, and I feel sweat trickling down my back. I undo the gold clasp at the top of my dress and fan my face with one of the tattered *Highlights for Children* magazines. There's a raccoon on the cover.

The room still smells the same, kind of musty like a basement, with something sweet underneath it. There was a time when these chairs were the right size for me. I would sit and eat generic orange cheese crackers and drink fruit punch from little Dixie cups. I'd color books of Bible stories like Jonah and the Whale, the Good Samaritan, Moses getting the tablets the burning bush, and Jesus in the stable, with gifts of frankincense, incense, and myrrh. With mismatched boxes of Crayolas I colored in all the miracles: Jesus walking on water and blind men seeing, the sick being healed, and loaves and fishes for thousands. The message seemed so simple. Be good. Believe. Have faith. And you will be rewarded.

The lies now astound me. I was skeptical after Dad died. I wondered if it were all true. I decided I could still believe after Dad died and even blamed myself. Maybe I didn't believe enough. Wasn't good enough. Didn't pray quite enough. Or maybe it was like Mom explained it: that sometimes things like this happen, and we can't explain it. It was nobody's fault, and it was just his time to go and God was there, helping us through the whole time.

But for it to happen twice is unforgivable. I cannot believe anymore or have faith in something so flimsy. I cannot believe in a faith based on a book with thin pages telling tales of fantastical events that I know never actually happened. I learned to pray and believe while sitting in this same chair I'm in now. I swallowed the lies and the blind faith, and it was fine when life was fine. But I just can't do it now. I cannot depend on those invisible things outside myself that I can't see or touch.

There is no omniscient presence taking care of me. This past year is my proof.

There is no God.

In the hallway and beyond, I can hear the loud echo of voices. There are hundreds of people waiting. All of them want to hug me, shake my hand, and look in my eyes to convey their condolences. And I will accept it and nod and say thank you, thank you for coming. I will convey with my eyes the very thing that I do not feel.

I am fine. It was hard, but I am doing OK. We are fine. Thank you. Thank you. Yes, I will let you know if we need anything. Thank you.

Three hundred thank-yous. Maybe four hundred. I don't know. If I am going to put my faith in anything, it will be these people. Their presence and kindnesses are tangible proof I can believe in without question. They are here, and I will not let their kindness go to waste. I will be fine for them. I will be fine for my brothers. I arrange my face, re-clasp the top button of my dress, and walk out to meet them.

Afterward, my face hurts from holding a smile. I find that if I paste my face with the same expression, it holds the feelings at bay. If I don't show a feeling, it does not exist. It is like a ghostly, dark ache in my chest that never makes it past my neck. It is there, but far away, where it should be.

When most of the people have left, Jonathan finds me in the church kitchen, leaning against the sink, drinking cup after cup of water. I am so thirsty. It is all the talking. No matter how much I drink, I still feel dry and hot.

"You OK?"

I look at him and put the cup down, leaning hard on the counter. I can hardly stand, and it isn't over yet. We still have a reception at the house and the burial after that with the family. I don't know if I can do it.

He nods at me. "Never mind. That's a dumb question. C'mon, let's get out of here."

He takes my hand and leads me outside. People are getting into their cars and driving slowly around the church driveway. Everyone who came from college is waiting next to Jonathan's car. It is a 1972 Chevrolet station wagon, older than all of us, long and dented and brown, with mismatched tires. It always smells like old socks, and the passenger side door doesn't work. We all call the car Aunt Martha. It is parked right in the middle of the sensible sedans and work trucks and minivans of the churchgoers. And I am overjoyed to see it in all its ugliness with my college friends leaning coolly on her hood. We pile in, with me bunching my dress around my knees so I can slide in on the driver's side, across the bench seat. Two more people plus Jonathan, as the driver, join me. We have room left over. The engine revs, and I roll down the window and let the cool air wash over my head. Jonathan finds one of the few radio stations and turns it up loud. Aunt Martha backfires as we pull out of the church driveway. It scares us like it always does, and we shriek and I laugh. It is out of my stomach and out my mouth, and it is a genuine laugh. I forgot that laughing was something that existed in the world.

Back at home, Jonathan parks Aunt Martha on the lawn with the rest of the cars, and we pile out. I motion for him to come upstairs with me. It's hotter upstairs, and the dress is sticking to the back of my neck. The sleeves are all of the sudden incredibly itchy. I unclasp the collar and struggle with the buttons in the back.

"Can you help me with this?" I ask him.

I turn around so he can unbutton the back. I try to pull it over my head, but it gets stuck halfway off. Jonathan laughs, then grabs the skirt, pulls it up and over my head and off. I stand in my underwear and bra and shrug my shoulders, pulling the sticky hair from my neck.

"I hate this dress. I'm never going to wear it again," I say. And I realize it is true. The person who bought the dress for her high school award ceremony, the national honor society, and graduation doesn't exist anymore. The dress was purchased for a stranger.

He holds it out in front of him and rubs the velvet collar between his hands and frowns at the brooch-looking clasp at the neck.

"Yes, I think that's a good idea." He walks it to my desk and stuffs the entire thing into the tiny trash can. One of the sleeves sticks over the edge, swaying like it is waving good-bye.

I pull on my favorite jeans and an old shirt. The burial is late this afternoon, but it will just be family and I am through dressing up. I put on my stonewashed jean jacket and clip in my nose ring. I bought it last year for Halloween at the shop down the road from the college that also sells bongs in assorted colors and sizes. "For tobacco use only" the sign above them said.

If I am going to make it through the rest of the afternoon, I need to be someone else, and that someone is hard and edgy and doesn't give a fuck about anything. I keep saying it to myself whenever I feel anything besides hard and angry.

I don't give a fuck.

I walk through the crowd to check the soda supply. The ice chest on the kitchen table is empty. We hadn't planned on so many people. The sandwich trays are picked clean as well. I rummage in the fridge and put out the rest of the cold cuts and a loaf of bread. If anyone feels like eating, they can make their own sandwich. In the fridge I find a few ginger ales and a six pack of Coke, all of which I dump into the ice chest. I notice some bottles of beer in the back of the fridge and go back to get one. I open it carefully with the red plastic bottle opener and ease my way through the crowd into the pantry, where I close the door and take four long swigs. It is awful. I have never liked the taste, but this one seems especially bad. It has probably been in the fridge since Jack's birthday in the spring. I take another two swigs anyway and belch terrifically, stifling most of the sound in the crook of my elbow. It is nice to be in the dark pantry alone. The gulps start going down easier. I finish the beer and get another one from the fridge. This time I open it and casually walk out to join my friends on the lawn, where they are sitting in a semicircle in the grass. They know I don't drink much, but they don't say anything. Not today. Joe raises his eyebrows at me but doesn't say anything, either. He is vehemently opposed to all substances and even lives in a substance-free dorm on campus. We've had arguments at parties when I've had a beer. I give him a small shrug and sit down.

I sip at the beer for the rest of the afternoon and carry it around with me blatantly, even after I know I've had enough. It makes my stomach churn and feel uncomfortably expanded. Nobody else is drinking, and my friends are respectful enough to only take sodas. So what. I am nowhere close to being legally old enough. So what. There is nobody here to tell me no. Nobody is here to watch out for me in that particular way anymore. Besides, I like the way it makes me feel. It makes the edges of everything less sharp. The sadness is there, but it feels farther away, like it is outside of me instead of inside, constantly slicing at my rib cage. It isn't less, just a duller, more removed feeling. The dullness is a relief.

I make it through the rest of the afternoon and three more beers. My friends all leave, piling into Aunt Martha and hugging me good-bye. I'll see them the following week at school. Seven days feels like a lifetime. It was another lifetime ago that I left school, and I can't remember what I was like then. I try to remember what that girl was like, what she thought, and how she felt. Maybe if I can remember about her I can go back to being her.

People leave the house in small groups, and each one, without fail, says to let them know if we need anything, anything at all. Soon, only the family and relatives are left. We drive in a long caravan of rental cars the half mile to the cemetery. The pastor meets us there and shakes our hands. She's changed out of her robes and is wearing a black wool trench coat. The late autumn sun is dipping behind the trees. I think about this morning and drinking coffee in the quiet house at dawn. This day will never end and I am so tired.

I am glad for all the faraway feeling and hope that my quick teeth brushing before we left masks the scent of beer on my breath. I stand next to Jack and focus my eyes on the trees at the back of the plot. I think of nothing and make my insides go blank. My eyes see things and my ears hear things, but they don't register. I see my uncle crying and his shoulders shaking with his breaths. I see Pastor Alice gesture to the small marble box full of ashes in the ground and see it lowered down next to an identical little box. I want to be away from here—away from this grassy area and the sad people standing around it. I look at the stone bench with my last name carved into it. It is waiting for me. That much I know, and maybe I shouldn't make it wait. I am so tired. I want to crawl under the bench and lie down against the cool marble of those two boxes and stay there. I feel Carm's fingers curl around my hand and squeeze hard—Jack's strong hand is in my other.

At night Beth goes back to Boston, having to return to work for a day after taking weeks off. Then it is just my brothers and a handful of cousins who are spending the night. I can hear them laughing downstairs, playing a game of dominoes. Despite the sound, the house feels empty. We are alone. There are no adults in the house. I realize that we are it; we are the adults.

I get the same feeling I had earlier in the day walking around brazenly with the beer. We are the adults. We are responsible for us. The thought had been a little thrilling earlier in the day, but now exhausted in the darkness of night, it is pure terror. Nobody is responsible for me except me. There are people who love me and will help if I need it, but ultimately it is up to me to be all right and I don't know if I can be.

I hear more laughter from downstairs. Instead of making me feel part of something, I feel all the more separate from them. How can they laugh? How can they do anything except curl up like I am doing and shake with fear? The headboard is tapping the wall from the shaking, and I grab hold of the bedside table to stop it. With my other hand, I press the pillow into my face just before the sobbing starts. I think of the cemetery and wonder how it looks at night with its gray headstones and shadows in the moonlight. The dirt under the bench will still be damp and overturned. I don't want to feel all this, and I don't want to be here. Maybe it is not too late to join them there in that peaceful place beyond all loneliness and fear and sadness. It would be such a sweet relief to stop it all. Then I remember Carm's hand and Jack's hand holding tightly on to my hands when we stood in the cemetery. I have to stay. I realize there is no choice for me. I have to stay.

Chapter Four

*I*t isn't hard to get in my car and go back to college. I can't wait to get back. I think maybe once I get there some of this sadness will lift. At the very least, everything around me won't remind me of Mom. After being away for almost a month, I miss all of it: my classes, my own little dorm room, my friends, and the busy schedule.

I think of Grandma, my dad's mother, holding me by the shoulders after he died years ago, shaking me. I had been crying and couldn't stop. She was trying to help. She gave me another shake and spoke loudly, almost yelling at me.

"He's done with the pain! Don't you understand? He's done with it now!"

I didn't understand. I didn't know why she was yelling at me and trying to convince me of something. But I get it now. I understand the relief of being able to stop waiting and just have the thing you dread the most happen. I understand watching someone you love suffer and wanting it to stop at any cost. Death seems like a small price to pay for ending that kind of pain. Or at least I thought it would be until it happened. Mom's suffering ended, and I am glad for that. But mine keeps going. I think there is an end to it, but I don't know where.

My first week back is awkward and quiet. My friends don't know what to say. I don't know what to say back. After they realize I'm not going to burst into tears, things become more normal, but I stop spending as much time with some of them. I can't tell if I'm different or they're different. Instead, I go to the studio with Jonathan to study while he paints. I like the garage smell of the acrylic and being around someone who is occupied in a task so I don't have to talk. I start spending more time with Lynn and Kenli, two girls on the floor below mine. I sit on the floor in their tiny room, and we study in amiable silence when we're not making each other laugh in a hysterical, falling-over, belly-aching way that reminds me of my summer camp friends. It is so good to laugh, really laugh, and it seems like I haven't done it in years. Sometimes I sleep on their floor when going back to my single room feels too empty.

I meet with my professors and catch up on the work I missed. When I can manage it, I love focusing my mind on the concrete tasks and studying. Once a week I forget all feeling during the four-hour organic chemistry lab. It is a balm to have directions to follow. Measure this. Add this. Set up this apparatus. Titrate this. Write down what you observe. Be as objective as possible. At the start of the semester, the professor spent half a lecture period describing the importance of objectivity in the lab. "Observations only," he said. He had gotten downright frothy about the importance of it.

"If you can't touch, hear, smell, or see it, I don't want to see it written in your lab reports! I don't want to know what you think about something, or how you feel about it. Nothing intangible! Only if it can be observed by another scientist is it valid!"

It made sense to me.

The crystal is light purple with a melting point of 58 degrees Celsius. It is soluble in a solution of four molar Hydrogen sulfide. When burned, it gives off white smoke and is nonreactive with water. Its ion, when viewed with a mass spectrometer, consists of seven different isotopes ranging from 91 to 100 mass/charge ratios.

The girl is five feet, seven inches tall. She weighs 165 pounds. She has shoulder-length red hair and hazel eyes. She goes to class from eight o'clock to two thirty on Monday, Wednesday, and Friday. She eats in the dining hall in the middle table, closest to the windows. She is usually seen in a group of two to five students, walking on campus or sitting in the dining hall. She talks. She laughs. She spends one quarter of every twenty-four-hour period prostrate on her bed, staring at the ceiling or sitting at the wooden desk in her room, staring out the window, an open book in front of her. At least twice a day when alone, her eyes produce tears, and her lower jaw trembles. This proceeds into increased breath sounds and a noise that she muffles with the red throw pillow from the single chair in the room. If the audible breath sounds and tears happen for more than twenty minutes, the noise will turn into a reflex contraction in the throat, and the girl will vomit into the black trash can next to her desk. When with other people, and not talking or responding to someone, her mouth is held in a line, facial features unmoving, jaw slightly clenched.

The girl removes one half cupful of cold vodka in the morning from the mini-refrigerator and swallows it with one multivitamin. She then brushes her teeth with Colgate, winter mint flavor. She repeats this action at 2:30 and again at 10:00 p.m. before going to bed. The girl weighs 160 pounds. Then 150 pounds. Dark circles appear under her eyes despite sleeping for sometimes ten or eleven hours a night.

Every night she tosses and turns although in a deep sleep. The observer can only guess at what are in her dreams, but if you asked her she would say:

"My mother. Every night. It is my mother I have dreams of. Sometimes she is the center of the dream and sometimes she is sick and sometimes she is well and sometimes she is about to leave me on a long trip and sometimes she is returning. The plot and setting change each time, but it is always her."

There is a knock on the door. It is Joe. I can tell from the way he knocks, softly, but insistently.

"Hey? You in there?"

"Yes," I answer dully.

"Come on, you weren't at breakfast. It's time to go to Orgo. Open the door."

I shuffle to the door. I am still in my pajamas. He takes two steps into the room and closes it behind him. He puts his backpack down and draws me into his arms. I go rigid for a moment, trying to hold back the wave, and then it crashes over me.

I bite back the tears.

"I can't do this. I can't do this," I say into his shoulder.

"Do what? You're doing it, whatever it is, right now. You're here; you're making it to class, mostly." He rubs my back. "You're doing all right. You're all right."

I push away from him.

"I'm not all right!" I hiss. His kindness makes me angry for some reason. "I'm a fucking train wreck. How can you even stand to be around me? Something must be seriously wrong with you to want me. We're not even together! Why the hell are you here?"

I hate him for being nice to me. I hate him for trying to save me. I hate myself for being mean to him.

He gives me a little shake, holding my shoulders.

"Come on, you can't miss today. We have that quiz. Please, get dressed."

He takes a sweat shirt off my desk chair and pulls it down over my head. I'm angry, but I'm too tired to resist. He kneels down and slips my loafers over my feet, hefts both our backpacks on his shoulders, and pulls me out of the room.

We hurry across campus, him dragging me up the hill to the science building. We make it just as the quizzes are being handed out. We sit at a table in the back. I look down at the paper. I can't read the words. Or rather, I read them, but they don't mean anything. I read them again and again. It doesn't matter. None of this matters. This is a quiz. We live in a world where people you love get sick and die, and this is a fucking useless quiz.

Joe reaches under the table and takes my hand. He slides his finished quiz from under his elbow. I know he can write out these reactions in his sleep, as if he was born knowing them, like a second language. I shake my head. I have never cheated. I'm not starting now on a fucking useless quiz. This doesn't matter anyway. He squeezes my hand. I turn slightly to look at him. He bends his head to me.

"You can't fail out. You need to be here. I need you here. If you go home, it won't be any better. You'll still be sad, just sad away from me where I can't help you and be with you."

The professor looks pointedly at us and clears his throat. Joe sits upright but keeps his eyes on me. His face is fierce. It's fiercer than I have ever seen it, angry even. He taps his paper twice with his index finger, hard on the table, then at my paper. I look down at my paper. I've never seen him angry before, and something about it snaps me into being able to see. The words and figures make sense. I scribble furiously for the last ten minutes.

Lynn's family has a small cabin an hour away, nestled in a little town just over the hills surrounding the college. We pack the car with enough food and booze to last our small party of six for a week even though we are just going for an overnight. We stay up late into the night, mixing awful drinks, and fall asleep huddled together in sleeping bags on mattresses pulled together on the cabin floor.

In the morning it's so cold we can see our breath, and Mike lights a fire outside, and we sit around drinking bad coffee made in an enamel pot. I pour some rum from the night before into mine, and it makes it better. I am feeling cagey. I haven't been around people for more than a few hours at a time. It has been a day since I cried last, and I can feel it building inside me. I wonder if this is what going crazy feels like. It reminds me of being thirteen and being constantly surprised at the force of my feelings and their ability to carry me away with them, like the emotions are something separate from me entirely.

I excuse myself and walk off into the woods and let the tears fall. I am so tired. Just doing the bare minimum of breathing seems to take enormous amounts of energy, never mind going through the motions of living. I stop walking. The sun is getting higher in the sky and starting to melt the frost off the leaves. There is a tall maple in a sunny spot, and I stand, fixated, staring at the ground at its trunk. There is something to see here, but I didn't know what. Then I see it. A perfect circle of frost remains, shaded by the base of the trunk, while all around it the fall leaf litter is illuminated in bright morning sun. I stand in the cold, shady part. I'm in the shade, I think. I'm in the shade but just a step away is warmth. I take one step to the light and am soaked by warmth. I sigh out loud. I step back into the cold to feel the difference again, then back into the light.

Just hang on, it says. *Hang on just a little longer. You'll make it. Hang on.*

⌒⟩

After the weekend, I return to my dorm. My room is in the quiet wing that is filled with the entire women's swim team. Apparently, they all wanted to live together, and the quiet wing was the only block of rooms available all together during the annual housing lottery. I don't mind. I like the anonymity of it, and they are relatively quiet. They have no interest in knowing someone who does not spend four hours a day soaked in chlorine, and I have no interest in them. They travel as a pack, go to bed early, and leave before dawn to swim their miles and miles. I hear them shuffling in the hallway when it is still dark—the zippers closing on their gym bags, doors closing and opening. I hear them, and it wakes me more gently than an alarm. It allows me to hold on to the images of my dreams for just a little longer. Sometimes in the early hours with the swimmers I can forget everything for just a few moments.

This morning, for the first time I was having a dream of both Mom and Dad together. That has never happened before. In the dream, they were on the back deck at the house, sitting in Adirondack chairs, holding hands. A boy was there who looked just like Carm, and he was dancing and making them laugh. The entire back field was in bloom, and there was light everywhere. Mom, Dad, and the boy all were backlit, and everything was warm. The edges of what I could see blurred to white, so it seemed we were in the middle of a space that went on forever.

When I'm awake, I think about the dream and feel uneasy as I get ready for my day. It's late enough that Carm and Beth are up, so I call them just to make sure. Carm answers on the first ring. I ask him how he is.

"Fine," he says and then I hear crunching. He must be eating cereal. "I have to catch the bus," he says through a mouthful, "can you call tonight?"

I hang up and measure out a drink in the ceramic coffee mug, the one that Chloe's mom made for me for high school graduation. As I'm swallowing it, I remember something that makes me intake a sharp breath, and I spit out the mouthful back into the cup.

Carm had a twin.

I cough and sit down on the unmade bed. I think I might be going crazy. It can't be good to dream about the dead like this, not every night. It can't be good to drink in the morning like this, but I need the way it blurs the edges of things for a few hours. It can't be good to have to wear a belt with all your pants because they slide off your hips, onto the floor without one. It can't be good to hate the people you love most for no reason.

I remember those kind nurses from hospice, how they would talk about anything and were always calm. They said there were people you could talk to, people who could help. I think that you have to be crazy or neurotic to go to a therapist, but that doesn't seem so far off the mark right now. On the way to class, I stop at the switchboard and rifle through the stack of phone books to find the most recent year. I look up "therapist," and it says "see psychiatrist." There's an ad in the margin of the page for suicide prevention. That's not a good sign. I flip to "psychiatrist," and there's an entire page of doctors and clinics along with phone numbers. Most of them are in town. Another margin has an advertisement for suicide prevention and the number for the Samaritans. Maybe I could just call them. But what would I say? "I'm not actually thinking of offing myself because that option is off the table, but I don't really know how to keep living. Do you have any tips on that?" I put the phone books back and walk to class.

Afterward, I walk by the nursing building. The nursing program is one of the most rigorous on campus, and the students, almost all women, travel in weary-looking packs. I follow a group of five of them into the building.

I ask at the front desk to see the department head. She points to Sharon Dettenrieder's office and says I'm just in time for office hours. I knock. Sharon gives me a firm handshake and asks me to sit. I sink into the couch. It is a great couch, the kind that takes your whole body and holds it.

"What can I do for you?" she asks from her desk. "Are you interested in the nursing program?"

The way she is looking at me with her kind, expectant eyes, it is obvious why the nursing students speak so highly of her.

I open my mouth. Nothing comes out. I am having that feeling again that if I say anything I will fall apart right here on this professor's excellent couch and actually never be able to get up. She is still looking at me with those kind eyes. I pinch the skin on the top of my hand, discreetly and hard, take a gulp of air, and try again.

"I'm wondering if you know if there's a local hospice group. I'm looking for someone to talk to."

"Talk to about what? Are you doing research or interested in volunteering or something else?"

"Something else." My voice sounds dumb and small. Why did I think that somehow I would be able to do this without actually having to say it?

"I think they have counselors there, at hospice I mean, that specialize in helping people who have..." I pinch my hand harder. "Who have lost someone."

She gives me a strange look and then she leans forward.

"Have you lost someone?"

I nod. Hold it together. Hold it together. Get the name. Get the phone number. Get out.

"Who?"

I can't do this. I can't say it out loud. Everyone I have been in contact with has known she died without my having to say it. I wonder if it would be awkward if I just stood up and said I made a mistake and leave. But I can't seem to get up off that couch or move out of her steady gaze.

It comes out in a whisper. "My mother," I say and feel everything shutting down, my insides going numb. I'm grateful and finally release the pinch hold on my hand.

"When? When did she die?" I am amazed at how brave her voice sounds. She can say the word "die." She doesn't even flinch at all. Just like those hospice nurses.

My voice answers and is so quiet I can't believe any sound comes out at all. "Thirty-seven days ago." I don't even know where that number comes from, but it is exactly correct. Somewhere in the back of my brain I am keeping meticulous, complete track of time passing without her.

Two tears manage to slide out of my eyes. One from each eye. I don't feel them until they soak into my collar. One wet dot on either side of my neck. Hold it together. I need to hold it together.

She nods and purses her lips together. It looks like she's thinking. When she does speak, it is slow and careful.

"In times like this, it helps a lot to have someone to talk to. You were right to come to me. I think what would be best is if we made an appointment with the college counseling service. Would it be OK if I called for you?"

The breath I am holding releases. She is going to call for me. I don't have to explain this over again on the phone to a stranger. I feel the relief all the way to my feet, like all the muscles had been tense and now they've relaxed.

"You wait here just a minute. I'm going to get the number and make the call. Do you have any more classes today?"

I shake my head.

She leaves and returns.

"I talked to Gary, the director of counseling. They have an opening at two this afternoon. Will that work for you?"

I nod although I am not sure. I thought maybe it would be weeks before I'd actually have to go. It is an odd feeling, knowing that I need something desperately but not wanting it at the same time. I am scared.

Sharon stands. "I have to go teach class now, but I'll be back in an hour. I want you to go to the dining hall and get something to eat or have a cup of tea and then come back here at quarter till. I'll walk over to your appointment with you and introduce you. Does that sound all right?"

It is all right. She is taking care of me. She walks me to her door. She touches my shoulder and looks at me with those kind eyes.

"Gayle, I know this is hard, and you did the right thing to come here. We'll make sure you get the help you need."

"Thank you," I say, my voice catching in my throat.

⟡

Sharon takes me to the third floor of the student services building, and after a brief introduction, she says, "I'll leave you so you can talk."

Before she closes the door behind her, she says, "Gayle, come see me again next week so we can check in." I don't hesitate when I nod and know I will.

I turn back to Gary. He's a tall man with glasses and a beard, and he motions for me to sit down on his brown couch. It's just a regular couch, not the kind you lie down on that I was expecting.

He tells me that everything we talk about is confidential and asks me if I've ever been to any therapy of any kind. I shake my head. I only knew one person who had a shrink. She was in my art class in high school and wore black with the same leather coat, every day, worn at the elbows, with safety pins all over it. Sometimes she'd take a pin off and poke at her fingertips during class. She left halfway through our sophomore year for two months, and when she came back, the leather coat was gone and her hair was short and she didn't talk to anyone. Every Wednesday she got called out of class, and everyone said she had to go to her shrink.

He asks me a series of questions about taking my own life. I think of my brothers and the bright red advertisement for the Samaritans in the margin of the phone book.

"No, you don't have to ask me those questions. I'd never do that. Ever."

"OK," he says and writes something on his pad. "Before we get started, do you have any questions?"

I shake my head.

"So, the first thing you should know about therapy is that it is going to feel worse sometimes. You'll leave here, and you'll feel worse than when you came in because we're going to talk about feelings a lot. But mostly after talking, people find they feel better and stronger. I just want to make sure that if you feel worse you don't give up on coming to see me. If you feel like you're stuck or we're not making progress or even if you feel like you'd rather talk to one of the other counselors, that's all right, too. But it's important to keep coming."

He's not selling this very well.

"How often should I come to see you?" I ask.

"I suggest weekly at first. When you're feeling better, we can go to every other week. Some students come in just once a month or so when they're wrestling with something they need help with. Most of what I see is academic stress and relationship stress. You're not alone though. I'm seeing another student who lost her mother a year ago and a few students who have lost siblings. It's unusual to experience losing an immediate family member so early, and most students say it's a pretty lonely place to be. So you need to know that you're not alone, and my job is to help you sort through all the feelings of grief you're having. Do you know what grief is?"

I know he's asking if I know what the word means, but it is so much more than a word. It is a black and endless hole inside you that will never be filled no matter how many tears you shed to try and fill it up. It's always there lurking in the background even when you're laughing with your best friends and spilling popcorn all over the floor. It's a force that makes you be alone when really all you want is for someone to take care of you. It's the thing that is lonely no matter how many cards and phone calls you get from well-meaning people. It's the thing that makes you feel like you are drowning and you can see your brothers drowning but can't save them because you're trying to save yourself. It's the thing that will make it impossible to ever be truly happy again.

"Yes," I say. "I know what grief is."

Our weekly sessions leave me red-eyed and sometimes shaking.

"You're going to have to confront these feelings sometime," he says. "Trust me, it's best to do it now instead of waiting ten or twenty years."

Afterward, I take my wilted self into the sunlight and squint and wander aimlessly around the campus. I'm useless for the afternoon to study. Instead I go to the ceramics studio where I'm dutifully fulfilling my art requirement. During the day I have the place to myself. The class is easy because of all the time I spent as a teenager in the studio with Chloe's Mom. In the aftermath of therapy, the warmth of the industrial kilns and the smell of dust is comforting. I prep twenty pounds of clay, kneading and working the air bubbles out, sprinkling water on the gray lumps to get them pliable. Then I sit at the wheel, and the lumps spin, sliding through my fingers. I hug the shape with my hands, centering it until it looks like it's not moving at all, then draw it up into a cylinder.

One after another I line them up behind me on the workbench, pulling bat after bat off the wheel. During one of the sessions, my professor sees what I've done and is impressed. She gushes about the importance of such practice and reminds me that all thrown forms on the wheel come from this. If you start with a centered piece, symmetrical and perfect, anything can come from it: plates, goblets, vases, mugs. Everything comes from this one perfect form. I wait until she's gone before stripping my work off the bats and dumping them into the recycling bucket. I squash them down into the soft clay of the bucket, deep beneath the water so there's no trace of them. I don't want beautiful vases or plates or goblets. I just want the calm that comes from centering lumps of earth in a warm, dusty studio.

Chapter Five

"Joe, I can't watch a movie with you tonight. I have to go to a talk for premed majors."

"I'll go with you."

"But you're not in premed."

"I know. I'll just go and sit with you and read my book."

"It makes me crazy that you hardly ever have to study," I say. I've been clear that we're no longer dating, but we still spend a lot of time together. No matter what I say or do or how mean I can be, he always comes back.

We walk to the science hall and find seats. The lecturer drones on about all of the "exciting and growing" fields available to physicians today. I sit at the end of the row, doodling in my notebook. Joe sits to my left. He's put down his book and has actually pulled out his Sociology homework. The rare times he does study, it is only for the humanities.

The lights dim and the presentation begins. In between slides I glance down at my organic homework, trying to memorize the reactions.

The presenter drones on.

"And this is the computed tomography, commonly known as a CT or CAT scan. The field of radiology is a growing one, as there are advances in the methods to detect various calcifications, tumors, masses, and bone trauma."

"Next slide please."

"And this is a radiation machine used to treat a variety of tumors."

I look up from my notebook. It is the same machine Mom had slid into every day for a month until she got burn marks on her head and felt so weak she could hardly walk. Riding home in the car, she'd hold her head. Beth took along one of the yellow Tupperware containers for when she had to be sick on the way home from the clinic. In the beginning it was all right. It was towards the last cycles when she could hardly move due to nausea. She'd hold her head and moan, retching into the Tupperware, and it would continue for hours after she got home. There was nothing that would make it better. We'd been warned against dehydration, and she'd sit bravely with one small glass of water in front of her, taking small sips in between bouts of nausea. Sometimes she'd lose it all, and we'd refill the glass and start again, over and over, just fighting to drink a goddamned little cup of water.

The room starts to spin. I feel a burning in the back of my throat and gag. I lunge out of my seat and just make it outside the building to the steps, where I deposit my dinner behind one of the bushes.

Joe finds me out there a few minutes later, my head down between my knees.

"Here, I brought your backpack."

"Thanks. I just needed some air."

He pats me on the back, looks worried.

"I'm dropping out of the premed program tomorrow," I say. "I can't do this. I don't want to ever work in a hospital or a clinic or anything having to do with sickness. I'm done. I thought I could be brave enough to do this and somehow make it a life mission to help people or whatever, but I can't. It was totally stupid to think that I could make a difference somehow. I just can't do it. I'm done."

⌣‿⌐

I finally tell Gary about the drinking. He smiles a little and shakes his head when I asked him if I am an alcoholic. This is embarrassing.

"The definition is pretty loose about what makes an alcoholic. I'd put you in the self-medicating category. I'm not saying it's healthy in any way, but it's pretty common when you're having big emotions that you don't know what to do with. Some people use alcohol, or food, or sex, or even video games to dampen what they're feeling in order to keep functioning. If you work through this, the pain will be less, and you won't need to dull it down. I think you've caught it early enough that you'll be fine."

He takes a sip of his coffee, then steeples his fingers together thoughtfully.

"Could you try something for me? How about you start by just removing your access to it? Get rid of what you have so it's not easy to reach for it. Instead, do some of the things we've been talking about, like going for a walk, or writing, or calling a friend. I think you'll do fine."

He has such confidence in me.

That evening I dump the beer in my fridge down the drinking fountain drain in the hallway, then run the water to get rid of the smell. I take the empty bottles to the basement recycling bins. This weekend someone will root through them and find the bottles and take them to the redemption center in order to buy more beer.

I carry what's left of my vodka stash down to the second floor, wrapped in a coat. Kenli answers the door, and Lynn is behind her, sitting at the desk.

"Would you guys hold on to this for me?" I hand her the bottles. They clink together in the coat.

Kenli looks at me with a question in her eyes and then seems to understand instantly.

"Of course. Sure. It's here for the next party, right?"

I thank her and leave and think of Gary's parting words after today's session.

"One more thing about drinking. It's something you may want to just be aware of in your life; just notice how much and when and why you're drinking so you make the good choices."

My chemistry professor raps his knuckles against the blackboard.

"Pay attention, folks. Your next exam is just two weeks away before Thanksgiving break, and this material will be on it."

Thanksgiving? Holy crap.

Suddenly Claisen reactions lose all their importance even if they are going to be on the next exam. There is something much more important. We have to make Thanksgiving happen.

I turn to a new page in my notebook and begin scribbling furiously everything I can remember from the year before. The recipe for the sausage stuffing. The potatoes.

Was the squash baked or boiled? Was I even in the room when she made the gravy? I know the weird plastic measuring cup is involved with the graduated spout and some flour, but what else? Maybe the jarred gravy isn't that bad. Where did Mom order the turkey from? Shit. I can't remember. I think it had a yellow label on it. Is it even too late to get a turkey?

I am sweating, and I wipe my palms on my jeans, then run my forearm over my face.

Joe is sitting next to me, watching. He passes a folded note across the table to me.

"You OK?" it says.

"I can't remember the recipe for my mom's T-day stuffing!!!!" I scribble back.

He leans over and whispers, "Do you need to leave?"

I shake my head. "I just forgot about Thanksgiving!"

The professor eyes us from the front of the room. I shrug and give Joe my "I'm fine—I'm always fine" look and lean back into my seat and get back to my lists. It is essential that I write down everything, every detail that I can remember from that morning a year ago that might help piece things together. I write as things come to me, in any jumbled order. I can organize it later. The important part is getting everything down.

Celery (2 heads?), chopped in the Cuisinart with the round attachment thing
onions—chopped
Stuffing mix—the bag was blue
Sausage—browned in the big flat frying pan
Broth, the kind in cans with the little house on the front. 4 cans, I think.

Rinse the turkey in the sink.

Put in big roaster pan—from the upstairs barn?

Put chopped garlic on it and some red spice. Paprika or Cayenne pepper or Mexican seasoning? not sure which.

Need to look up how long and at what temp to cook a turkey. I think we put it in at 5 am?

Do I call the Motters and invite them or do they know to just come?

Find the silver polish

How stupid I am. How dumb to think she would always be here. How naïve to think that for the rest of my life that wonderful stuffing and perfectly cooked turkey and all those sides would just show up on the table each November. Why on earth didn't I think of this sort of thing when she was sick and have her write them down? I am the only one who has ever witnessed the cooking of some of the dishes, and I only saw it once.

Dammit to hell.

I scribble for all I am worth. The class ends, and I don't get up. It seems more important than any exam or test I've had in my life. My family's tradition relies completely on my recall ability, and I am determined to get it right.

I can sense Joe sitting patiently next to me. He'll be late for his next class, but he doesn't move.

The room starts to fill up again with people from the next class. Finally I put my pen down and drop my arms at my sides. This is all I have. Three pages. I hope it will be enough to piece it together.

I run back to my dorm room and call Beth. We have almost daily phone calls about what and how much to buy. To my relief, turkeys are still available. We work out lists and spreadsheets like we are preparing for a complicated military operation. There are schedules for how and when to cook everything, and I make phone calls to the good cooks I know for recipes to fill in the gaps where I'm not sure. I comb the hobby section at the college library and finally find a cookbook that has a formula for how to figure out turkey cooking times, both stuffed and unstuffed. I check the book out and cradle it in my arms as I carry it back to my dorm. It is the holy grail of information I have been needing. Maybe the day won't be a disaster after all. Maybe we can actually pull this off.

We do the calculations for the turkey and realize if we're going to meet the target time for when the Motters will arrive, we'll need to get the turkey in at three. The night before Thanksgiving, we each choose a time, every hour on the hour, for when we'll get up for basting duties. In the darkness of Thursday morning, Beth and I both get up and set backup alarms, just in case. Three hours later I'm back in the kitchen. I can't sleep. In our family, Thanksgivings have always been sacred. Christmas we changed it up each year and sometimes even traveled, but Thanksgiving is ours. Always in our home. Always with Jack's godparents. Always the same foods in the same bowls at the same time. It has been this way for longer than I have been alive, and I am determined to keep it going. It represents stability and wholeness, two things that we are all needing so badly. So it has to be the same.

In the morning, over coffee and bagels, we start preparing the rest of the food, and Jack and Carm set out newspapers on the kitchen table and set to polishing the silver. The Motters arrive, and for a moment while they are taking off their coats and handing over pies and everyone is hugging their hellos and talking over each other, it feels the same. This is what I wanted. This is what I needed. We need to prove that one thing has not changed in a world where everything has.

Twenty minutes before the meal, our preparation becomes frantic. There doesn't seem to be enough stove burners to get everything hot at the same time. Jack and Carm shuttle dishes to the dining room as they are done. Beth puts the mashed potatoes in the wrong bowl, and I can't breathe until she scrapes them out into the blue ceramic bowl where they are supposed to be.

"It's OK, it's OK. Look, all better," she says in a tone that you might use with a hysterical child.

"Sorry," I mutter. "I know I'm being crazy. You gave up being with your own family to be here, and I'm being crazy."

"It's all right, there's no place I'd rather be than here."

We get all the food onto the table. I know the turkey is dry and the gravy is lumpier than it should be. I think the potatoes need more salt. But everything is here. The menu and the setting are complete. We haven't missed anything.

Jack lights the small candle that was a gift from a hospice counselor. It is a white tea light in a gold-colored holder and sits next to the woven cornucopia filled with random food out of the fridge because I didn't have any gourds. There are two apples, an orange, and some onions and potatoes. I'll add gourds to the master list for next year.

"For those that aren't here," Jack says simply.

We hold hands and say grace. First in Norwegian. Then in English. As always. The last line sticks in my mouth.

For health and strength and daily food we praise thy name, oh Lord.

I still won't thank God for this.

But I say the words anyway and feel a warmth inside me that hasn't been there for a long time. The feeling is, appropriately enough, thankfulness. Gratitude. Beth was at my side through the hours in the kitchen, Carm and Jack hovered nearby and lit the woodstove, polished the silver, set the table, peeled potatoes. The Motters still came; I had thought for a while that maybe they wouldn't want to. But they are here, as always, with their gentle, calm and memories and pie.

We have what we need, and we have each other.

We sit down and eat.

Over Christmas break we all collapse. It seems all we do is sleep and eat cereal and spend long afternoons in front of the TV watching Christmas specials and reruns. I get together with my high school friends a few times, and while I am with them, I remember the person I was. It is like living in a different version of myself for a few hours that is lighter and younger. I make one attempt to go into the attic and get out decorations but am immediately overwhelmed by all of the boxes and retreat back downstairs. Jack, Carm, and I fly to Oklahoma to spend Christmas with Mom's sister. I know we can't stay in our house.

My grades for the semester come in the mail, and I stand in the post office, reading the envelope. It's no longer addressed to "The parent/ guardian of." It is addressed to me. I wait to get home to open it, then have to run my fingers over the numbers. I've met my required GPA, but only by a small margin. The score seems too high because the only thing I can remember about the semester is the long afternoons lying on my bed, looking up at the map of the Adirondacks on the ceiling, tracing the blues and greens with my eyes. I can't recall a single detail of anything that I studied.

A year ago when my grades came from college, they were tucked in between a stack of Christmas cards, and there was a letter included stating I was on the honor roll. Mom made a big deal out of it and put the letter on the fridge under the wooden magnet shaped like a duck, like I was in grade school.

"Mom, c'mon," I muttered. "You don't have to put that on the fridge."

"Yes, I do!" she said with unhampered enthusiasm. "This is a big deal! We need to put it up!"

Now, looking at my grades, I can't even tell if I should be disappointed or happy about them. I guess somewhere in between. I think Mom would be pleased, even though they are lower. I wonder when I'll stop wondering what she'd think. I'm just glad that I passed and kept my scholarship. Maybe next semester I'll do better. I crumple the grades and put them into the woodstove, where they immediately flare up and burn away.

Spring semester passes, then another starts in the fall. I am halfway done with college. I still have days when it all seems pointless, but I'm going to finish what I started and leave with a degree. My fears of failing out and losing my scholarship are gone. Since I made it through last year, I know I can do two more years.

On the one-year anniversary of Mom's death, I call Jack.

"It's been a year," I say.

"Yup."

"You OK?"

"Yeah. You?"

"I'm all right."

And it's true. We're all right. I called Carm, but he was at his soccer game. Beth goes to all of his games and cheers from the sidelines. She brings big bags of peanuts to share with the parents on the bleachers. When I was home a few weekends ago, I went with her and noticed how all the parents there cheered for their own kid and also for Carm. He has a whole brigade of parents, and it made me inordinately glad. I got a lump in my throat when he assisted for a goal and his brigade stood and cheered for him, spilling peanut shells everywhere. I still feel guilty for not leaving school to be with him, but the truth is that Beth and the brigade are doing a far better job than I ever could.

I made sure weeks ago to make a therapy appointment for the anniversary. Gary congratulates me.

"It will keep getting easier after this," he says.

I don't believe him. There have been many days that feel harder than the day before it and others that feel easier. It is unpredictable and doesn't make any sense.

After the appointment I walk up the hill behind the campus, into the woods. I need to mark this day somehow. I went walking here a lot when I was a freshman. I came here when Mom was sick, and afterward when being around anyone was overwhelming. Sometimes the football or lacrosse team will run by during their practice, but mostly I have the place to myself. Since it is fall, the view is stunning, and I wonder if I will miss this, the view from Oyaron hill when I graduate. Immediately after I have the thought, I know I will miss it. It is sad to miss something and feel nostalgic for it when you still have it. But maybe it is just because this is an anniversary day and I know that no matter what happens, time keeps passing even when it feels like it should stand still for you.

Chapter Six

"A cell phone?" I ask. I am sitting in front of the open package, holding it up. It is small and black. Only a few people I know have one.

"You're driving back and forth so much, we thought it would be a good idea for you to have one. Happy birthday!"

Jack is always thinking of things like this to take care of me.

"Wow, thanks!" I try to muster enthusiasm in my voice. I'm not sure I want to be seen on campus with a phone. Most of the kids that have them drive Land Rovers and BMWs. I'd look ridiculous driving my old 1982 Rabbit, talking on a cell phone.

Jack seems to sense my hesitation. "You can always just keep it in your car and use it to call home. The prices just came down, and it's probably cheaper than using your dorm phone."

I test it out that Sunday on my drive home and call Joe at the radio station.

"Wait, so you're really talking to me from your car right now? That is so cool! Call me again when you can get me on the radio, and I'll play songs for you."

I drive through Albany and turn onto Route 88. Just before Cobleskill the highway rises out of the valley, and at the top the entire Susquehanna valley spreads out beneath me. It is breathtaking every time. At the bottom of the rise, just after the rest stop, I turn my dial to 88.9, WXLO. Within a mile the static clears, and I hear Joe's voice clearly.

"And here's an old favorite from They Might be Giants going out to the night shift."

"Birdhouse in Your Soul" starts playing, and I dial the station's number. After two rings Joe answers.

"I can hear you now," I say. "And why do you keep talking with that strange accent? It sounds like a cross between an Irish brogue and a preacher."

"It's my thing. It's the Father Joe Show."

"You're so weird. It doesn't make sense. There's nothing religious about your show at all."

"Well, my fans like it. Besides, I thought you liked weird."

For the next half hour, I have my own personal DJ. The sounds of Joni Mitchell, Madonna, and Billy Joel fill my car. It is one thing to have your favorite song come on the radio, another thing entirely to have favorite after favorite play in a long stream punctuated by the voice of someone you love. The buds on the trees are just coming in red and green, and my Volkswagen has a full tank of gas. Route 88 could take me all the way to Ohio if I wanted. I open the window and turn the radio up. I feel most home here in the between time, alone on the highway, neither at home in Hardwick or at my second home at Hartwick College. I feel the most at home moving and being nowhere in particular. It is the staying still in one place that doesn't seem to work.

"Gary, I'm just so sick of feeling removed from everything and not normal," I say.

"There's no such thing as normal, trust me. All you students, all of us as human beings, all struggle in some way or another to varying degrees. Really, there's no such thing as normal."

He purses his lips and steeples his fingers in the thoughtful way that he does.

"But I do have an idea to run by you. There's another student that I see, a young woman a year ahead of you who lost her mother four years ago in a car accident. She said she'd be glad to meet to with you if you'd like."

Talking to a complete stranger about something so personal would be terribly awkward. Gary seems to read my mind. "I know it might be uncomfortable at first, but I could introduce the two of you. You could meet here initially and see how it goes. Sometimes seeing someone who is going through a similar experience really helps. It's the entire foundation of most support groups."

He sees my hesitation.

"Think about it; we can keep discussing it."

The next session I agree to meet her. I decide I do want proof that there's someone else who might possibly understand what this is like.

We meet at Gary's office, and he does the introductions. Her name is Anna. We walk to the campus center for coffee. I'm inexplicably nervous and try to come up with interesting things to talk about. My sentences come out choppy and don't even make sense to me.

We talk about classes and majors for twenty minutes before Anna says, "So, I don't know about you, but this feels terribly awkward. It feels like a bad first date or something."

Relief floods me and I laugh. "I was just thinking the same thing!"

We talk for the next two hours—about our siblings and loneliness and feeling old. We talk about holidays and what it's like to even try to take your mother's place. We meet once a month. We have no classes together and no friends in common, but nod and smile whenever we see each other on campus. Once a friend asks how I know that girl. I don't know how to answer. I consider telling the truth and saying that we're part of small club that meets to drink lattes and talk about death.

Saying that "my therapist introduced us" also sounds too strange. I've only revealed to a few people that I even go to therapy.

"Through student services," I say. She seems satisfied.

"You have a lump in your right breast."

"What?" I say.

"There's a lump, right here," she points underneath my right arm.

This is a routine physical. There aren't supposed to be lumps. I am lying on my back in the exam room with the paper gown pulled down to my waist.

"Here." She guides my hand to it, and it is unmistakable. It is the size of a golf ball. *How could I have missed that? Well, easy,* I think. *If you're too afraid to do self-exams because of what you might find, of course you won't find anything. I thought this might happen someday; I just didn't think it was going to happen so soon. I thought I'd make it to at least thirty. Damn.*

The appointment stretches into hours. They try a needle biopsy and find it is a solid mass. The mammogram reveals the same.

"Most likely just fibroid cysts. Really, nothing to be concerned about, but we should take it out to be sure."

Nothing to be concerned about? Are you kidding? I want to scream at them. *This is my life we're talking about.*

They schedule a day surgery in two weeks.

I tell Beth about it before I go back to school after spring break. We share a bottle of wine on the back deck, bundled in coats against the cold April night.

"I'm not telling the guys," I say. "No way. I'll tell them if there's anything to worry about. But there's not. It's just cysts right now." My voice sounds more sure that I am. At all costs I want to protect them from this kind of worry. I want to tell Joe, but we're taking a break from each other. My choice, of course. My stupid choice. I never know whether to call him my boyfriend or not and I thought that seeing him less might make our relationship less confusing. I picked a terrible time for a break. I ask Gary about it during our next session.

"You need to get some support on this one," he says. "Tell your friends. Don't do this alone."

I tell Lynn and Kenli, and they are great. They offer to drive me, and I insist I'm fine with it; I just might need some help when I get back.

"What can we do? How can we help?" they say over and over again.

I think for moment. "Honestly, I just want to get fantastically drunk."

We go downtown.

I remember walking downtown to the bars; I remember dancing to ABBA, I think. I remember trying something in a little shot glass called a snakebite.

Later, Kenli smoothes down the hair on my forehead. Lynne takes off my shoes.

"Gaylie, we'll be right here." The words give me a flood of relief. I can't face waking up alone in the dark if the sadness comes. We moved in together at the beginning of the year and I can't count the times hearing their breathing from across the room made the night less dark. I'm flooded with love for them—unreasonable love. I start crying a little. Between tears, with slurred words, I choke out, "You know, you're my Tacy and Tib."

"What?" Lynn asks.

"You're my Tacy and Tib," I repeat louder. "I'm Betsy and you're Tacy"—I stab one finger in the air towards Lynn—"and you're Tib." I gesture towards Kenli.

They looked confused .

"It's from a book I read when I was little." I lean over and dry-heave into the trash can Kenli has put by the bed. She holds my head. Both my mouth and the trash smell like fermented beer and lemons, and that makes me wretch harder. After a few minutes, I lie back and take a sip of water and continue. I have to explain it.

"They are three best friends who live in Minnesota." My head hurts now, and I am frustrated that they don't understand.

Kenli eases me back on the bed while Lynn pops two Tylenol into my mouth and hands me the cup of water.

"It's OK. You can tell us in the morning. Just go to sleep now."

I close my eyes and hear the familiar sounds of them opening drawers and turning off the lights. Like we do every night, we all exchange "goodnights." I'm half asleep, but the last thing I hear from across the room in the darkness is the smile in Lynn's voice as she says, "Sleep tight, Betsy."

A few days later, I drive the four hours to the hospital and am surprised to find out I need a ride home afterward. I hadn't planned on that and have to get back to school that night.

"It's policy for general anesthetic," the nurse says. "No exceptions."

"Can you just do it under local?" I plead. "Please? I'm fine with it. Please, just check with the surgeon."

She leaves and returns a few minutes later.

"He agreed, but he said to warn you that you are going to feel it. There's no way he can get enough Novocain in there so you won't."

"It's fine. Thank you."

Soon, I am strapped to a table, my arms outstretched in a cross, with a thick strap around my waist. There is a sheet curtain around my neck so that I can't see what is happening. The nurse is right, I do feel the needles going in, but after that it isn't so bad.

They keep asking how I am doing.

"Fine, thank you," I answer.

Towards the end I feel the surgeon prod the wound to pull it closed, and the room wobbles, then spins. I feel his fingers on my ribs under the skin deep inside me. I swallow hard and pretend that it is someone else's body on the table.

The pain starts halfway back to school after the Novocain wears off. The label on the Vicodin says to not drive while taking it, so I hold off as long as I can. I'm still twenty minutes from my dorm.

I did not plan this out well.

I time the next three days around taking Vicodin and staying coherent enough to study. One night I drink two beers with it to see what it will do, but it just makes me tired.

A week later the call finally comes. I take my phone into the hallway and make the nurse repeat the answer twice. It's fine. I'm fine. Just a cyst. No cancer. I had been waiting for her to hand me a death sentence, at which point I would need to completely rearrange my life. I don't have to move across the country in order to avoid having my brothers see me sick. I don't have to. I am healthy. I am going to live. I didn't realize how much I wanted to until there was the possibility that I couldn't anymore. I have five metal staples and an ugly pink scar on my breast. Pity, I was just starting to like them—their weight on the front of my body and how they look under tight shirts. But I don't care. I don't have cancer and that is all that matters.

I share the good news with Lynn and Kenli. I call Joe later that night, and he comes over. We talk until almost dawn. I need to stop this cycle of on-again, off again. We only have one year of college left, and I'm going to make a go of it with him. He's stuck by me through everything and has always been there no matter how hard I tried to push him away.

⟋

I invite a group of friends to come home with me for Easter weekend. Although we haven't spoken it out loud, Jack, Carm, Beth, and I have a consensus that we're going to celebrate holidays, but do it in our own way. So each Easter, Fourth of July and birthdays seem to follow the same pattern. They begin with cars of friends arriving and people claiming space in the spare rooms and couches. We've added some permanent mattresses stored under beds and put as many beds in one spare room as possible. Now the house sleeps eleven in beds and four more on mattresses. There's room for ten more on couches and floors.

I don't know if we are trying to fill in the missing by adding people, but it seems to work. We take turns grocery shopping and cooking. Easter morning I come to breakfast wearing the pink rabbit ears Mom made for me to deliver May Day baskets when I was nine. I can't believe they still fit.

We all drank too much the night before and down cup after cup of water followed by strong coffee, then devour an enormous pile of pancakes. Later, we check the Jell-O eggs that Beth made the night before. The first batch oozed out of the molds, so for this batch she tripled the amount of gelatin. We run them under hot water, and they pop out of the molds easily, perfectly formed. They have pretty psychedelic translucent colors—garish blues and greens—and look more like alien eggs. Although we try to eat them, they are inedible. We're all in a fun mood; it's another three-day party. Jack gets the idea to launch them off the back deck with a water balloon launcher. We take turns sending the eggs flying out into the back field. If they hit something, they make a satisfying splat sound. Carm runs to the road and retrieves one. Remarkably, it is still intact. He finds more, and we have a round two.

We spend the rest of the afternoon making games that involve the launcher and the eggs. Jack puts on the pink rabbit ears and runs into the field.

"Hit me!" he yells. "Just try to hit me!"

We try but he can anticipate the path of the egg projectile and leaps out of the way. To make it more challenging, he takes off his belt and cinches it around his ankles so he has to hop. With every hop the rabbit ears flop up and down, and I hope a neighbor drives by to see this—a man hopping around a field in pink bunny ears. On Easter. More than that, I hope there are kids in the car. An entire minivan filled with kids. It would make their day.

Finally, one hits him square in the chest, and he yells something un-intelligible and falls into the grass. He comes up kneeling.

"Son of a bitch!! That hurt."

We're laughing too hard to stand.

Later, we get out our books and pretend to study for upcoming mid-terms, but mostly we just sit in the March sun and talk. The day is broken up by a collective nap and meals and various games. We joke about how it is a lot like summer camp with scheduled activities and meals and minimal adult supervision. Some of us are barely old enough to be camp counselors, but the name sticks. Camp Huntress is born.

In May, even though it's the week before finals, Jonathan comes home with me to see Carm off to the prom.

Carm comes downstairs in his T-shirt and dress pants, holding a comb.

"I can't get my hair right."

"You want me to help?" asks Beth. Her hands are deep in a bowl, mixing fruit salad.

"Oh, let me do your hair," says Jonathan.

Carm hesitates.

"I guess so. As long as you don't make me look gay."

Jonathan rolls his eyes.

"Looking gay and looking good are almost the same thing," he says, pushing Carm towards the bathroom.

Twenty minutes later Carm comes down in his tuxedo, his hair gelled and parted perfectly. He struts around the fireplace, then presses his back up against the mantel. He hums two bars of the James Bond theme song and makes his fingers into a gun. We laugh and Beth straightens his bowtie.

We take pictures in the yard next to the yellow forsythia. Beth can never remember the name of it, so it's become the "school bus" bush to all of us.

"Look serious for one," she says.

Carm's smile disappears, and he turns his head and stares intently towards the top of Sessions Road. For a moment I can see the features of the man he is becoming: his jaw more square, his shoulders angular, and his brown eyes intense and kind.

The missing catches inside me like a hiccup. I cough to clear it. Mom would love seeing this. I love seeing this.

The four of us drive to the town common that is already teeming with the other families. The girls are giggling and tugging at their dresses, and the boys are holding plastic boxes of flowers out in front of them with both hands as if they might explode. Carm's date is pretty and blond in a tight dress. He pins the tiny corsage to the top of her shoulder strap. Beth made him practice in the car. The other boys struggle with theirs before they line up in a row for pictures.

The four couples look like they've stepped out of a *Prom Dreams* magazine. I could have never pulled off a look like that when I was seventeen. Probably still couldn't.

The limo arrives and parks next to one of the old stone hitching posts. A red-faced man whose stomach pushes out against his cummerbund opens the door and gestures grandly towards the velvety insides. Parents shake his hand, and I hear one mother ask to make sure the liquor cabinet in the back is empty.

"Sodas, only," he says and chuckles. "Don't you worry." He says it like it's something that is actually possible.

We all stand and wave to the limo until it's out of sight. Jonathan takes my arm as we walk back across the common, and I link my other arm through Beth's.

"I'm glad they have a driver tonight," I say.

"Yeah," says Beth, tightening her arm around mine.

Chapter Seven

I'm slightly hungover, but not too bad. I saw one guy throw up in the bushes as we were marching out. Classy. I just hope his mother didn't see.

We file in a long line to our seats and sit in full sun for the ceremony. I can feel my face getting burnt, so I tilt the cap low on my forehead for shade. So the mortar boards are good for something after all. I make it up to the stage and get my diploma; my advisor hugs me and it's over.

Afterward, we walk in the opposite direction of the crowd headed to the quad for watered-down punch and cookies. Instead, I take my family to my car, where we pile in and drive to the bird sanctuary that, along with the woods behind the campus, has been one of my sanctuaries many times over the last four years. I came here a lot to walk and get up to the top of the hill to get a different perspective. I was here a week ago to walk and think about graduation when I realized that I didn't want to be anywhere near the quad afterward with all the proud moms and dads.

I talked to Gary about it.

"What if I decide not to go to the graduation reception? Is it some kind of cop-out to avoid it? Should I be facing it bravely or something?"

He shook his head. "No, I don't think so. Find what works for you and your family. That's the brave thing to do here, whatever it looks like."

So champagne and birds it is.

This morning I packed a cooler and a paper bag, so when we get to the top, I pass around cheese and crackers and bottles of lemonade. It's way better than bad punch and food-service cookies. I pour the champagne out into paper cups for a toast. We even let Carm have one too, then tip our paper cups together in "Cheers."

I load up my apartment and move back home. I think it is less of a defeat to move back home when that home technically belongs to me. I settle into a rhythm of sleeping late and spending the afternoon working on the house or the yard. The yard seems to need mowing every three days. Everywhere I look I see things that need to be painted or fixed. I make almost daily trips to Aubuchon's hardware. I joke with my friends that I'm living the life of an old retired man.

Throughout the spring I watched friends send in graduate school applications and line up internships, and, for some, a real paying job. I didn't have it in me to do any of it, I was so worn out. Still, now, I'm so tired. It can't be right to be this tired and be twenty-two.

Friends come and stay in the extra bedrooms at Camp Huntress— some for weeks and months. It's like a halfway house for those in their twenties. We have a really good time, but we're all in limbo between jobs and homes and relationships. Everyone is either in graduate school or in an entry-level job that is awful.

This is not the life I imagined. I imagined some kind of career that had meaning, working with interesting people, and maybe even making a difference somehow in the world. I pick up some odd jobs for the summer, but mostly I sit on the lawn tractor and drive in circles around the acres, thinking about what's next. Getting through college was my blueprint for the last four years. Freshman, sophomore, junior, senior. It was a clear and linear path broken into neat semesters. I was so focused on graduating and staying connected to my family that I never thought about what was to come after the diploma.

In the spring when I was contemplating what life might look like after college and coming up with a blank, I talked to Gary about how lost and directionless I felt.

He nodded and said that most every senior that was in his office that year was having similar feelings.

"When you've had a big loss or challenge in your life, it can be really easy to use that as an excuse. Try not to do that, OK? If your parents were still here, you'd still have problems and challenges. They'd just be different ones. Your life would not be perfect and easy with them here."

I know he's right, but it's hard not to imagine an alternate reality where life is easy and happy. In that reality, my parents would be waving from the doorstep, and I'd be trotting off to medical school, happy and ambitious, knowing exactly what I wanted. I'd have a white coat to wear for my internships, with my last name embroidered on the breast pocket. The white coat would probably even be ironed.

Before we had our last session, Gary talked about ways to find a new therapist wherever I ended up. I can't imagine starting over with someone else and having to tell the entire story over again to a complete stranger. It keeps me from calling anyone.

"Now is one of the few times in your life when everything gets dismantled," he said. "You're going to leave this college community, and all your friends will scatter all at the same time. This won't happen out in the real world. Friends will come and go, and you'll change the place you live, but it will never be one full, clean sweep like graduation is. Make sure you get some support."

He's right, but still I can't bring myself to do it.

In midsummer we start planning a huge party to celebrate my graduation from college, Carm's from high school, and Jack's from graduate school at Boston College. We hadn't had a big party event since Jack turned twenty-one and we all decide it is time to revive the tradition. We print up the invitations and call it the "Camp Huntress Tri-Grad Party."

We set up the barn as a contingency plan, but the weather is perfect and people stream in, lining Sessions Road with cars from one end to the other.

One hundred people come; some relatives fly in from across the country, but mostly it is the Hardwick community and our school friends. We invite everyone. The bedrooms are all full, and tents get set up in the yard.

Joe brings his music collection, and we rent a big sound system and set up twinkle lights. Carm borrows trampolines from friends and sets up three in the backyard, and we bounce wildly from one to the other.

At dinnertime, the music stops and Jack takes the mic and gives a short thank-you speech to everyone for coming and bringing food. He thanks everyone for being so supportive of our family over the last four years. Pastor Alice says grace and we eat.

Late in the night when we're dancing under the stars and the kegs are almost empty, I have the strange urge to take my diploma out of its frame and cut it up into confetti and give everyone a piece of it. It belongs to everyone as much as it does to me.

Joe shows me his summer sublet. It's a duplex—nicer than any of the places we stayed in college. It looks almost like a real house. I haven't seen him since the party because his doctorate program started so early.

We talk for a while, but it's awkward and halting. I can tell he's watching me closely.

"How are classes?" I ask.

"They're good. Lots of intro stuff, intro to research and the thesis process and stuff. I think I know who I want to work with; hopefully I'll be done in five years. Four if I'm lucky."

I nod. Five years seems like forever.

"Are you happy you chose it over Notre Dame?" I ask.

"So far."

I choose my words carefully and say, "I need to know again that you didn't choose Amherst so you could be close to me. I need to know that you chose it because it was the strongest program."

"I did; you know that. We talked about it a million times this spring."

I nod and can already feel the sting of tears in the corners of my eyes. I wonder if he knows what's coming. After all these years breaking up with him multiple times, I wonder if he can feel it or if he knows this time is different.

"We can't be together," I say quietly, trying to keep my voice steady.

"I know," he says.

"I still love you."

"Me too."

He looks so sad. I want to take it all back but can't.

"You know, I wish you weren't so kind. It makes this really hard. Can you be an asshole just a little, or just pretend to be one…If you're not, I don't know if I can go."

"Um…you're a bitch?" he says in the kindest tone possible with a question mark at the end.

"Yes, I am, I say. But for some reason you can never see that."

We sit in silence, both staring down at the floor.

"This is different than the other times, isn't it?" he finally asks.

"Yes, I think so. This is for real."

"OK," he says.

"I can't see you for a long time. A year, at least. It's the only way I'm going to be able to get over this…over you."

I step out into the sun, and it hurts my eyes that are already puffy. He doesn't follow me to the door and I'm grateful for it, but I can sense him behind me, still sitting on the couch. I walk as fast as I can to the car. If I hesitate at all, I might turn back. I might go back to him and bury my head in his shoulder and beg forgiveness for leaving and say that I love him and we'll make it work somehow. But we won't.

I know with certainly that nobody will ever love me like he did with that level of unwavering devotion. But I need something else, or, rather, someone else. So does he. He deserves someone who can love him with the same level of devotion, and I need someone who challenges me. If I stay with him, I'll always rely on him to relieve some of my sadness and emptiness. I have a vague sense that if I stay with him I will never become the person I'm supposed to be, even though I have no idea who that might be. All I know for sure is that I need to know what it feels like to be on my own. The certainty doesn't make it easier though. I drive away and try to calm the pressure building in my chest. It is an awful thing to know that your heart is breaking as it is happening.

The house has had multiple layers of paint over the years, but paint can't cover up 150 years of New England weather. With houses as old as this, there's no way to figure out when they got their last facelift.

We have a family meeting and all agree that we're going to try and keep the house for a few more years—at least to get Carm through college. We say that it's important to have a home base to go to when you're in college, but we don't say that it is as much for us as it is for him. Plus, I don't know where I'd go. Not having this place, this home, to be the hub for our family is unthinkable. When I was young, I used to think that moving was the worst thing that could happen to someone. I remember the handful of classmates who came and went through the years: the girl with the funny accent from Georgia and the one that I gave stickers to on the bus because she was moving away to Springfield. I couldn't understand why she didn't seem sad to be leaving her home and moving to a city. I kept asking her, "So you're just leaving and never coming back?"

"Yeah," she said. "But we're taking all our stuff with us."

"But what about your room and the grass in your yard and your favorite trees?"

She shrugged and said in a tone that implied it was enough of a full explanation, "My mom says the new house is bigger."

It was raining that day, and I was wearing my favorite purple rain poncho. The stickers I had in my pocket were damp, but I pressed them into her hand anyway. They were the neon-colored smiley faces we got for spelling tests.

"Take these with you," I said.

I felt so sorry for her. Maybe she didn't understand what moving meant and how awful it would be to leave your home.

I still feel the same way about it, and I'm baffled by people who pick up and go to a new place without a second thought. I can't imagine ever feeling about another place the way I feel about this home and this land.

It is so much a part of us that it is like another family member. I'll take care of it as long as I can—more now than ever. This is the only thing I know.

We take out a home equity line, and I gladly take on the role of general contractor. I don't know anything about construction, but none of us does. I'm the only one not working or not in school, so it makes sense in a way. This becomes my new job. Renovating.

We hire a carpenter named Chip who lives in the next town. He smokes small cigars with white plastic holders that he balances between his teeth while he works. He says it keeps him warm.

He and a younger guy who doesn't say much come every day it's not pouring rain. They work all fall and into winter, even on the coldest days when I can tell their tools have frost on them. They often work without gloves, and their chapped, red hands make me want to feed them.

I collect quick bread recipes, and soon I can get a banana bread in the oven in ten minutes. When it's done and cooled, I stand on the porch and yell "Coffee's on" to the guys. I serve it on the tray with matching cups, and they hold the porcelain cups with their big hands with black fingernails. They remind me of the men I knew when I worked at the farmers' co-op, like Russell. Men who do hard work. Good men.

After coffee break, I go out with them and look for places to help. They seem glad to have someone for the grunt jobs. Some days I help them tear the clapboards off the house when they're trying to beat the weather. We wedge crowbars under the boards and pop them off. The wood cracks and splinters. I collect the hand-forged square nails and put them in an old coffee can. It doesn't seem right to throw out something that took so much work to make. The steel galvanized nails that will replace them look flimsy and cheap. The new clapboards and windows take away some of the strange angles it had, and Chip even props up the drooping roofline.

In the spring as soon as there's no more chance of frost, I start painting. I like the rhythm of moving the paintbrush back and forth, watching the house look like itself again, but better. I discover books on tape at the library and find an old Sony Walkman in the office closet to play them. They have a few books on CD at the library, but they are new and hard to get. But there are plenty of books on cassette tape, especially the classics. The twenty-five tapes that make up the unabridged audio version of *The Grapes of Wrath* get me through almost two full sides of the house. I'm good at it, if one can be good at such a repetitive task. I move the paintbrush back and forth, spreading an even coat of Olympic Stain in Gray Sandalwood, and the Joads travel the dusty roads from Oklahoma to California. Ma and Pa hold the family together, and Tom stands up for his ideals, and they all refuse to be broken by circumstance.

⁓

I run up Ruggles Hill, a half mile uphill in semidarkness. The air is searing my lungs, and the back of my throat tastes metallic. At the half-way point, the road curves to reveal more hill, and it's a disappointment every time. The second half is steeper than the first half, and my legs scream to stop.

But I can't. The dawn chorus is still going strong, and the tree canopy is alight with birds and morning sound. The grayness of the woods starts to take on shapes and different shades of new spring green.

I feel everything and nothing at the same time, and this hill is why I take this route. I put one foot in front of the other. I breathe. I don't think because there's no room left for thought in a brain completely crowded out with physical sensations. And it makes each sensation more intense because when I run this hard, there is nothing else.

At the top, finally, Ruggles Hill evens out and I take the turn fast onto Ridge Road and the flats. The sun is red and just coming up, mostly still hidden, and the sky is pink over the trees to my left. The air smells like wet earth, in the way it does in early April when everything turns to mud.

And then it happens. My legs start striding on their own as if they know where they are going. My breathing turns from ragged to even, and I am flying down the road. The white church steeples look pink in this early light and point out of the trees in the middle of town back where I'm headed. Two more miles, and I'll be home.

I can't believe I went this long thinking running was something to be avoided and a punishment. I remember the forced laps around the ball field in Little League when we weren't paying attention or didn't sell enough raffle tickets and how I detested each lap. There are lots of days I don't want to go out to train, but now I seem to need it. It's the only time that things fall into place and make sense, where the objective is clear and simple: just run.

Later, I try running six miles. Then eight. The day I do ten, I know I can do twenty and sign up for a marathon. The books and articles about training are so simple. It is an equation. If I train and run five miles, then the next time I run five miles it will be easier. If I add intervals next time, I will be faster. This is a clear effort where results are guaranteed. This is a part of myself I can understand—my body as an equation.

In October I need new pants for the winter. I pick out a stack of pants in my size and carry them into the dressing room. I undress and pull on the first pair. They fall off my hips to the floor. I go back out to the racks and get the next size down and then the next. I stare at my body in the mirror. I haven't looked at myself in a full-length mirror in half a year. I had no reason to. How did this happen? It is not my body there, reflected back. My hip curves out from my waist. I have ridges on the sides of my torso, and I poke them with a finger and realize they are ribs. I move my nose inches from the mirror to make sure it is me looking back. It fogs and my reflection is ghostly. I wipe it clean.

Part IV

Chapter One

June looks at me from her rocking chair, pulled up close to the sofa I'm sitting on. When she met me at her door moments before, she said "Welcome" and swept her hand through the doorway to indicate how welcome I was. At least she didn't try to hug me. I don't like it when someone I just met tries to hug me, especially not a therapist. I think there should be a separation between client and therapist, and I can tell she's probably someone who is an over-hugger. She has on a long, embroidered tunic over jeans and is wearing sheepskin slippers on her feet. She had me remove my own shoes at the door, and I'm glad I'm wearing good socks today; I didn't even think of that. Her earrings are long and dangly, and her hair is short and gray, cropped just below her ears. I can't tell if she's wearing make-up at all, but her eyes are bright and almost clear blue. They are the eyes of someone you know is always watching, even when they aren't. We settle into our seats and I wait. I think she's supposed to start by asking me a question. So I wait.

"How can I help?" she asks.

I can feel her eyes on me, and I look up at her and then away. They are kind eyes, but it is hard to be looked at with such intensity.

"I'm having…" I begin but don't know how to finish the sentence. I thought her first question would be something easier, like my age, or profession, or marital status and I could answer succinctly, as if filling out a form.

1. Twenty-three

2. Office manager for a software company

3. Single, one previous serious relationship

"I need some help with…"

With what? With not feeling so bad all the time? With having some direction? With being less broken? With patching all the holes and emptiness?

"It's all right not to know the answer to that question," she says. "Let's try a different one. How about, what brought you here to see me?"

Good, that's an easier one.

"You came highly recommended as someone who is unconventional but knows how to really help people fix problems they're dealing with."

For some reason I see humor in her eyes when she asks the next question. "OK. And what's the problem you're trying to fix?"

"Well, it's not a problem, exactly. I just feel like I should be happier or better somehow."

"Tell me more," she says.

"Well, life, my life, didn't go exactly how I planned it, and I feel pretty stuck. I don't know what to do next—personally or professionally or otherwise. I've been to therapy in the past, back in college. And it was really helpful in a lot of ways, so I thought I'd try it again?"

I try not to raise my voice at the end of the sentence to make it into a question, but it happens anyway. I wonder if there is a right answer. I tuck one leg under me on the couch and run one hand through my hair, hoping it will make me more comfortable. It doesn't. I think it was a mistake to come. I'll just get through this session, write her a check, and be done with this. I was stupid to think that someone else could help change my internal landscape. The darkness is just the way I am and the way I feel. I think maybe the lightness of living only belongs to children and those who have had life happen the way they expected. It's not so bad, the way it is now. I live in a home I love with Beth and sometimes with my brothers and all of the assorted people that come to live there, long and short term. Jonathan drives out from Boston almost every weekend, and we do house projects together and cook elaborate meals with Beth and whoever happens to be around at the time. We have fun. We take care of each other. Between Jack and me and Beth, we have enough income to take care of the house and pay Carm's tuition. A lot of people don't even have close to that, and I should leave the therapy for people who have real problems. I'm OK. I don't really need this.

June's voice brings me back into the room. "Gayle, you just disappeared for a minute. What were you thinking about?"

I want to tell her that I was thinking about something that happened yesterday or a grocery list, but I'm here because I wanted to tell someone what's going on in my head, and it defeats the purpose if I lie.

I look at the floor. "I was thinking that it was a mistake to come here and that maybe I don't need to be here after all."

"Oh, I see. Well, you can certainly leave at any time. Since this is our initial session, this is like an interview to see if you and I are a fit. If you don't think we are, I encourage you to maybe try somebody else. I have a list of names of colleagues in the area that I could refer you to."

I don't answer, and she continues, "How about I ask you questions about the type of person you'd like to talk to, and that can help narrow down the list of references."

"That's not it. I mean, I think we fit fine. It's just I think that maybe, well, I don't need therapy at all." I describe to her all of the ways that my life is working out. It seems like I talk for a long time. "So, things are working pretty well, for the most part. I don't really have real problems," I conclude.

June nods and looks at me thoughtfully. This is the way she must be, I think, lots of thinking and nodding and pausing before talking.

"I can see that you are a successful and pretty driven person. But I get the sense that you know that something is missing in your life. What is that, do you think?"

I answer before I think it out and filter my answer.

"Happiness."

And the word hangs in the air, and I know it is the truest thing I've said.

"So, you came back," says June as we settle into our seats. I into her big sage-colored couch and she into her rocking chair. It's chilly today, and she has a knitted shawl around her shoulders.

"After our last session, I wasn't sure if you would."

"I didn't think I would either, but I liked some of the things we talked about."

"Like what? What made you change your mind?"

"I guess it was thinking about what you said about happiness, although you called it joy. I liked what you said about it happening from the inside out.. That made sense to me. The external ways I try to make everything OK don't seem to work, so there must be something else."

"I wanted to ask you about that," she says. "What kinds of things do you do to, as you say, 'make everything OK'?"

"Well, I guess I kind of do lots of things. I keep really busy with work and social things and volunteering. I read a lot. I fill my days until there's not a minute to spare. I keep things really organized. I wouldn't say I'm a control freak or anything, but I like things to be even and steady."

"Are either of your parents like that?"

"My Mom was," I say. "She had lists upon lists and almost never stopped moving. She served on lots of committees and boards and was involved with the church. She went way beyond being an active member of the community; she was the hub of all sorts of things."

"You said your mom 'was,'" says June. "I assume she's no longer with us?"

That is a strange way to phrase it, I think. The euphemisms for the word dead are astounding.

I nod. "Right."

I don't offer any more, and the silence hangs in the room. I can hear the grandfather clock in the corner ticking.

Finally June says, "I can see you're not quite ready to talk about that. We can come back to it. Hmm…Why don't you tell me about your work?"

I tell her about my job at the software company and how much I enjoy working with the guys. I think they are brilliant, and we turn out a great product for chemistry education. I can't keep the pride out of my voice, and I much prefer talking about this.

"Can you meet me at the bank?" Jack asks. "We need to extend the equity line against the house for Carm's tuition."

"Sure," I say.

On the appointed day, Jack drives out from Boston, and I meet him at the bank. I am ushered into one of the back offices where Jack is already waiting. He stands and I peck him on the cheek. I turn to the woman behind the desk, and she stands and shakes my hand.

"Gay Ellen, nice to meet you," she says.

"Just Gayle is fine," I say, settling into the chair.

The woman, Beatrice, is in her mid-forties, I think. She has short brown hair and wire rim glasses. She's peering through them now at the stack of papers in front of her.

"So, you're taking out a loan against the property at—she consults her papers—forty-four Sessions Road. Is that correct?"

"Yes," says Jack.

"And you've lived there how long?"

"Um…about twenty years," says Jack.

"And you two are the only owners on the deed, correct?"

We both nod.

"And this loan is for the purpose of college tuition for your dependent, D. Carmody?"

We both nod again.

All of a sudden, she looks up and peers at us over her glasses. Then her face takes on the expression of someone doing long division in their head. She's trying to figure something out, and I wonder why she doesn't use the calculator that is right next to her elbow. She opens her mouth to say something, then closes it again. She shuffles through the papers on her desk and squints at them.

Jack and I exchange glances, and he shrugs.

Beatrice looks up. Her face is red, and she blurts, "I'm sorry, Mr. and Mrs. Huntress. This just doesn't add up!"

"Oh!" I say, pointing back and forth between Jack and me. "Oh! We're not together!"

"Siblings!" Jack says, horrified. "We're siblings! Carm is our *brother.*"

Beatrice sits back in her chair and fans herself.

"That is such a relief," she says. "I just couldn't figure out how you both could look so good and be in your forties."

I take off my coat and settle on the couch, and June brings me a cup of tea. I choose peppermint this time, and the heat feels good on my hands as I cradle the mug.

"How have you been?"

I start talking and telling her about the last two weeks.

She listens attentively for a long time and then says, "And how have you really been?"

The question catches me off guard. It's like she can see right into me.

I take a deep breath and leave the week's events behind. "I thought about what you said during last session—about either dealing with my feelings piece by piece and unpacking them slowly or going deeper all at once."

"And?" she asks, more curious than impatient.

"I think I want to keep doing this incrementally."

"All right, we can do that." Her tone is businesslike.

I feel the need to qualify. "I'm sorry, I wish I could be braver in this, but I'm just not. I can barely make it through what we're doing now. I'm just not very comfortable in this realm."

"No, don't apologize. The important thing here is that you know what you need and have asked for it. And again, my job is to support you in any way that you need." She doesn't seem disappointed, and I'm relieved.

"I do have one question, though, that I was thinking about," I say. "When things get really emotional, how do you keep people from, well, being totally overwhelmed and consumed when they go into the big feelings? Like, what do you do to prevent that? It's such an internal thing, and you're outside that, so I don't see how you can help. I guess that's the thing that scares me the most."

She nods as if she's been expecting the question. "First and foremost, I won't turn away. I will witness and respect whatever it is you're feeling without judgment. And I've been doing this long enough to know when someone is getting overwhelmed. I'll say words or hold your hand or do whatever it takes to pull you back away from the feelings again if it gets too much. I'll even shake you if I have to, although I've only had to do that once for someone."

I can't picture her shaking anyone. I'm baffled by what she does for a living.

I blurt out, "What is it like to have a job that is to be with people when they are in emotional pain? It sounds so awful."

June laughs.

"Oh, no, just the opposite. I can't imagine anything better for me to do. I guess I do have certain gifts and intuition that I was born with, and they help me see beyond the surface of things to help clients. I also believe that everyone has these gifts—it's just some of us cultivate them in order to be in healing professions. I really do love what I do. It is the greatest honor in the world to see someone reveal vulnerabilities and support them. It really is."

"Well, I believe you, but it still sounds awful," I say.

We talk some more, and then in a lull in the conversation, she says very quietly, "I'd like to talk about your parents. Are you ready to do that today?"

At the mention of them, my eyes fill with tears. I knew this was coming.

Damn it.

I nod anyway. I haven't really talked about them in any deep way since I did with Gary. There's something about having to tell the story again from the beginning that undoes me. I haven't been able to do it yet.

I swipe at my eyes with the heel of my hand. Incrementally, like she said, I can do this.

June reaches up with her slippered foot and pushes the box of Kleenex across the coffee table towards me.

"You know," she says, "I have boxes and boxes of these."

There is summer sun streaming in the window. I've watched the view from that window go from winter gray to spring green to lush summer green, like single snapshots in time-lapse photography. I feel like I've spent hours on this green couch, entire seasons, spilling my guts out. I don't like it, but it is doing something I can't describe that I do like, and I keep coming back.

June leans forward, elbows on her knees, so she's lit from the side by the sun. I feel the drop in my stomach. I know she is about to tell me something important and something I'm probably not going to like.

"As your therapist I'm technically not supposed to do this. I'm not supposed to advise you or tell you what to do but lead you to figure this out for yourself. But I think you've struggled with this one for a long time, so I'm just going to come out with it."

She takes a breath and looks at me.

"You're missing out. From what you've told me of your childhood, I think your essence is one of joy and engagement. You lost that somewhere along the way when you decided that life was not to be trusted and you had to hedge yourself against the sadness after your dad died. This was reinforced after your mom died. The very reason you're sitting here in my office is because you know, deep down, that something isn't right. Something is missing in your life. And the thing that you're missing is the full range of your feelings."

She sits back in her chair and continues.

"You can't selectively not feel things. In order to not feel the sadness or the anger or the frustration or any of the other 'bad' feelings, as you call them, you also damp down your access to the other feelings. So while you're busy keeping all that sadness at bay, you're also damping down a whole lot of joy."

I think for a moment.

"So you're saying that feelings fall on a spectrum, like a spectrum of colors? And I'm only seeing a few of them, and there're a whole lot more to see, or feel?

She nods and I continue, "It's like I'm only getting the red and the orange, and there's five more cool colors I'm not getting?"

"Gold star for you!" she says, smiling. "Great metaphor. I couldn't have explained it better myself. You got it."

I sit back on the couch, thinking. I remember that feeling as a kid, of feeling happy and knowing that nothing bad was going to happen. I remember feeling like I was protected and unafraid and not so careful all the time. Everything she said feels true to me. Keeping things even and steady is what I do. "Damped down" is exactly how I feel most of the time.

"How do I get it back?" I ask. "I want the full spectrum. How do I get it back?"

June leans forward again into the sun, and again I feel the drop in my stomach.

"We are going to have to unpack all those feelings. You're going to have to feel them in a deep and full way to get the full spectrum back. Are you ready to do that?"

I don't think I'm ready at all, but I'm going to try anyway.

I'm trying to focus on my breathing. The brochure said this morning's yoga class was for beginners. In a font that looked vaguely like something you might find written on papyrus, it claimed that "the growing popularity of yoga is due to its ability to bring every person, no matter what age or shape, greater flexibility, reduced aches and pains, and improved athletic performance. In addition, regular practice can bring a reduction in stress and an overall sense of well-being."

I'm not exactly sure what they mean by that, but I want it.

I want to feel like a well being. June said getting to feelings through the physical realm might work really well for me after hearing about how much I enjoy running.

I still get out and run, but on the coldest days and the days like today when the there's a storm and a thin film of ice everywhere, I do my miles on the treadmill at the gym. Today all the treadmills are full.

So, here I am, breathing, or, rather, being reminded to breathe by an instructor who looks like she subsists on lettuce and herbal tea. She elongates all of her vowels when she talks. I think it is supposed to sound calming.

"Breeeeathe," she says.

"Ooopen your heeeeart," she says.

"Feeel the stretch in your haaaamstriiing."

I arrange my limbs to match the way the woman in front of me is standing, one leg forward and bent, arms outstretched, then move down to the floor. It's like a push-up, except my butt is way up in the air, and it's called "downward dog," like a dog stretching, I guess. We come to this pose over and over again. It makes my arms and shoulders ache, so it must be doing something.

At the top of the hour, the instructor floats over to the CD player in the corner of the room. Chimes and chanting waft out from the speakers, and she instructs us to sit in meditation, cross-legged on our yoga mats, backs straight, palms on knees.

"Thanks for your work in class today. I want to reflect on the fact that there are a million reasons to do yoga. Your goal might be to be healthier, or recover from an injury, or bring more peace and balance and mental clarity into your life. These are all destinations. And just like you can use all sorts of modes of transportation to get to a physical destination, there are lots of ways to get to your goal. Yoga is just one way. I think it's one of the quickest because it focuses the mind and body in very specific ways. But the truth is, yoga is about involving the mind and body fully, being present, feeling everything. You can do yoga while you're doing the dishes or driving a car or talking to a loved one. The asanas, or postures we do, are just one way to do yoga. Yoga is another name for how to interact with life."

I reflect, but I have no idea what she's talking about.

"Mmmm," the woman in front of me says, as if in agreement.

"Let's close with three 'homes,'" the instructor says.

She rings a little tea saucer, and everyone around me says in unison, drawing out the vowels just like the instructor, "Home. Home. Hooooome."

That makes sense, I think, as the last syllable echoes off the walls. What better way to bring a sense of well-being than invoking home. I think of Camp Huntress with its wide beams and the smell of wood, all the people I love filling up the rooms.

As I roll up my yoga mat and wait in line to put it into the wood cubbies lining the back wall, I resolve I'll come to another class.

I advance from the multipurpose room at the gym to fancy studios with beautiful wood floors surrounded by Ficus trees and classes filled with trim people in actual yoga outfits. I did not know that yoga had its own clothing, but I suppose eventually every activity does. God knows I have a closet full of various running gear and at least a dozen pairs of trainers. I learn that we end class with "om," not "home," but by then I've already decided that maybe yoga is more than glorified stretching. Maybe it's not all bullshit and there is some spiritual part of it and millions of people aren't misguided, but just searching. Maybe if I keep doing it long enough I'll find it myself.

I pucker my lips in the mirror and run a tube of gloss over them. Lynn leans in close on my left and brushes her bangs. Kenli gets half her face into the mirror, applies mascara, then hops to the other side to get her other eye. The door cracks open, and Jonathan sticks his head through the crack.

"Ladies, we need to get going. Stop primping. You're hot enough."

"We are, aren't we?" I say, twirling in my long, blue velvet dress. I found it in the back racks at Salvation Army, and I'm pleased with it.

"Seriously, we need to go. I need to get the hot hors d'oeuvres into their warming pans." He comes in the room and takes Lynn's eye shadow brush out of her hand. "Here, let me." She closes her eyes, and Jonathan holds her chin in one hand and swipes the brush over her eyelids in quick, expert arcs.

We grab our handbags and meet in the kitchen, where Beth, Jack, Carm and their friends are already milling around and picking at the remnants of dinner. Rebecca and Beth are standing at the sink, working through a mountain of dishes. With only two bathrooms and a dozen people, getting ready took longer than we expected. We'll fill all the beds and couches tonight and overflow onto sleeping bags on the floor.

"Pictures, quick," says Beth. She balances her camera on the ledge in the kitchen and motions with her hands for us to squeeze in tighter. We drape our arms around one another. It's the entire Camp Huntress crew.

The camera beeps, and the red light blinks.

"Say, 'Happy New Year!'" she says.

We pile into cars for the short drive to the town hall. Jonathan has gone ahead and greets us at the door, balancing a tray of stuffed mushrooms in each hand.

"There're already twenty people here," he says. "Beth, I took their tickets and showed them where the bar is. The DJ is all set up."

"You're the best," she says.

The main hall looks even better in the dark with the lights low. It didn't look all that festive when we decorated in the afternoon, but now with the flickering candles and the disco ball in the middle of the room it looks fantastic. The music is quiet, then the DJ puts on something louder. I watch in delight as the dance floor fills with my college and high school friends and adults in town who I've never actually seen dance. It's a multigenerational gyration. Jonathan walks by and takes my hand and twirls me around the floor, then dips me dramatically. My forever perfect date.

Chapter Two

I 've been seeing June for almost two years. Sometimes it seems like we make so much progress that I can actually feel the pieces of myself falling back into place. Sometimes it seems like no time at all has passed, and all of my broken pieces are as broken as they ever were.

"You're thinking of this in a linear way," June says one day. "It doesn't work that way."

"What do you mean?"

"It seems like you think that if you come to therapy and do all the right things and read the right books and write in your journal and do yoga that eventually you'll get to a place where this doesn't affect you anymore. That might happen for you; I don't know any of my clients well enough to ever tell them the way their healing is going to happen. But for everyone I've ever worked with and in my own experience, it just doesn't work that way. It's going to be hard for a while and you're going to feel stuck and then you'll get to a point where everything feels good. You won't feel 'broken,' as you call it, anymore. You'll wipe your hands and think, 'Oh, good, I've put that behind me. I'm all set with that.' Then weeks or months or even years will pass, and then it will come back again. It's a cycle, Gayle. Grief isn't linear."

I trace a circle around my knee, and I think about it.

"You look really disappointed and sad," she says.

"I am. If it's just going to come back again, then what's the point of doing any work at all on it? Why even try to feel better or more whole?"

She looks at me evenly.

"I'm not going to answer that for you," she says. "Think about it for next time."

I get up to leave and resist the urge to slam the door of her office. Sometimes I wish she would just tell me things. I get in my car and drive back to work. The red lights aggravate me. The car in front of me that forgets to put on its turn signal bothers me. I want to lay on the horn when it makes a sudden left into a gas station, but the car is long gone.

"Fuck you," I say to my windshield.

I'm ready for the next session.

As soon as I have my coat off and we're sitting, I say, "June, I have a working theory. I figured it out last week walking down the street by a jewelry store."

June clasps her hands together, a rapt audience. I feel like I'm ten and showing off a school project I'm proud of.

"I saw a nautilus shell hanging from the store window. It was cut in half and inset into a stained glass circle. So one side you could see the shell side and the spiral on the other."

"Aaand," I continue, drawing out the word to make it dramatic, "I think that's the answer and why I think I need to keep working at this."

"Because of the spiral?" she asks.

"Exactly. I don't think that grief is cyclic—that implies a circle: the same thing around and around again. And that's not how it feels to me.

"It is definitely more like a spiral—like a perfect nautilus shape but with some dents and imperfections in it." I draw a spiral in the air with my index finger to demonstrate. "Not exactly adhering to Fibonacci principles, but close to it."

June laughs. "That's the first time anyone has brought Fibonacci into a therapy session, but I like where you're going—continue."

"So anyway, you start at the center in the dense part, the darkness. And you start moving out along the lines of the spiral. At the center, it's still pretty frequent and dark. But it changes. It gets lighter and more expansive. But you keep moving. You keep getting more space in between the lines. I guess it is the same thing, the same line you're on over and over again, but, unlike a circle, you're actually moving towards something. I don't know what that something is, but you, or I in this case, have to do it. Because I sure as hell am not going to spend any more years in that dense, dark part in the center."

June claps her hands together. "I love it! That is such a great analogy!"

I smile with her, then get more serious.

"Why couldn't you just tell me something like that last week when I asked? Why couldn't you just tell me?"

"I could have, but I could tell you were pretty angry and probably wouldn't take it in. Things like this have a lot more meaning when you figure them out for yourself. Am I right? Were you angry?"

"Yeah, I was angry. I still am, I guess. I'm just angry at having to deal with this; this is the deal I got. I know it's childish and useless, but I guess I'm mad at having to work so hard to be OK. I just feel so damaged sometimes."

June slowly puts her tea on the coffee table and leans forward.

"Time for a life secret," she says. "Everybody—and I mean *everybody*—is damaged somehow. You can't make it through life without it. Yes, some people have things happen that you might consider worse than others, like death or abuse or addiction or major illness. But even if you don't have those things, maybe you had to live through a divorce of your parents, or being teased as a child, or being left by your first love.

"There's no scale to measure the hard things in life. What is hard for one person, the thing that they spend the rest of their lives getting over, might be just a walk in the park for someone else. It's impossible to judge how deeply something might affect or not affect someone. In my years of practice, I've met clients who have endured the worst abuse imaginable and all sorts of trauma and tragedy, and they're OK. They worked through it and took responsibility for themselves and their lives and are no worse off than anyone else. In fact, the ones that had to go through the worst are often the ones that end up more stable and happy in the end…Let me give you a metaphor."

She pauses to think for a minute.

"It's like they've had to go into the blackest darkness you can imagine alone, and they've gotten out. The only reason they do is because they have found the light inside them needed for the journey. From that point forward, they know it's always there to draw on should they need it, because they've used it before.

"It's what we're doing right now, in all these sessions. You're finding the light again. Can you sense that or feel that on some level? That things are lighter than when you stepped into my office two years ago?"

"Well, yes, things are definitely better. But I still feel damaged. I still feel broken. I feel like there are all these people walking around who got the secret manual about how to be successful and happy, and I didn't get it. I don't know how to *do* this."

"Do what?" she asks.

"Do *this*. Do life. Make decisions. Move forward. I'm so stuck. I don't know what I want, and I don't know how to decide."

She has that knowing expression on her face.

"OK, ready for another life secret?" she asks.

I lean forward on the couch to listen. I think she should write a self-help book called *Life Secrets* or *What You Should Have Learned by Now But Didn't*. It would sell millions. Or maybe just a few copies. I don't know. Sometimes it seems like everyone else knows things I never caught on about.

"Making a life takes practice. Some people seem to be really good at it and make choices, and things seem to work out magically for them. But it's actually a learned skill. Just like you take for granted the fact that you know how to eat well and get enough sleep and exercise and generally take care of your physical needs, there are full-grown adults, some even in middle age, who never really learned how to take care of themselves."

"Really?" It seems so basic. How could anyone not be able to do that. It's the most basic part of survival.

"Really," she says. "It's hard for you to imagine because you've been doing it for long, and you had good models in your family for how to do it. But other people actually have to learn it. They have to learn what works best for them and their bodies and through trial and error figure it out."

I am incredulous. "No kidding?"

"Creating a life is exactly the same thing. You just need to make best guesses based on your intuition and what you think might work for you, then execute those decisions. Pay attention during the process to see how it makes you feel."

She makes it sound so easy, and I know it's not.

"But what if I choose wrong? What if I completely mess it up and make a wreck of my life?"

She smiles at me, amused but not unkindly.

"You will. I guarantee you'll make mistakes. That's the whole point. You need to start practicing choosing things for yourself and take some time to really consider what you want in your life. With your relationships, your work, your family. Don't live a life of default, Gayle. That's the worst mistake you could make. Choose. Make mistakes. And then choose again and choose again. Go for what you want, and ask for what you want. That's the way to do life."

We sit regarding each other from across the coffee table. I realize I have tears in my eyes and take a Kleenex to wipe them away. I always think I might be able to get through one of our sessions without turning into a puddle, but I never seem to make it.

Her voice goes gentle.

"Hon, this…this deciding what you want and choosing it is hard for you because you didn't get what you wanted. There's a little girl in you who wanted something very badly, and it didn't turn out the way she wanted. I wasn't there, but from what you've told me, that was a big unexpected blow to you."

I nod and then as usual, she asks the question that takes my breath away.

"What do you think that girl wanted?"

Now the tears are really coming. I give up dabbing them away and just let them run down my face. I'm about to say the thing that of course I wanted, but have actually never said out loud. I've actually never admitted how disappointed I was by what happened. My voice comes out in a shaky whisper.

"I wanted them to get better. I wanted them to live."

She holds me in her gaze and nods. It was such a given—wanting something that I didn't get—that I overlooked its importance somehow. By never acknowledging it, it's like I never really accepted the hurt of it. And it's as if the coil of springs inside me unwinds and relaxes for having said it, like releasing a breath I've been holding for a long time.

In the way that makes things more true, June repeats it back to me, her voice steady, "Yes, you wanted them to live."

The room is full of windows overlooking the valley. When it gets dark, you can see the lights of the city in the distance. I watch beads of sweat drip off my nose steadily like a leaky faucet. I don't think I've ever sweat this much. Ever. At the end of two hours I am spent. The instructors keep talking about the spiritual part of yoga. They don't shut up about it through the whole three hours of each session. They talk about the yoga of presence, of breath, of just being with the moment. I stifle my smirk when the instructor says for the eighth time, "Foster openness; keep breathing." I've allowed myself secret eye-rolling at all these reminders to breathe. All I can focus on is the drips of sweat and the burning in my legs. Why don't they talk about that?

After four days I feel like something is melting from me with all of the sweat and effort. I've never done yoga like this. This is impossibly hard. I can't wait for each session to be over. In between sessions I walk in the lush gardens and sit in the chairs overlooking the valley, drinking as much water as I can hold. I decide doing vacations for personal improvement isn't really a vacation. I'm wondering if I'll make it through the week. In the afternoon on Wednesday, I just can't do it anymore. I talk to myself in my head, like I do on a hard run facing a big hill or three more impossible miles.

You can do this.
Just get up.
Power through this.
You can do it.
One more pose.
Don't fail at this.
Get up. Get up!

I stand and arrange my limbs into a loose approximation of those around me. Warrior Two pose. My legs are shaking, and my arms feel like they have sandbags tied to them. Gravity is stronger than it normally is. My legs buckle and I come down to my knees. I just can't do it anymore. A sense of failure floods over me. Everyone else is still standing, sweating, performing, strong in Warrior pose. I just can't do it. My body feels slumped and weighted. I can't move. I feel stuck to my mat. The feeling of defeat starts at the top of my head and flushes out to my skin. I have to get out of this room. Somehow I stand and stumble out the door and fall onto the prickly grass outside the studio. I put my head between my knees and start to cry. I can't tell if it's tears or sweat streaming down my face. It doesn't matter. It all is just salt water. What's wrong with me? Why am I being so sensitive? It got hard and I fell apart.

I sense someone next to me, sitting down on the grass. It is one of the instructors.

"I came out to see if you're OK. Are you?"

I wipe my face with my arm and shrug. "I guess so. I just reached my limit."

She nods. I know she sees I'm upset but is completely unfazed and matter of fact. We sit in silence for a few minutes.

Then she says, "Sometimes when you go to your edge your body just releases. There is a theory that memory and emotion are stored in us— not in the brain but in the cells themselves. So if you work your body hard enough, it comes out. I've had it happen to me before. It's a really good thing. You're going to feel lighter after this. It's like a surrender—a letting go of emotions you've been holding on to.

"This isn't failure. You simply reached your limit for today. There's no shame in that. In fact, you can still do the yoga but not the poses."

I give her my skeptical look. It sounds like some kind of Zen Koan riddle.

"No really. You can. Remember, the yoga is about the presence. Just being with it, not hiding or trying to stop the emotions. It's not really about the poses, although most people think it is."

I run my forearm across my face and nod. It doesn't really dry anything but does move around the sweat and tears, the salty soup drenching my face. "I don't know if I can go back in there."

She reaches out and rests two fingers on my shoulder.

"You can do it. Come back in. Do Child's pose. Do Shavasana. Just sit there if you need to. The yoga is the noticing. The yoga is the being. Your yoga today went beyond the poses and went internal. That's the most challenging type of yoga there is."

She doesn't say anything more but I realize I'm holding my breath. I don't know if I've breathed since I left the studio. My first breath comes out ragged and the instructor puts her whole hand on my shoulder again and squeezes it until the ragged sounds even out.

OK, breathing, it is.

Thursday evenings I drag the trash barrels out to the street. On my way back to the house, I pause in the yard in the waning light by the miniature crabapple. Every year I climb it in early spring and prune back the gnarled branches. We've all touched this tree at some point, even Beth, following the decades-old scars with pruning shears repeating the same cuts. I touch the other plants as I pass them: forsythia, rhododendron, myrtle, holly, sedum, dogwood. I know them but have been completely lost for names in other gardens. I only know about what needs attention in my own yard. Dad knew the names of all plants and how to care for each one. I think about his broad back, brown and bare in the summer, when he kneeled in the dirt. I think about him standing tall, how he seemed as tall as the trees, when he rose to stretch.

Now I kneel in the damp grass in the semidarkness and push some mulch back into place. We spread it by the wheelbarrowful when Jack and Carm were home last weekend. When we work together taking care of the house, we fall into a wordless rhythm, handing tools back and forth, holding back branches, stepping aside for a shovelful of dirt. Beth once threw down her trowel in exasperation when we stood in silent union to move to the next section of the yard.

"You gotta talk to me and tell me what's next!" she said.

I didn't realize we hadn't been speaking.

I stay on my knees for a while in the darkness, inhaling the scent of things growing. The lamp in the TV room goes on, and I can see Beth settling into the couch. The yellow light from the windows splays out over the yard in wide arcs, and I stand because it pulls me towards it like a moth towards a flame. Warmth. Home.

Chapter Three

I wonder what this man will be like. He had a kind voice on the phone, and we talked about his outdoor company. I'm thinking of doing some part-time work in addition to the software job to get outside more. I read through my résumé again. I have lots of experience despite the fact I haven't been working in the field for a few years.

I lean up against my car, and it is hot against my back even though the day is cool. I look up and squint into the sun, and there is a man walking towards me across the parking lot. The afternoon sun is behind him, and he is backlit so I can't make out his face, but I know instantly that this is the man I have been waiting to meet—not just today for this interview, but maybe always. A voice in the back of my head echoes from a place I have never heard. It is inside of my head but not coming from me.

"Oh, it's you," the voice says.

"Hi, I'm James," the man says.

I extend my arm, and then he wraps his hand around mine, and it sends a jolt of electricity up my arm.

We have lunch and talk about the various trips we've taken and led. Throughout lunch I study him between small bites of my chicken salad. I know he is older—maybe thirty-something—and he's not wearing a ring. He has a disarming confidence, and I have trouble eating and carrying my side of the conversation at the same time. I wish I had put on make-up today. I give up on eating and have the waitress wrap what is left of my lunch. He insists on paying as a business lunch, and we shake hands good-bye in the parking lot. When our hands wrap around one another, instead of a jolt of electricity, there's a spread of warmth. I let go of his hand even though I want to keep holding it. I don't know what to say. I feel like I have too many arms, and I'm not sure where to put them. I put my hands in my pockets, then take them out again to give him a small wave as he walks away.

June's new puppy greets me at the door. Lucy is an adorable golden retriever, and this is our third meeting. She sniffs my shoes, then runs away into the living room. When she tries to stop, her paws splay out on the smooth wood floor, and she yelps then rolls over to her back, wiggling with all her paws in the air.

I'm laughing as June comes in to hug me.

"I feel better already," I say. "Lucy is really doing a good job as therapy dog."

We settle in and June asks, "So, what's happening in your life?"

Before I answer, she squints at me from her rocking chair.

"Wait a minute, are you in love?"

My face gets hot although I don't know why I'm embarrassed.

"Yeah," I say shyly. "It shows, huh?"

"I could tell something was different from the minute you walked in the door," she says, clasping her hands in front of her. "Oh, this is exciting! Tell me everything!"

I tell her about meeting James and how I had an instant feeling of something electric the first time I saw him. I tell her how I've never felt this way, but I'm not sure I can trust it since I've only been in love once before, and that was different from this. This time it's uncomfortable, and he puts me off-balance. Our interactions send me spinning towards new thoughts and feelings I've never had.

"I don't know; this just feels more real somehow. I can't really explain it."

"You don't have to," says June. "Falling in love is its own thing entirely that defies explanation. This is wonderful news!"

It's dawn. It's not light yet, but the birds have started their morning chorus, calling out to the first rays of sun that are streaming over the trees. People are sleeping everywhere. Some are in tents, but some just lay down where they were and fell asleep—in lawn chairs, on the soft grass, on the trampoline. Most have sleeping bags, but some are covered with a beach towel or have a jacket tucked under their heads as a pillow. I walk among the sleeping people and pick up beer bottles, then unplug the lights in the dance area, picking up paper plates as I go. I do one final lap around the house. The fire pit where the spit was set up for the pig roast is still smoking and smells faintly of barbeque. I turn off the slushy machines, still churning the remnants of bright-red strawberry daiquiris. Throughout the night there was a line of people waiting for them, outdoing the line for the keg. In the front yard, someone in one of the tents is snoring. I am the only one awake.

I need to go to bed. In a few hours, everyone will be up. Beth will fill the party carafe with strong coffee. I'll put out bagels and juice and a bottle of aspirin for those that need it. We'll spend the morning cleaning, breaking into small groups to get the work done. We'll play the radio loud, dragging around trash barrels and taking the lights down. It's an odd thing about these parties: the preparation and the cleanup are almost as much fun as the party itself. In the afternoon we'll eat leftovers and fall asleep in lawn chairs and maybe play a languid game of volleyball.

I walk through the silent house to my bedroom and step over Lynn, into bed. She's sprawled out on the floor in a sleeping bag. She's still wearing that same brown T-shirt she wore to sleep in college—now even more threadbare. I pull the corner of the sleeping bag to cover her and feel a wave of love. Both she and Kenli are in graduate school, but we try to get together once a year. We still talk on the phone weekly, but it's not the same. I miss them.

I lie in bed and close my eyes, but I can't sleep. It was such a good party. One of our best. I think we even topped the Tri-Grad Party three years ago. There were so many people I loved in one place tonight: the community and neighbors, high school and college friends, and people from work. If I go to sleep, it means the night is over, and it was so good I don't want it to end.

I had been waiting all afternoon for James to arrive. With each new person walking down the driveway, I had squinted, willing it to be him. Later, I was in the backyard at the buffet tables, and I looked up and there he was, standing on the porch. My heart leapt and I followed it, bounding up the two steps into his arms, kissing him in front of everyone. Later, we danced under the square of yard lit with Christmas lights, and then when the band finally stopped, I walked him to his car. He hugged me tight, and I loved the feeling of his tallness and his arms around me. He pressed his lips to mine, my back pressed into the hood of his gray Volvo, and the soft night pressed in around us. Our mouths moved together, and our arms and legs tangled but still seemed to have a place. Eventually he stood me back up and let our lips touch slowly, almost chastely, before getting into his car. I stood in the darkness and watched the Volvo's taillights disappear over the hill of Sessions Road, then I floated back to the party, my body tingling.

On the way, I waved to the leaving truck carrying the band and their equipment away. They were good: part-country, part-rock. Beth is dating the lead guitar player. I watched the way she watched him play tonight on the little stage. It is a good thing to see love made visible like that. They are planning on moving in together in the fall. Jack and Carm are living in Boston and come home every few weekends. The visits are becoming less frequent as girlfriends and their work take them to a life outside of Hardwick. I am splitting my time, too, and feel the pull of a different life away from here. Tonight feels like it is the end of something or the beginning of something, or both. I need to sleep but still don't want to. I want to hold on to the night just a little bit longer.

⌒⟩

"So, James and I passed our one-year anniversary," I say.

"You don't seem very enthusiastic about that," June says.

I shrug.

"I guess I thought it would be different than this. The nine months or so was pure bliss, then something happened. I don't know what's going on. We don't feel as close as we did in the beginning. I'm really emotional a lot of the time, and we have to talk about things a lot; the conversations aren't really light and fun. They're hard—really hard…" My voice trails off. June has heard this all before. We've been talking about it for months.

"Hmmm," says June. She's got her yellow legal pad out on her lap where she sometimes takes notes. There's a lot of writing on it, so it must be from our previous session. She taps the pad with the eraser end of the pencil. "There's a piece here I think you are missing, and that is that love, or rather a relationship, can be very, very uncomfortable."

"You mean it's supposed to feel this way?" I make a face like I just ate something unpleasant.

"No, not supposed to. But it can, especially if you're working through some of your own issues. Do you remember when we first started working together and we were talking about feeling the full spectrum of your emotions?"

I nod.

"This is the same thing. You're going to feel sadness and anger and resentment and boredom and all manner of emotions in your relationship in addition to the ones that feel good.

"But in a relationship it goes one step beyond that. In addition to actually feeling those things, you must say them out loud to share them with James—even the bad ones. Especially the bad ones." June does little bunny-ear air quotes with her hands around the word "bad" whenever she says the word.

"You're going to have be open in a way that I know is really scary for you."

"Why?" I ask. "Why do I have to share the 'bad' feelings?" I do exaggerated air quotes when I say "bad" to mimic her.

"The sharing, my dear, is where intimacy comes from. You get to be who you are and express the full range of yourself and still be loved. The closeness you're missing is because of lack of sharing."

"OK, but what about my girlfriends? It's so easy being with them. I love them, and I don't feel this same discomfort with them. It's fun, expansive...just easy."

June nods in agreement.

"You're right. There's something about a romantic relationship that is different. It just is. Your friendships don't have to weather the stuff of life. If you were in a relationship with anyone where you had to negotiate things like finances, fidelity, sex, family, and make all those decisions that sharing a household entails, you'd have to deal with all this. The beauty of friendships is that you don't have to; friendships exist in a narrower context, and you can easily skirt around difficulties or differences. In a romantic relationship, especially if you're living together, you're confronted with the issues on a daily basis. I think it's easier sometimes to love friends because we don't generally put so many expectations on our friendships."

"It doesn't really sound appealing when you describe it that way. And we're not even living together yet. Why not just be single and have great friends?"

"You could certainly do that. I have a few single women friends who do that and are very happy; I think it's more of an option for women than it is for men since we're generally better at forming and maintaining those really intimate friendships that can sustain our emotional selves."

June crosses her legs and sticks one foot through the arm support of her rocking chair. I'm always surprised when she does this. It doesn't seem like someone of her age should be that flexible. She puts her palms up towards me.

"So, it's an option...You can walk away from this relationship with James and avoid these issues. Maybe even find someone else who is 'easier.' But avoiding them doesn't make them go away. They are still there. I think the most beautiful part of human relationships is that we get to be hurt and upset and feel the entire spectrum of emotions and work it out. It will lead you to a greater understanding of who you are. For most people, forming intimate relationships is the best chance we have for becoming our best selves."

June puts her other leg up so they are both crossed in front of her in the chair.

"If you're serious about this man, it is going to take a tremendous amount of courage. It is going to push you, and it is going to bring up all sorts of big feelings."

"I don't know if I'm ready. It seems kind of irresponsible to me and to him when I'm not sure I'm ready."

"Well, as with everything, it's your choice."

I nod sadly.

After a long pause, June adds, "But, for what it's worth, from my professional opinion: I have faith in you. You're at the point now where you've done enough work that you can deal with it. It is going to make you more of a whole person if you let it. I encourage you to try."

Snow is falling outside the window, and Lucy is sleeping on my feet, keeping them warm. The room seems extra cold, but maybe it is because we are talking about death.

June asks, "Do you believe in heaven or some sort of afterlife? Or any sort of idea where somebody's spirit or love remains after they die?"

"Nope," I say. "Heaven seems kind of like a childish idea to me. Just like God does. It is like putting your faith in a magical unicorn, but a magical unicorn that lots of people seem to illogically buy into. It doesn't make sense to me."

"But you had a religious upbringing?" June asks.

"Yes, very much so. My parents were fervent believers, but it didn't seem to do any good. In fact, sometimes I think it made it harder for them to face the reality of what was happening to them. I remember my mother's prayers on morphine, her insisting she was being healed. I don't know. Maybe it just brought comfort in some way and that was enough." I shrug.

"I'd like you consider something, and it's a big something," June says. "I'd like you to consider that your definition of God was and still is a bit limited."

"What do you mean?"

"You have this image of an all-powerful being in the sky either helpless or indifferent to your plight. There's nothing wrong with that; it's what you were taught. But I'd like to give you a different perspective. Would you be willing to hear it?"

I nod.

"When you talk about that time in your life after your mom died, it seems like you feel like God abandoned you."

I nod again, and my jaw involuntarily tightens.

"I'm going to ask you to try on another perspective. Imagine that God is not a thing separate from us, but something inside us, all of us. Imagine that God is love, simple as that. Ultimately, love is what all religions point to. They each call it a different thing and explain it in different ways, but in the end it all usually boils down to love and divine spirit. When you talk about that time in your life after your mom died, you also talk about all of the people who cared about you—about how you put your faith in them. You've told me about all the people in Hardwick who watched out for your family. What if the thing you were putting your faith in is actually God? What if the kindness and love of all those people *is* a manifestation of that divine spirit? What if you were seeing God all along, every day, in a million different ways and just didn't know it? What if God was coming through all those people?"

Her questions send a shiver down my spine. The world seems to tilt on its axis, and I put my hand down to June's couch to steady it. It is as if all of the pieces of a jigsaw puzzle I've been holding get broken up and reformed to make a new picture.

We sit for moment in silence, then June taps her chin with her index finger.

"Can I give you some homework? I want you to research some other religions: what the basic beliefs are and what are their views on death and the afterlife. See if you can find some common themes about divinity, and see if any of them fit for you, now, for where you are. I'd like you to take a special look at Buddhism because it gives some practical tools for how to get acquainted with your thoughts and feelings and how those things get generated in a person."

I open my eyes into a slit and look around the meditation hall without moving my head. It is an odd thing to sit still and even odder still to do it with fifty other people. We are evenly spaced on floor cushions, with our backs ramrod straight. I find it's not too uncomfortable if I remember not to slouch my shoulders when I sit. Some people have shawls or blankets around their shoulders, giving them a triangle look. The hall is still lit by the candle sconces reflecting off the tapestries, but the rectangles of the windows are now dawn-gray instead of black. The session must be almost over, and my stomach growls for breakfast. I think of coffee like I do every morning and am disappointed when it's not there. It's dumb to still hope for it, because it's not allowed, but I do anyway. Afterward, I'll scrape crusted oatmeal out of a stack of bowls higher than my head. I'll do it in silence, standing next to the man with a bushy beard who is also doing the same thing. I don't know his name, but it doesn't matter because we can't speak, although we have developed a shorthand of charades to ask each other for more soap or a new sponge. It will be my favorite part of the whole day because I get to do something. I get to work and have a purpose, even if it is just completing a stack of dishes. I kind of wish I could do work all day. I wouldn't even mind doing it silently side by side with nameless people.

It is the sitting that is the worst, and it is the sitting that makes up most of the day. For those hours and hours, I despise having to sit still and having to watch the gymnastics in my head. Eventually the thoughts tumble wherever it is that feelings begin, and then I have to watch them try to wrap their strong, spindly arms around my heart and squeeze. Sometimes I win, and the feelings run through and melt away just like the Dharma teachers said they would. Sometimes they win, and all the sensation and darkness that I've been trying to keep away grows inside me. It is all I can do to stay put as my muscles twitch and my skin itches to get away. Sometimes tears slide from the corners of my eyes. I try to remember the inside stillness that the teachers keep describing, the place they say you can always come back to no matter what is happening. I twitch and hurt and come back. Feel and melt and come back. Again and again, a million times a session.

I know what I will tell June next time I see her. I will tell her that she was right about meditation. I'll tell her I now understand and I am acquainted with my feelings, but we are definitely not friends.

Chapter Four

*J*une's window is open, and I see a film of pollen on the screen. The green outside is spring-like, and its brightness seems to mock me.

"I hate this holiday," I say. "It's not even a real holiday. It was just invented to sell more greeting cards."

"I assume you're talking about Mother's Day?" asks June.

"Yes."

"It sucks," I add.

I'm in a rotten mood today. I shouldn't be taking it out on June, but the great thing about her is that she always seems able to absorb my moods, whatever they are. She'd probably call my rotten mood authenticity or have some other kind word for it.

"You're right. Holidays can suck pretty badly for people who are missing loved ones."

I'm amused that she said "suck." She looks like a proper grandmother in her rocking chair, taking a sip of tea.

"You can see this as something that sucks. In a lot of ways it does. But you can also see it as an opportunity to create your own traditions and make the holidays work for you in a way that makes them not suck."

She continues, "One of the parts of being an adult is taking a look at your traditions and reevaluating them, not just to keep doing traditions because they are traditions. Does that make sense?"

"Yeah."

"Listen, let me give you an example. I have a client who has a difficult family and for years he'd go be with them and there'd be a big family fight and he'd leave with leftovers and a heavy heart. We examined his favorite parts about the holiday and found out what he loves is the tradition of the meal and watching football, uninterrupted. So now, he goes to a local restaurant and gets a take-out dinner, complete with turkey, for himself, sets up the coffee table with a full place setting and candles and linen napkins, and has a wonderful afternoon relaxing and eating and watching football—alone, because that's the way he wants it."

"That sounds awful," I say.

"Well, of course," says June. "Because you're you. And to you and your family right now, the holidays mean being together and cooking together and having your traditional meal. But that's not everyone's cup of tea." She holds up her steaming cup to me as if to illustrate the fact.

"When you came in, you mentioned that Mother's Day is a greeting card holiday. Is that what you miss?"

"Yeah, I miss going to the store and picking out the right card with the right words and having someone to send it to."

"OK, so you like picking and sending out a card to someone who is special to you?"

"Yeah."

"How about this? How about you still get to that that? Just because your mom is gone, it doesn't mean you have to stop doing that. You could still pick out a card for her and bring it to her graveside."

"It sounds more than a little crazy—buying a card for someone who is dead."

"Who's to judge?" says June, putting her palms up in a shrug.

I shrug back. "I guess so."

I get an idea.

"Wait, what if I could buy a bunch of cards and send them out to the people who are like mothers to me, like Gram and my aunts and some mothers of my friends?"

"Bravo! That's a great idea. You need to keep remembering that you're in the driver's seat here when it comes to making your life work. Your parents aren't here to provide a lot of things for you, but that doesn't mean you get to give up and just not have them. That's not OK. Instead, it means you have to figure out how to provide them for yourself or ask for those things."

I leave the appointment and drive into town. I'm excited to go to CVS now and comb through the racks of cards. How instantly things can change on June's couch.

I give a long sigh and put my tea back on the coffee table. We've been talking in circles. I take a surreptitious glance at my watch to see if the hour is up yet.

"You seem frustrated," says June. "Or is it bored?"

"I'm sorry. I guess I'm sick of hearing myself talk about this. Sometimes I feel like I have no right to feel sad. I've been given so much: a happy childhood, awesome parents, great brothers, friends, family, community. Not to mention resources. I've always had enough; sure, it's been tight at times, but we've always had plenty of food, clothing, shelter and knew there were people we could call on if we didn't. I don't want to squander all this; I feel like I've been given so much. I'm just not doing a very good job of it."

"Of what? What aren't you doing a good job at?"

"Of being successful and happy and a good person. I still feel mean and sad and angry and all sorts of other awful things. I just think I should be doing better."

June's mouth upturns in the way she does when she's amused. It's like teasing but it's not unkind.

"So, you think that maybe there's some other version of yourself in a parallel world that has a better life? That version of yourself has made different choices, has the perfect relationship that always feels wonderful, a career that is one hundred percent fulfilling, her house is always clean, and she's probably thinner and more beautiful as well, right?"

Damn. I hate it and love it when she reads into me like this.

"Well, when you describe it like that, it sounds pretty ridiculous, but yeah, I feel like I'm in the wrong world sometimes. In that parallel world all the people are totally happy and doing all the right things."

"Oh, sweetie. There is no other world, no other try at this. You only have this trip. You're doing fine. Most people are, but think they should be better in a thousand different ways. There is no better. Just this."

June reaches down to run her hand along Lucy's side, who is sprawled out at the foot of the rocking chair. June gives her a final, vigorous scratch.

"Just this, right, Lucy?"

Lucy looks up briefly at the mention of her name, then lays her head down again and gives a contented sigh.

June straightens.

"Listen, I want you to consider an important question."

"What if the measure of your success is not happiness? Not perfection? Instead of making the goal to be happy and feel good all the time, what if instead you changed the goal to be engaged? Just engage with what's in front of you, not try to change it, and see what you can learn from it. That goes for situations, people, and even your own emotions. Notice, accept, and then decide how you want to engage it."

"That sounds exactly like what my yoga teacher says when we're sweating through a hard pose or what they say is the reason for meditating."

"Exactly," says June. "Both traditions are trying to give you ways to deal with your own human experience in a healthy way that works."

I make my back straight and my breath even and wait. The morning sun streams in my bedroom window and splays out over the rug. It is an odd thing to sit cross-legged on a pillow alone in a room and do nothing except be still. But I keep trying. Sometimes the stillness inside comes, and sometimes it doesn't. When it does come, my thoughts and feelings slow down and arrive one at a time instead of in a jumble, each one separated into its own partition of a moment. I don't know how to make it happen, but it seems to happen more often when I'm meditating with other people. I've asked June about it, and she says there is power in people meditating together; it lets you be supported in the energetic sense. I have no idea what she means by this. She seems to share a vocabulary with my yoga teacher, who also names the ephemeral with words like "empower" and "soul" and "flow" in such a convincing way that I almost believe they are real. When I asked June for proof of how one knows these things are happening and how she knows they exist, she just shrugged and said, "Intangible mystery!" Now, it's become a catch phrase in our sessions when we depart from the world of the senses. When she says it, it's my clue to accept whatever is happening without needing an explanation of why or how it works.

"Stop trying to figure it out and pick it apart," she says. "Just rest in it."

"How's the relationship going?" June asks.

"Good. He asked me to move in with him."

"What did you say?"

"I said yes. I think I'm ready…we're ready."

"And what are you going to do about the house?"

"That's the million-dollar question. My brothers and I have talked about it ad nauseam, but we're just not ready to sell it yet. It doesn't make any sense to keep it, but still, I find it so hard to imagine a world in which it's not there, not ours."

"How so?" asks June.

"Well, it's like my safety net. It's my Plan B. If life doesn't work out in some way, I can just move back to the old house and go back to my old life and be fine. It feels like everything will always be OK if I can go back there."

I pick at a loose thread on the knee of my jeans.

"What else?" prods June.

I sigh. "Even though it's a happy time to be moving in together and everything, I guess I have a lot of doubts about the relationship. I watch friends of mine jump into living with people or even getting married, and the whole relationship thing seems so risky: to put all your eggs in one basket like that."

"You mean, it's risky to love one person intensely?" asks June.

I shrug. "Yeah, I guess. I just feel like I always have to hold back a little and not give my whole heart over, you know?"

June bites her bottom lip and looks at me intently. It sometimes unnerves me when she does this, like she's reading something. Finally, she says, "You're looking for a guarantee, aren't you? You're looking for assurance that he won't leave or he won't die, and then once you have that guarantee, you'll commit."

"Yeah, that would be nice." My voice has an edge, and the edge sits in the air for a few minutes, so I glue my eyes to the floor.

"You realize that's impossible, right?" June's voice is quiet, and the sharp edges I feel go soft. Tears spring to my eyes and I nod.

"We don't get guarantees. Not even you. You're not exempt from loss. Nobody is."

The wave crashes over me. My voice is choked and comes out just above a whisper. "But what if he dies, June. What if he leaves me?"

"Oh, sweetie," she says and pushes the box of tissues towards me across the coffee table. "When a person leaves or dies, they don't take their love with them. I know it can feel that way. But it's actually not true. Their love gets planted in you, and you're the one that tends it and helps it grow regardless of their presence in your life."

I swipe at my eyes and shake my head slowly.

"It's not true, those are nice words and I wish it were true, but it's just not. Maybe it's true for other people, but it's not for me. They're gone, June. Have been for years."

⌒⟶

I brush the rain off my shoulders, onto the tile in June's foyer and slip off my muddy shoes. I got wet in the few steps between the car and her door. It is a steady, relentless rain. In the kitchen I choose chamomile tea, and June fills my mug with steaming water.

We talk for a while before June says, "I was thinking about our last session and your feelings about loss and how that relates to your life currently. I have something I'd like to try. Would you be willing to do an exercise with me?" she asks.

"Sure, I guess."

I don't necessarily like her exercises, but I know they can take me places I can't go on my own, or won't go. I'm not sure that she knows how much trust I have in her—that I'll follow her just about anywhere she wants to go in the emotional landscape.

"OK," she begins, "I want you to close your eyes and breathe."

I'm ready for this part and realize I have already closed my eyes and I'm taking exaggerated breaths.

"What are you smiling at?" she asks.

"It's just funny; all of your exercises begin like this."

"Hmm…I guess they do, don't they?" I can hear the smile in her voice. "I actually do have some that involve movement, but we've never tried those. You move enough in your life; I'm trying to encourage you to be more still and inward."

She continues, "So, are you with me? Breathing? Eyes closed?"

"I'm with you," I say, taking a huge breath and letting it out slowly.

"Keep going," she says, and I can hear her breathing with me.

"OK, I want you to think about your dad and think about what it felt like to be around him. You're ten, he's healthy, you're with him. What do you feel?"

I feel nothing. I refuse to. I hate having to remember this. It makes the emptiness feel larger, and I want to avoid it.

"It's OK. You can go there to that feeling and it will feel hard at first, but then it will get better. I need you to name it and feel it, and then we can move on."

Getting this over with sounds good, and I try harder. Still, there's nothing. "I'm sorry, I don't have anything," I say.

"I think there might be something in the way," says June. "Keep your eyes closed, and focus on where in your body there might be something in the way."

I run my attention down my body, like in a yoga pose, searching for tightness. "I think it's here, in my chest," I say, pointing just behind my rib cage.

"What color is it?" she asks.

Color? How can a feeling have a color?

"I don't know," I say.

"Well, what if you were to take it out of yourself and examine it, say under a microscope? Describe to me what you'd observe." It is a weird request, but I do what she says anyway and envision my rib cage opening and revealing what is inside.

Surprised I say, "It's black. It's knotted, sort of oblong and round. It's heavy like it has a high density."

"Good, good. Now, imagine you can let that be and breathe around it. Feel what it's like to have your dad with you."

"I feel"—and the word comes to me in an instant, obvious and clear—"safe. I feel like someone is watching out for me and keeping me safe. Nothing can hurt me. He's there and I'm safe."

"Great. Now I'm going to ask you to do the same for your mom. Imagine her. Imagine her in this room with you. Imagine the feelings she has for you. What do you feel?"

I open my eyes and shake my head. "No," I say.

"What's the matter?"

"I can't go there."

"Why not?"

I search for the words, thinking. "You're asking me to remember and feel what it was to have her here before she died. If I feel that, if I remember, it will remind me of what I don't have any more. It's too much. It's too big. I can't look at it, and I can't feel it. I'm sorry. I just can't."

I rub my forehead and look outside, where the rain is abating a little. I feel bad. I know I've let her down. I'd do this if I could, but it's just impossible.

"What do you think will happen if you do?" June asks.

"I'll be lost—swallowed up by the enormity of it. Listen, you're pretty understanding, but I don't know if you get how big it is. This is one thing you just don't understand." I'm angry now, and I don't know why. I sit back on the couch and cross my arms. I feel childish, and I don't care.

June leans forward. "Gayle, I've been working with you for quite a while, and this is the one big ouch in your life. I do see how big it is for you. I know this is not easy. You might be feeling some anger right now because you're afraid I'm going to push you into something. Remember what we talked about in our first session a few years ago…What we do here in this office is completely up to you. It's your life and I won't push you into anything or be disappointed if you to. Only you can know what you're ready to do. My job is to things, feelings, out of you and support you in examining them.

She pauses and reconsiders. "Well, for you I would say it's more to draw out your feelings and actually feel them; I think you do enough examining them on your own." She does not say this unkindly, and I am grateful. Her words are so gentle it's impossible to hold on to the anger.

"Listen, my other job is to not let you get lost in your grief. Sometimes when we have feelings that are so big, it does feel like they will swallow us and never let us go. But I won't let that happen. I promise. I'm here to witness it and make sure you don't drown in it, remember?"

I'm struck by her word choice, "drown." I've thought of it that way many times although never said it out loud to her.

"Yes, that's it. Drown. I feel like I'll drown if I feel these things all the way. It's OK to take them out in bits and pieces, a little bit at a time like we have been, but to feel them all at once..." My voice trails off.

June nods. "If bits and pieces is more comfortable, that's how we can keep working through this. But I do want you to think about it before our next session, if you would. I, as your therapist and as someone who cares about you, think you're ready for this next step. I think once you face this sadness head on it will release some of its grip on you. I'm not saying it will go away, but it will become more integrated inside you and a healthier part of you—instead of something inside you that you're afraid of."

I agree that I will think about it. As I'm driving home, I have the thought that there's nobody else in my life who asks me to actually contemplate the impossible.

I lie on the floor like June instructs. One of the pillows from the green couch is under my head. It's pretty comfortable on the throw rug, and there's afternoon sun from the window streaming down, warm on me. I could fall asleep here.

"Are you ready to try again?" asks June.

"Yes," I answer. We've been working at this for months.

She leads me through the breathing and tells me to put my hands at my sides.

"You're safe," she says. "I won't let you get lost in this."

More breathing.

"Think about your dad. You're ten, he's healthy, you're with him. See him next to you. What do you feel?"

I repeat my answer from the other times because it is the same every time. "Safe," I say. "I feel like someone is watching out for me and keeping me safe. Nothing can hurt me. He's there and I'm safe."

"Good, now I want you to really feel the safe feeling."

I do and June asks, "Where in your body does it live, and what is it like?"

"Here." I put my hand on my stomach. "It's like a comforting weight or something here."

I hear the rustling of June coming down to the floor next to me.

"Keep your hand there, and now I'm going to put my hand on yours, OK?" she asks.

I give a small nod into the pillow.

"This is the safety feeling." She presses her palm into my hand gently. "It's always here. It's like a gift your dad gave you. You can always come back to it."

My ears feel wet, and I realize my tears are running into them. June presses a Kleenex into my palm, and I wipe down my face.

"Do you want to keep going?" she asks.

I nod into the pillow again. This is farther than we've ever gotten. I can hear my own pounding heart in my ears.

"Breathe, Gayle. Breathe. Now, think of your mom. I want you to imagine her here with you. She's right here. What do you feel?"

My answer is a choked sob.

"OK, OK," says June. "I know it hurts. Stay with it."

I squeeze my eyes shut and turn over to my side and curl my knees to my chest, gulping in air between the sobs. June presses her hand into my heaving shoulder. Her palm is warm.

"I'm here," she says.

My breathing evens out, and I roll over to my back again and wipe down my face with the crook of my elbow. My chest is still heaving with breath, but my heartbeat is steadier.

"Now, feel into your mom's love as if she were right here. Go slowly, keep breathing."

My heartbeat is even, and I focus on my breath as if I'm meditating.

"Where is it in your body?" asks June.

I can actually feel the warmth, like a bright coal, just behind my breast bone. I touch my fingertips lightly to the center of my chest.

"Tell me the color. What does it look like?"

"It's white. No, wait, it's more than white. It's colorless. Just light. It kind of pulses, like a heartbeat, but it's more constant, less beats."

"Good. Breathe into that place you just found."

And I do. When I breathe and focus on it, it radiates out and feels bigger than my own body. For a moment I start to wonder what it is and what exactly is happening. The feeling starts shrinking immediately.

"Stay with it, stay with it," June coaches. "Just feel it. Breathe. You can do this."

I go back to the still place and feel the warmth in my chest spread again. It gets bigger. All of a sudden I see my mother's face, bright and smiling, her kind brown eyes. It's like she's in me and around me at the same time.

A gentle voice floats in. "Stay, stay with it. What does the feeling want you to know?"

My voice is choked but in between breaths I manage to say the words out loud. They come in a flood, forced staccato sounds in between wet breaths.

"Keep loving. Don't be afraid to love deeply. I'm with you.

"Oh. It's here, she's here. Right here.

"Love is still here.

"You can do this. You can love fully!"

My tears turn to laughter, and then I'm laugh-crying. I open my eyes, and the light is too bright. June is smiling widely above me, kneeling, and she claps her hands together and starts laughing with me.

"I can love fully," I say again, resting my fist on the center of my chest.

"That's it! That's it," June says. She helps me sit up and hands me a glass of water that I gulp down. She gets me another glass, then we talk some more, and when I finally stand to leave, I see I've been here nearly two hours. I awkwardly ask her if I can pay her for two sessions. She waves it off.

"I had a feeling we were going to do some longer work today, so I left the afternoon open. You did well today. In the therapy world, this is the kind of thing we sometimes call a breakthrough. But I want you to know that it won't be all roses from here on out. There's still more to do, but for now I just want you to enjoy this feeling and be proud of yourself for the work it took to get here. I know I am."

I feel immediately shy.

"Thanks." I can't look at her.

She hugs me again.

"Take care of yourself today—that was a lot on you. Drink lots of water, and don't do anything that requires a lot of concentration or physical effort. I know you have to go back to work, but take a walk outside beforehand if you can to settle."

I take her advice and drive a short way to a nearby park. At this time of day in the early afternoon, it's still mostly empty. I walk around in the bright sunlight and kick leaves, look up at the trees, and marvel at the color of the leaves against the sky. It's as if I'm seeing it all for the first time. The whole world seems brighter and clearer than I remember. Every dozen steps I have to stop walking and stand to take it all in.

Holy shit.

The intangible mystery.

Chapter Five

The picture shows Jack smiling, and his arm is around Heather. The light of the city reflects off the water behind them.

"She said yes," he says simply.

They plan a small wedding in an elegant room in the State House in Boston. I find him getting ready, just in time to help him with his cuff links.

"Are you nervous?" I ask.

He shakes his head.

"Why not?" This seems big to me. The kind of thing that would make the ground shake and world tilt a little differently. I feel my own world tilting at the prospect of adding another person to our family and Jack having a family of his own that is not us.

"I want this, and I'm ready," he says.

I wish I could figure it out myself and be that certain about James, about anything really. Maybe I'm just not built that way.

⁓

I lean forward on June's couch, put my elbows on my knees, and rub my temples.

"What's wrong?" she asks.

"I'm frustrated. It seemed like we made so much progress at first and now…" My voice trails off.

"Now what?"

"I guess I feel stuck. I think I've told you everything and we had that breakthrough and I made a lot of progress in my life and my relationship. But now, I don't know what else to say. And I still feel like there's something still there—more stuck grief or something else inside me that I can't talk out or process."

"Describe it to me. Tell me what it feels like."

"It's like a hard knot or a ball. Something with a lot of mass and weight that's right here." I move my hand in a circle around the center of my torso.

June purses her lips together and nods, like she knows something.

"It's really great that you can feel that and sense that. A few years ago you wouldn't have been able to say something like that. You were really ready when you started coming here, and that readiness created a lot of progress in the beginning. Now things are moving a bit slower, and you're frustrated by that?"

"Yeah, think I got spoiled at first because it was like I was having these revelations on a weekly basis. But now I guess I feel like no matter how much I talk it out, or breathe, or do any of the exercises we do, it's still there. I know this grief thing will come and go, but it seems like there are pieces of it I just can't reach, even with your help."

I shift on the couch and run a hand through my hair.

"I don't know. It's like it's preventing me from…" *From what? What are you talking about?* "From doing something or being something," I finish, still not sure.

June takes a sip of her tea, then uncrosses her legs so she can lean towards me in her rocking chair.

"OK. There are ways to reach what you're talking about, but I probably can't provide it for you. Usually, it involves work in some sort of a group setting."

"You mean like group therapy?" I ask.

I'd rather not share personal things with strangers in a musty church basement with watery coffee. I'll do it if it is the only way, but it sounds awful.

"No, I wouldn't call it that," June says thoughtfully. "Do you remember how you told me about a year ago about that yoga retreat you went on, the one where you got overwhelmed and had a sort of emotional release?"

"Sure." I had been doing yoga regularly since then but had never had it happen again. It was helpful, but not earth shattering and didn't seem very significant.

"Well, what I'm talking about is another kind of retreat that does something similar, except in a very targeted way."

She stands and goes to the bookshelf against the back wall and scans it. She pulls out a book that has a piece of paper sticking out of it.

"Here it is."

She sits back in her chair and copies from the piece of paper.

"Here are the names of a handful of organizations that run the sort of programs I'm talking about."

I scan the short list. Most of them have "women" or "womyn" in the name somewhere. I am skeptical. It sounds flaky.

"What kinds of things happen there?" I ask.

"They are all a bit different, but all are intensives lasting from just a day to a full week. All are in a group setting, so you'd be fully supported by trained facilitators. I have other clients who have gone and even some friends of mine who are therapists who have done facilitation at them. They'll use a mix of different technologies to help participants get what they need."

"I don't understand." I know she's not talking about cell phones or lasers. "What do mean by 'technology'?"

"Oh, I forgot you work in software. That's probably not a great word for you since you have so many other associations with it. What I'm referring to is the original, ancestral technologies where emotional soul knowledge is applied for practical purposes."

All I can imagine now are cell phones made out of pewter and stone, but I know that's not what she means.

"It sounds kind of voodoo or medicine man sort of stuff," I say. "Do these programs happen to take place in the desert in tepees and involve peyote?"

"Yes, some do, but I didn't include those on your list there." I can't tell from the smile on her face if she's joking with me or not. "I know you wouldn't like those."

⟿

I chose a program from June's list months ago, and I arrived yesterday to this place in the woods off of a series of dirt roads that were hot and dusty. I expected it to be like camp; after all, the packing list required we bring a tent and a sleeping bag and warm clothes and said we'd be outside most of the time. I liked that. I felt comfortable with that. But now, I don't feel comfortable at all.

I did not expect the silence and the somber tone. I did not expect the welcome I received when I arrived from the woman in black at the end of the road asking me if I was ready to die. I want to find her again in the faces of the staff, break the silence and tell her, "No, I want to change my answer! You've got it all wrong. I came here to get unstuck, and it has nothing to do with death, don't you see? It has to do with life!"

⟿

We're standing in a wide field in a circle, and I regret my choice to come here. We're asked to breathe and take the hands of the woman standing next to us, and now I am in a field holding hands. Everyone else is wearing floaty skirts and tops with lace and flowers. I didn't know there was a dress code. I look down at my cut-off jean shorts and scuffed Nikes, and I want to run. I want to let go of these clammy hands and run back through the field, past the main building, to the dirt parking lot where my car is parked and be out of here in ten minutes. I could be out in less than that if I leave my tent and all my stuff behind.

They claim this is another ritual to make it safe for us for when we do the deep dive into our "healing places." They actually call it that: "healing places." This, whatever this is, is not going to work for me.

None of what they talk about here is real. They have created a world of make-believe that defies logic. They talk about energy and healing places and Mother Earth as if they are tangible things. I'm trapped in a world of make-believe with these women in floaty skirts.

The crystal rock that is being passed around is almost to me. We're supposed to hold it and let good energy seep into it. It comes to me, and I clench it in my fist, try to look calm and serene, and fight the impulse to fling it out into the surrounding field.

June's word's ring in my ears. "Don't try so hard to figure things out. Lots of things are unexplainable and can't be put into words or even thoughts. A feeling perhaps, but not words. We're not meant to understand it, just live alongside it. Remember, the intangible?"

I will try. It is only a few more days. I will go back home after this is over to the world where everyone understands that cars and computers are the real things and energy means electric bills. I squeeze the crystal, warm from the other hands, and pass it to my left.

I am expecting a teepee for the sweat lodge but instead, in the middle of the field, there's a dome covered by blankets and quilts. Next to it, there's a roaring fire, and a woman is sitting next to it. She is wearing a skirt but is naked from the waist up. As we get closer, she is introduced as "The Elder."

She stands to welcome us, and the skin hangs off her like it is melting off her bones, and her breasts lay like triangle flaps on her sunken chest. There are two feathers woven into her long gray hair.

"We need to cleanse to get ready for the journey you are going on," she says. "It is time to get ready."

We all strip down to our waists, and the woman chants a prayer, and we follow her motions, turning to face the four directions as a group as she does. I wonder what someone would make of this: a group of half-naked women standing in a field all facing the same way. I have never done a sweat lodge, but the way it is described to us it sounds just like a sauna.

We enter the lodge by crawling through an opened flap in the blankets and fill the lodge in concentric circles. The last woman is the elder dragging red hot stones behind her on a blanket. She chants over the stones and then wraps each in a towel and places it in a hole in the center of the dirt floor.

"Close it," she says abruptly.

And the flap above the doorway falls immediately, putting us into complete darkness. I bring my hand in front of my face and it touches my nose, but I still can't see it. Within minutes the air begins to feel hot and close. I can hear women shifting and breathing around me. After a long time, my eyes adjust and I can see the dim outlines of a few heads at the center where the rocks are smoldering. I can feel my pores opening and sweat running in small rivulets down my back and between my breasts.

The silence and heat go on and on.

I don't know how much longer I can take it. It is such a little space with so many people and so much heat. I look towards the center. The woman who is the elder is right above the rocks. Her face is barely lit by the smoldering rocks and looks ghostly and lined. She ladles some water from the bucket next to her onto the rocks, and they sputter, then steam a white cloud around her head. A moment later the steam reaches me. It is like something physically solid. She keeps ladling, and wave after wave of solid heat buries me.

This is not a sauna. It is a heat like I imagine hell to be. I hear some muffled sobs and then a wail from one corner. There's no way I can get out of here. There's a wall of women between me and the exit. Sweat is dripping off me as if a spigot has been turned on above my head, and my heart is racing as if I was pacing out a mile. This can't be good for a body. I feel dizzy and rearrange my limbs in the cramped space to get my head below my knees that are hugged to my chest.

The elder woman starts to chant. I strain to hear the words through the heat and then realize it's not English. Her wrinkled face looks disembodied and floating amid the steam. The chanting is louder and fills the entire space until it sounds like it is in my own head.

Then in the darkness, I see other faces in a feverish haze. My mother, my father, and the boy who is Carm but not Carm: his twin.

Oh, God.

I cry out and a hand slick with sweat slips into my own and squeezes. I forgot I am not alone in here.

The faces float in front of me, and I don't understand how I can see them without light. One of them speaks, and it is my mother. Her voice is kind but directive and clear.

"Stop being afraid to live. You can do this. Stop being afraid."

The chanting stops abruptly and I hear the elder woman say, "It has ended. Open it."

A square of bright white appears, and we are flooded in light. I squint and see that everyone's hair is wet and plastered to their heads. Almost everyone has streaks of mud on them from the dirt floor, and their skin glistens with sweat. One by one we crawl out in the same order we came in, the concentric circles unwinding. When I am out, the air is cold against my skin although it is a hot summer day. We all collapse into the grass outside of the lodge and gulp the water that is offered to us. As my eyes adjust, I stare up into the bright sun. The cool air dries my sweat, and I feel completely awake but I do not understand what is happening here.

(⟶)

Each session starts the same way. The facilitators have everyone breathe and then they ask, "Who is ready?"

One by one the women raise their hand and go to the front of the room. They share their stories. More than half have been abused: sexually, emotionally, physically, or in other unspeakable ways. Listening to them I feel sick inside. I can't imagine being treated that way. I don't think I belong here at all. I haven't been hurt, not like that.

As each story unravels, the woman reliving the telling unravels with it. It is scary, the sounds and expressions that happen for them. They don't hold anything back, and nobody is trying to soothe or quiet them. To the contrary, the facilitators coax them to scream and makes sounds and kick pillows and punch a heavy bag in one long stream of unfiltered emotion. I am transfixed. It is terrible, but I can't look away. At the end, when the screaming and crying are over, the woman looks up, and her face is red and puffy and covered in wet tears and snot. But below that her face is calm and, then an unfiltered smile spreads out. It is a smile of certain triumph. I don't understand what is happening, but something significant is changing inside them. It is some kind of transformation. I am swept up in it and want to cheer for what I see, as if the women are in a race they are about to win.

"Who is ready?"

The facilitator with the white linen pants and red bandana tied around her black hair looks at me with her piercing blue eyes.

My head nods before my mind catches up.

Wait! No, not ready. Not ready at all. I can't feel that much. It will swallow me.

Somehow my legs unfold and I stand. My legs are shaking, and my stomach is in my shoes.

I half walk, half stumble to the front of the room. I stand facing the facilitator, and every sinew in my body is rigid, every muscle tightened and ready. I clench and unclench my fists, ready, as if for a fight. She waits a long time before she speaks, and then the room goes away and all I see are the piercing blue eyes and all I hear is the question.

"What needs to be healed?"

I start talking. There are more questions and more words, and those floating, piercing blue eyes are always in front of me with a shock of red above them, holding me. Now that I've started I can't stop. Soon, the words are coming out in chopped, wet breaths. I am going down, down into that endless blackness. It is beyond thought and beyond reason. I've known it's there but never really intended to go near it. Now, I am in it.

My mouth is forming words and sounds, and I think maybe even sentences, but I don't recognize the voice because these are the things I never intended to say.

The room spins, and there are people around me and holding my arms, and then a figure under a black cloth rises up in front of me. It is the thing I have been talking about, now right in front of me. It is death. It took so much from me. I hate it. I hate it with every piece of me. I push against the arms holding me and already feel the bruising as fingers dig into me, holding me back.

I hear a sound like a demented animal might make, long and loud without words. There is sound everywhere inside my head and filling the whole space of the room, and it is me. It comes from deep inside, below my lungs and heart and belly. There are not thoughts anymore, just blackness and something uncoiling and the scream. It goes on and on, and it will never stop. It is an endless emptiness. Down and down. At its end there is still nothing, and at this deepest point something breaks. In a final explosion of sound and breath, the black figure disappears from in front of me, and the piercing blue eyes take its place. My throat is raw, and I choke on the final vibration of sound and start to gag. I sink to my knees and heave violently. I can't stop gagging, and then there's a bucket under my face and I vomit into it.

There are hands on me, holding my head. A cool washcloth is pressed to my forehead, a glass brought to my lips for a sip of water. I rinse my mouth and swallow, and then everything goes blank.

I am lying on the grass. It is cool and not bright, so I must be under a tree in the shade. I see spots of red in the dark green. It is an apple tree. I sense someone sitting next to me. I open my eyes wider and rub my face to focus. It is one of the facilitators. It was the one from earlier who was dressed in the white linen pants and red bandana.

She is so close, I could reach out my hand to touch her knee. She has her legs crossed, and her hands are resting on her knees, the fingers of her thumb and middle finger making a circle. Her eyes are closed and face expressionless. I can see her chest moving as she breathes in and out. I realize my breath cycles are matching hers. She is backlit by the sun, and those tiny white seeds and insects are swirling around her in the golden light. Against the backdrop of the apple tree and grass, she looks like something from the cover of a yoga magazine.

She hears me stir and slowly opens her eyes.

"Hello," she says.

"Hello," I say, coming up to one elbow.

Wordlessly, she moves a mug of tepid tea and a small bowl of grapes and orange segments towards me.

I take the mug and drain it. She refills it from a plastic bottle, and I drink again.

"Eat some fruit," she says.

I suck on an orange segment. The juice, sweet and cold, feels wonderful on my raw throat. I take another, sit up fully, and move onto the grapes. They taste clear and sharp.

"Where is everybody?" I ask.

"They're inside. Still working. We'll go back and join them when you're ready."

There is so much I want to ask. What happened in there? Did I really throw up in front of all those people? How much of what I remember was real, and what was imagined? I don't trust anymore what my eyes saw. Visions and illusions seem to be an acceptable thing here, and nobody questions it as being abnormal.

I feel lightheaded and notice that my hands are shaking as I hold the mug. She sees me looking at them.

"It's OK. Memory and feeling are stored on the cellular level. You just released a tremendous amount of energy. It will stop soon once your body evens out again. It's good. Really good."

I don't know if it is good that I can't hold a mug steady, but I feel like I have just been asleep for a very long time. I look out across the orchard and field. The grass is greener than I remember, and I take in details without actually seeing them. There is a bee crawling on a lily four feet to my left, and it has pollen stuck all over its back. A cardinal flies in a dipping line at the edge of the field, bright red against the evergreens. I can feel the air touching my skin and going into my lungs. I can smell dinner cooking and the ripening fruit above our heads. Each sense is clear and separate and at the same time seamlessly part of the whole picture.

"It will wear off soon," she says. "But in the meantime, enjoy it. Feel."

Chapter Six

I stomp the snow off my boots at June's door. Lucy comes over and licks my hand as I'm untying the laces. She follows me into the studio room, where June is already perched on her rocking chair. I sit on the couch and invite Lucy up with me. She looks overjoyed in the way that dogs do and rests her head on my thigh.

"You look pensive today," says June. "What's on your mind?"

I give Lucy's head one final rub, then look up.

"We, my brothers and I, decided to put the family home on the market."

June's eyebrows rise in surprise, and she says, "Wow, that's big. So you're ready?"

I contemplate her question.

"I don't think 'ready' is the right word," I answer. "I think it's the right thing to do, but it doesn't make it easy. We've had some renters and some friends live there over the years, but it is so much to take care of. My brothers' lives have taken them elsewhere, and mine is, too. But I still feel its pull on me, the old and familiar and comfortable. I guess part of me still wants to go back there and stay." Even now, in June's office, I feel the tug. I wonder if it is possible to feel at home in more than one place or if your childhood home always tugs on you, like a magnetic north.

I continue, "It's so strange, but ever since we put it on the market officially, I've been having dreams about it almost every night."

"Tell me about them."

"Well, it's a variation of the same dream every time. I'm always in a house with lots of rooms and hallways. There are fireplaces and doors with wrought iron latches, big beams, wood floors. In the dream I wander the rooms and go outside to find more buildings that magically appear out of nowhere. The barn has somehow multiplied into four buildings, and the old chicken coop has been resurrected. Everything in the gardens is blooming all at once. The lilac bush, the daffodils, and the dogwoods are all flowering out of season. It's so weird."

"What's the feeling you have in the dream?"

"Well, there's a feeling of anxiousness and searching. I need to find something, and it changes with each dream. Sometimes it's a suitcase or an article of clothing. Sometimes it's a person; my mother or father or a friend or co-worker. It's essential that I find the thing or the person before I have to leave, and the clock is ticking away. Usually I have a flight to catch, or a meeting to get to, or a car is waiting for me out front."

"Sounds like your subconscious is working a lot out during the night."

"Yeah. Doesn't take Freud to interpret it, does it?"

"No. But I am curious. What do you think you're searching for? In the dream, I mean."

"I think I feel like time is running out for me. I have to find peace or my sense of home or something. It's the next thing I need to do to move forward. I think it's related to how stuck I've been feeling for the last few years."

"Hmm. Do you know much about archetypes?"

"They're like characters, right? Or characteristics that show up in a lot of different stories?" I say, remembering something about studying archetypes in a literature course in college.

"Exactly. They represent common human traits or characteristics that get repeated in stories regardless of the culture. One of the common archetypes is the hero's journey. Did you ever read *The Odyssey*?"

"Parts of it, but not the whole thing. But I remember the story."

"Good. Odysseus is one of the classic representations of the hero's journey. He's called to go on a journey, and he has to decide if he wants to leave the comfort of Ithaca to do so. Essentially, he has to decide to leave the known and launch into the unknown; that theme shows up repeatedly in hero's journeys. But in a nutshell, he decides to go, adventures and mishaps ensue, and he does what he needs to do. Because he goes, he gets the treasure that often shows up in stories as gold, or learnings, or secrets, or gifts."

"You're being called to the unknown here. You're being called to leave the comfort of what you've known and go into something else—a different home, maybe marriage, a life separate from your family, all pretty big changes."

"It seems kind of grand," I say. "I mean, I know this next step in my life feels difficult for me, but I'm not going out and slaying dragons or anything."

"I wouldn't be so sure about that," says June.

I dig out the bike pump and fill the tires of Beth's old easy rider. I try it out in the driveway, and the tires hold the air. I pedal up the road towards the center just like I used to, no helmet, no spandex, no biking shoes. I can smell the fried dough as soon as I pass the town barn. When I pass the ball field, I can hear the music and noise of hundreds of people at the fair. Cars are lined up all along one side of the road and parked at odd angles around the library, taking up every available space. When I get there, I'll see person after person that I know and be reminded of my mother stopping to chat over and over again, with me impatiently tugging her hand. Only now do I understand the joy of seeing someone you haven't seen in a long, long time and needing to connect with them.

My visits back to Hardwick are infrequent since we've had renters living in the house, so coming back for the annual fair seems like revisiting something essential and fleeting. I have the feeling a lot these days: of wanting to take it all in and bottle it up to save it. I want a visual snapshot, but I also want to capture the way the air smells in August, dusty and heavy with ripeness. I want to save the sound of the cicadas and the feeling of warm wind on my bare arms. It's been the same since I was a child, and each year the memory gets more ingrained because it's been reinforced for so long—like a river carving out a deep canyon, over and over throughout the years. It's managed to be mostly the same for two hundred years and perhaps will be unchanged for the next two hundred. Sometimes, small towns and dedicated people can keep traditions like this going indefinitely. I hope so.

Once I visited some ancient ruins, and the information center had a resource booklet showing a photograph of the ruins from different angles. You could flip a page transparency over each photograph to show what the town looked like when it was intact and bustling. Each transparency had line drawings, and when it covered the photo, the ruins were rebuilt into grand buildings, busy streets, and houses. My memory of Hardwick is like that little booklet. I see the town the way it is now, but I also see thirty years of memories overlaid on it. It's impossible for me to untangle all that history. It's melded together. Many of the people who inhabit the overlays aren't even alive anymore, but to me they're still here. In addition to the memory of them, there are also different versions of myself embedded everywhere I look. I can see myself as a five-year-old playing on the common after church. There is me as a ten-year-old riding my new bike, and me as a teenager watching Jack's Sunday afternoon pick-up football games and writing letters while sitting on the grass. For better or for worse, Hardwick is where all of my ghosts live. A poet friend of mine calls hometowns the "substrate for memories," and I think he's right. What he means by that is that it takes the physical presence of objects to conjure the memories. The loss of that substrate is what worries me the most about selling the house and leaving town for good. If the house with all of its familiar creaks and walls and smells and furniture goes away, do those parts of me go with it?

June disagrees with this. It is not the things, she says, but your own memories you get to have until you choose to stop remembering them. They are yours no matter what goes on in the external world. But I don't know. I've never tested it—I've never been without the physical substrate for any significant amount of time. It seems important to keep it and be able to revisit it to keep it alive.

I see Pam and Ray Robinson at their cheese stand on Hardwick Common and sit with them behind the booth in the shade to catch up. They invite me to the Time Capsule party that's the following day. I look at them blankly.

"You know, the time capsule?" Ray says.

Pam rescues me. "You were probably only eight or nine," she says, "and don't remember. But in 1982 Ray had a big party at the pond and buried a time capsule. Your whole family was there."

I was five in 1982 and don't remember, and it intrigues me that I don't have any memory of it or haven't heard it spoken of since. I know that some of my memories aren't mine at all, but memories I've formed out of other people telling me about my own history.

But I do remember the Robinson's pond. We used to swim there, before Dad built the pool. It required a short car ride and picking your way down a path, towel draped over neck and Mom trailing behind with the big canvas bag filled with juice boxes, blankets, and apple slices. I remember being scared of the water snakes whose turtle heads and winding bodies appeared out of the black water near the marshy edges. And also of the mucky bottom, not so much for the cool muck but for the fear of having my feet come across something slimy and unknown within the muck. Still, when you got past the muck and into the center, you could take a deep breath and go under to the cool layer, beneath where the sun had heated up the water. And holding my breath in that cool darkness on the hottest August days is what I remember most.

By the time I arrive, the party is in full swing. People have brought beach chairs and coolers and a small blue awning with a table underneath. I do a round of hugs, put my cheese and crackers on the table, and get a beer from a cooler. Behind the party there are holes dug every few feet, and two of the Robinson men are leaning against spades. They haven't found the time capsule yet and have been digging for hours.

Perched on a picnic table is a MacBook with a slideshow showing pictures from the 1982 party. The pictures have that slightly grainy, scanned quality of old photos. I wait as the photos scroll, looking and waiting, and then there they are: my parents looking impossibly young. Jack looks tall, but maybe it is just because all the other kids are so small. He's tan and his hair is almost blond. I am wearing a lime-green bathing suit that is either stretched out or too big, because it droops around my waist. In one photo we're eating hot dogs off of paper plates. In another all the kids are grouped together and making funny faces at the camera.

Cell phones are produced, and calls go out to others who were there that day. Vague directions are relayed about the big rock and a clump of birch trees, of trying one spot near the pond and changing the location due to a big piece of shale. We all peer closer at the MacBook photos, trying to decipher the location of the hole from the surrounding area. The trees are now thirty years taller and, the screen porch has long since fallen down and reclaimed by the forest.

John from down the road, who has a backhoe, arrives later, and they start digging in earnest, making gaping holes in the area where they think the capsule is. Every few minutes there are shouts when they hit something hard, and the men descend to hand dig. At the end of an hour, all they have are a big pile of rocks and torn-up ground.

Someone jokes that a lot of beer and a lot of pot was consumed on that day, so it's no wonder that nobody can really remember where the damn thing is buried.

The men shrug, and they get more beer out of the cooler and put down their spades. Maybe this is how the true past really is. You can try to bury it away in a safe place so you can revisit it just as it was whenever you want, but years later when you go to retrieve it, no matter how long you dig, it still eludes you. And in the end, maybe it's not that important, since the present is the only real thing there is.

Thirty years is a long time. Since then Ray and his first wife have divorced and each remarried. Almost all of their grown children and stepchildren have married, and some of their grandchildren are here today. Ray sits under the blue tarp and sips a beer so cold it sweats. One of his grandsons runs over and hands him a red plastic truck, then runs back into the water at the edge of the pond, splashing and laughing.

"How's the house sale going?" asks June.

"It's been on the market for months. It's an odd thing. I want it to sell, and at the same time I still don't want it to happen. I think it will be really hard when it does."

"It might, and it might not be as hard as you think."

"I guess the good thing is that it might take some time, even years," I say, "so I can get used to it. The housing market is pretty dismal right now, especially for old houses."

"So what else is going on in your life?" asks June.

"Remember how we were talking about a year ago about me maybe volunteering?"

"I remember. You wanted to maybe do some work with hospice, right?"

"Yeah. I looked into it and decided that working with them might be too intense. Maybe at some point in my life, but I'm not ready yet. Instead I found this other place, a camp for kids who have lost a primary family member...so, I've been to the training, and I've been accepted."

"That's great! Do you feel ready?"

"I do; I'm not going to be doing any counseling or anything. They have licensed therapists to do that. I'm just going to be one of the 'big buddies' who hangs out with the kids during the regular camp activities and is there during the group sessions. Besides the sessions, it's a lot like regular fun camp, you know, with games and songs and campfires and stuff."

"That's so great!" June says again. "How about we schedule an appointment for you the week after it in case anything comes up for you?"

"I'd like that," I say. "I'm a little nervous about it, I guess. But I really want to do it. I know it would have made a big difference in my life if I had something like this."

⌒

During one free afternoon, my camper asks to go canoeing. We make our way to the waterfront with a big group of kids and adults. Adults are paired with their campers according to similar losses at similar ages. My camper lost her father a few years ago when she was nine. The brilliance of the pairing method isn't lost on me.

We wait our turn and are soon outfitted in a little red plastic canoe and life jackets and are paddling around the small pond. I think of my days in Canada and how this flimsy boat wouldn't last a day on those big lakes and wild rivers. I tell her about my trips, and she likes the story about a wildfire I saw. I paddle us over to the edge of the lake so we can see the turtles and frogs. If this kid is like other kids, she'll love it. I'm correct and she squeals when we see a turtle sunning itself on a log. We both laugh when she tries to catch it and almost falls out of the boat.

Later, when we're floating lazily in the middle, she turns to me. "Do you still miss your dad?" she asks.

They had said in the training that this might happen. They said kids can move in and out of grief more easily than adults, so often questions come out of nowhere. I think before I answer.

"Yes, but it's not every day, the way it used to be. I guess it's like missing him never goes away, but it kind of becomes a part of you and it's OK. I never thought that it would feel all right, but it does."

I'm not sure how to explain the next part but try anyway. "It gives you things," I say. "It makes you know what's important and what's not. It makes you older in a lot of ways, but you probably already feel that. It can really help you make good decisions and be a better person if you let it."

"Oh," she says. She looks down at the water and swirls her paddle around a lily pad. I can tell she's thinking.

She looks up and brightens, "That's good. Hey, do you want to go look for more turtles?"

"Sure," I smile at her, and we paddle off to the edge of the pond.

I sit down on June's couch. The windows are open, and the curtains move in lazy billows.

"So what's going on for you today?" says June. "How are things?"

I think for a moment and look out the window. There's a bird on the wooden feeder, hopping on the roof.

"Nothing, actually. I was thinking in the car on the way over about what I wanted to talk about, and I don't have anything." I shrug. "I guess I just don't really have anything to talk about today."

"You seem confused or surprised by that."

"I am. I'm here and I don't feel like I have anything to work on or anything that's bothering me. Isn't that strange?"

"Not all. Tell me about what it feels like."

"I'm kind of..." I search for the right word and am surprised at the one that comes. "I'm happy." I shrug again. "It feels weird to say that out loud. But it's more than that. I guess 'happy' doesn't quite describe the feeling. It's more. I feel like my life means something and there's going to be sadness and ups and downs and it's all right. I guess I'm just so glad to be here, getting to be alive and live and love. That's enough."

I don't know what else to say.

June leans forward, and I think she's going to give me one of her profound questions or life's secrets. Her face is very serious. Instead she says, "It sounds like you may not need me anymore."

I wasn't expecting that. I try to read her face to figure out if she means it or if she's using this to lead to something else.

"Really? You mean I should stop seeing you?"

She nods. "Yes, really. Only you can answer it for sure, but it seems like you're all set for now. You've done a ton of work here and outside this office. I'm really proud of you, Gayle."

My face turns hot, and I look at the floor.

"Now wait, don't get embarrassed. Take this in. Can you look at me and take it in?"

I make an effort to look up into her eyes.

"I am proud of you," she says slowly and clearly. "If ever you have an issue or problem, you have my number. But for now, you're done."

She stands as if to make it final, and I stand to hug her. This has got to be the shortest therapy appointment ever. June has a wide smile as she walks to the door.

She says, "Do you know that my favorite days are the days when my clients don't need me anymore."

"Huh," I say. "My mom said a similar thing about being a mother. She said her job was to work herself out of one."

"Smart mom," says June. "But we already knew that."

Chapter Seven

There are multiple messages on my phone from Jack.

The first message is breathless and announces that his wife Heather is in labor, then there's a second one saying the baby is coming now, and then shortly after, a third message announcing that I'm an aunt. On the drive to Boston and then walking through the long hospital corridors, I feel the presence of Mom and Dad. It has happened before. I feel it when I'm very quiet or when a great change is happening, and sometimes it comes like a subtle nudge forward towards something. This time it's the feeling that a great change is happening. This is huge. I duck into a waiting room to collect myself and breathe. I let my insides go soft and quiet, and the feeling is there. It's inside me and in the air touching my skin as well as part of my breath. It is gratitude and presence and joy for all that is and for what is happening right now.

After more long hallways and two elevator rides, I find their room and then I'm in a bear hug embrace with Jack and we're both crying. Or rather, I'm crying, smiling with tears streaming down my face and soaking into my collar, and Jack's eyes are moist. Heather looks good, but tired. And there's the little plastic cart with high sides and a bundle of blankets inside. I meet Gavin and he's in my arms, a little head with a hat on top poking out of a mass of blue plush. I look down at his sleeping face. I wasn't an aunt, and now I am. My brother is a father. My parents would be grandparents. We have another generation. This little seven-pound person with his very existence has bestowed on all of us new titles and made us more than who we are. He's made us more. That's how it feels when his little hand reaches out from beneath the blankets, opens and closes, opens and closes, finds the hem of my shirt and holds on tight. *Take it*, I think. *Take it, I'm yours.*

I find Carm waiting on the stone steps with the groomsmen. He looks nervous. Or maybe I'm nervous. I don't know.

"Walk with me for a sec?" I ask.

We take a few steps, and I stop to take off my shoes. This is no time to sprain my ankle walking on soft grass in heels. I hold his shoulder for stability. I lift the hem of my bridesmaid dress so I don't step on it.

"Are you doing all right?" I ask.

"Yeah. I'm nervous. I just don't want to lose it up there."

I nod. "Just remember that all these people here love you. It's fine even if you do 'lose it.' Here, take these." I hand him the earrings. They are small and flat and made of tarnished silver.

"Dad gave these to Mom. I thought it might be nice for you have something of theirs to have with you. Jack held them for his wedding, too."

"Thanks, sis." He slips them into the breast pocket of his suit and pats it.

A voice behind us calls out, "It's time."

"You'll do fine," I say quickly. "No shame in 'losing it.' We all love you, and tears aren't a problem." I smile a little to myself when I say it.

If only I knew that before I spent a decade trying to hide them. If only I knew years ago that there is no use in locking them up, pretending that "OK" meant not showing it. If only I knew it was all a necessary part of having a heartbeat.

"I'll be up there with you," I add. "Find my eyes if you need to."

He hugs me quickly, and I leave him at the stone steps.

The music starts, and one at a time we join the groomsmen at the front. We are all assembled under a blue sky in a wide meadow. I'm gripping my flowers so hard my knuckles are white. I don't know why I'm nervous now. Carm looks at me from his place at the front. All of a sudden the reason for wedding attendants becomes clear to me. It's not about throwing showers and bachelor parties. It's about being able to stand with someone you love as they go through something important, something momentous. I am glad I'm on the bride's side opposite him so I can see his eyes. He looks nothing like the kid I once knew, and at the same time I can see all of the ages he has been. Maybe it's because he's my kid brother and I feel the passage of time and events more acutely, but already I can feel the tears welling in my eyes. It is something about still seeing that little boy in him, the awkward teenager, the handsome grown man all rolled into one.

The bride comes, lovely and barefoot. I look at the guests seated in neat rows, and it practically undoes me. I feel so much, so differently for every person all in one place at the same time. My rib cage feels like it is cracking open, but it doesn't hurt. It's just opening, that's all. I focus on my breathing and looking at the bright sky. James catches my eye, seated in the front row. He mouths the words "I love you." He holds me in his eyes, and it steadies me.

People say words and the songs play and the vows are exchanged. I try to take them in, but mostly I just stand there and feel. Towards the end, Carm repeats his vows, and as he finishes, two Canada geese fly over, honking wildly. It's not a flock, but just two of them, flying in formation together over the ceremony. They are straight overhead like they came here on purpose as their destination flyover. I try not to make meaning out of meaningless things, but I can't ignore this one. I look at Carm over the top of the head of the woman who is now his wife. He pats his breast pocket and nods at me once with tears in his eyes. I don't try to stop the ones that slide down my face. It's not sadness so much, although that is a part of it. It is more gratitude. More of joy. More being opened to the waves of happiness and the waves of sadness. More of holding all of it together all at once, all of these things that make up love.

Christmas Eve James and I go on a walk. It's a mild, clear night, and the stars are out; I can see their pinpricks through the dark branches above the wooded trail. I hear a stream, and soon we're at a small waterfall. At the base, there's a small campfire burning, and in the glowing light James kneels.

I know what is happening, and at the same time it feels dreamlike and other-worldly. He says the words, and I hear "wife." I am going to be a wife.

I say yes. A million times yes.

I mean it.

Yes to the possibility of loving him for five or twenty or forty years and losing him. Yes to quiet mornings around the kitchen table. Yes to sinking into our community and making it ours. Yes to making a home with him. Yes to arguments and discomfort and anger. Yes to sickness and health and all the rest. Yes to making him my family. Yes.

When we get to the big barn with its metal roof and gray slat sides, James nods at me and mouths the words "This is it" when the real estate agent has her back turned. I can tell from the way his eyes are lit and how he's moving faster, running his hands along the wood and walls, that he's latched on to an idea. It reminds me of my mom when she had an idea in her head and was determined to make happen.

After the barn, I ask to see the house one more time. It's a medium-sized modern Cape Cod style. Everything about it is average from the size of the rooms to the worn wall-to-wall carpeting. It's a fine house, but not what I pictured. We finish the tour and get back in the car. James doesn't start speaking right away, which surprises me. We're out of the driveway before he says, "I think we just found our house."

I nod noncommittally.

"I can tell you're not wild about it," he says. "But listen, it has everything we've been talking about: room for both of our offices, acreage, a barn for equipment, room for family and friends but not too big. We have to do some renovations, but we could make it really beautiful."

I try to imagine it as beautiful and can't. I know this is where he is gifted, and I have a blind side. I am not a visionary.

"It could be a great home for us," he says. "Trust me on this one, please?"

And I do.

We close on a warm day in May and as soon as the papers are signed and the real estate agent leaves, James starts pulling up the carpets and dragging them onto the front lawn. By the end of the week, he's also torn down all the doors and trim. He works at that pace for three months. I bring over lunches and dinners, and sometimes I can get him to stop long enough to eat. Friends come over with hammers and paintbrushes and, remarkably, know how to use them. In a world where hardly anyone works with their hands anymore, I marvel that almost all our friends have some sort of skill. The house takes shape, and I can see hints of the beauty James saw from the beginning. From old carpets and dull paint, the polished wood floors and bright skylights emerge in carpentry alchemy. Maybe it's not so much carpentry alchemy as community alchemy. It's the people in our lives that have made all this happen.

It's odd that the most important lessons are often the ones that are never talked about but get filtered down through living example. My parents never talked about community in my memory, they just did all the things that made it happen. They went to church, showed up with casseroles when neighbors went through a hard time, hosted the parties, attended the potlucks, served on committees and raised the money. They showed that community is not a noun. It's a verb. It's created with a thousand little actions. Sometimes the actions are so small it's hard to see it while it is happening. Now my community seems like it was created out of thin air by divine luck.

During a weekend in July, we move in with the help of fifteen friends. In half a day, we pack up our old house and get it loaded. Boxes and furniture get carried into the new house at an alarming rate. With all the people working, it looks like a cartoon in fast forward. I go outside to watch the trees in order to see something that is still and calm. As I'm standing on the back porch, someone turns up the stereo where I have my iPod plugged in. Bruce Springsteen's voice comes out the screen door, singing about a dream of life coming like a catfish dancing on the end of a line. I hear the voices of our friends talking above the music. Looking up, I calculate the path the sun will take in the evening, sinking behind the tree line, and how beautiful it will be to sit on the back porch here. I can tell this is just one time of many we'll have these friends here and how much we'll share in the years ahead. I can almost feel my feet getting heavier and planting here. We're in this place for the long haul, rooting down deep.

On a quiet Sunday, James is working for the day, and I take my laptop to a nearby outdoor café for good coffee and uninterrupted writing time.

I've heard other writers say that writing saved their lives. I don't think I can claim that. My life-saving belongs to a network of people and a heap of grace. But still, part of that grace came through the words and stories others wrote down, so maybe in a way writing did save me.

I choose a table overlooking the river and take a sip from my steaming mug. The coffee is good and dark. I look out at the river and the rushing water, the white eddies of foam around the rocks. The trees are not turning yet, but any day now they will. We've been in our new home for a little over two months, and I'm looking forward to seeing what the land does when the seasons change. It will be like getting to know a new friend in all of her colors and moods and seasons.

I turn back to the screen and watch the cursor blink. I write a few sentences, then erase them and watch the cursor blink some more. I've written and revised as much as I can. There's more to write, but I don't know what happens next; I have no idea what the next chapters will be about and how to end the story of my life and my family. The true ending won't come for decades, but still I have the feeling that there are more chapters to this particular story. I look up from the screen to watch the river some more. Endings are their own intangible mystery and could be represented by a blinking cursor. There's just no way to know what's next until it happens.

My phone vibrates on the table, and I step away from the table to answer it. It's Jack.

"We have an offer on the house," he says.

Within a week the terms are agreed upon. Eagle Hill School up the road buys it to serve as faculty housing. It is the same small New England boarding school that lured my parents away from the Midwest as fresh college graduates to work as first-time teachers. I had imagined a family living there, and I suppose it will still happen, just in a different way than I imagined. It seems full circle for Eagle Hill to have it now.

We'll sell it to them, put the paperwork through, and then have two months to clear everything out. The night before the papers are filed, I dream of my old tree fort in the side yard, the one Jack put together with scrap wood he found in the barn. It had no roof, so really it was just a platform with a rope ladder hanging over the side.

In my dream I am on the platform, but instead of ten feet off the ground, I am hundreds of feet in the air. I have to get down, but I can't. I reach my feet over the side, and there's nothing solid in reach, just air. I scream at the people below who I think are my brothers. I don't know how to get down. I'm stuck and I can't leave.

"Just try," Jack yells. "Take a step; shift your weight."

The platform is swaying in the breeze, and I lean over with my whole body.

Then there's a sound like rushing wind, and the entire tree bends like a winter sapling and gently places me on the ground.

"See, you could get down," says Jack. "You just had to want to."

I wake up sweating and kick the comforter off the bed. It's 3:18 a.m., the witching hour. I call it that because I always have my scariest and most profound dreams between three and four in the morning. James is snoring lightly next to me, and the cat is curled in the crook of his arm. It's such a scene of domestic coziness that I lie back in the pillows and watch them both breathe for a while and try to match my breathing to them, willing myself back to sleep. Eventually I drift off, and when the alarm goes off three hours later, I'm in a deep, dreamless sleep.

In the afternoon I print out the stack of documents and sign them at my desk. After each page, I pause and wait for the feeling to come. There's nothing. When I imagined this moment, it wasn't like this at all. I imagined sitting in a lawyer's conference room in thick leather chairs while biting my lip and trying not to get tear stains on the deed. In reality, this it is so much quieter. I feel nothing.

For the first six years after Mom died, we put so much effort into keeping the house and making a home for each other. First there was getting Carm through high school. Then getting him through college. Then having a home base as we each made our way through careers and relationships while figuring out where to settle down. Then another seven years of having it be half a home and trying to decide with any sense of permanency what home meant for me.

I drive the paperwork to the local stationery store and get it notarized, then I treat myself to a new notebook and a really good pen. I address the FedEx envelope to the attorney, and for some reason I feel the need to sign my name once more to make it final. I dig out my new pen and use it to scrawl my signature in big letters in the white space between the FedEx logo and the words "The World On Time."

How appropriate. Maybe it is the world on time.

Chapter Eight

I pull in the driveway, and the gravel crunches. I notice how over-grown the front yard has gotten. It needs so much care. Now that it's technically not ours, I can see the house with fresh eyes. It's not ne-glected yet, but it's starting to look that way.

I sit in the driveway for a few minutes. I can't tell if I'm steeling my-self against the task of sorting through forty years' worth of memories or letting myself feel them.

"Breathe," June would say. Her voice comes even and steady in my head. "Steeling yourself against emotion only puts it off. You're really not dealing with it that way, just stuffing it away. You can always unpack it later if it's appropriate, but think about what it would be like to feel it right then and there."

I find Jack upstairs in his room. The closet door is flung open, and there's a pile of books and clothes on the bed already. He hugs me but averts his eyes.

"Are you all right?" I ask.

"I was, until I found that." He points to a children's book on the bed. It's the one about the mother who sang to her son after he was sleeping about how much she loves him. In the story, all of the boy's actions are chronicled, from his flushing watches down the toilet as a toddler to being a wild teenager. Mom gave us each our own copy with the words crossed out and rewritten in permanent marker about all the things we had done growing up. We were teenagers when she presented our versions to us, and they were accepted with some eye rolling.

"I don't know why," Jack says, "but I just thought it might be better to start with one of the hard rooms first." His voice cracks, and he swipes at his eyes.

I push a stack of Hardy Boys books aside and sit down on the corner of the bed, not sure what to say. Jack reaches back into the closet and pulls out two coats that he stuffs into a trash bag, then two more.

"I get it," I say finally. "There's a big part of me that just wants to power through it and get it done. But I think there's another way to do this or, rather, another way to be while we do this. It's really OK to just stop packing and sit for a while. There's a lot here. We don't have to rush. We'll get it done."

Jack straightens up and looks at me.

"OK," he says. "OK. I'll try."

When I get home, I'm exhausted. I had hoped to get in a few hours of work tonight, but that's not going to happen. James is gone for the evening, so I have wine and macaroni and cheese. I throw in some broccoli as a gesture to health, but really it's just the comfort I'm after. I climb the stairs to bed.

My dreams of the house come back. In them I am driving around in the old Volkswagen I owned years ago, trying to get somewhere. The roads all look vaguely familiar but don't lead anywhere they are supposed to. As I drive I pass swamps and junkyards of all my old possessions. Sometimes they are piled up in heaps and other times strewn out in a field. And I'm just driving around and around trying to get home.

Carm has been sending email updates, but I haven't seen him in months. We arrange to do a video call. When his face fills the screen I resist the impulse to reach out and touch the glass.

"You've lost weight," I say.

"Yeah, we both got a bit sick but we're fine now."

Behind him, I can see a hotel bed, a rickety standing lamp and gauzy curtains framing a window with darkness outside. I see Nicole's trekking pack on the bed next to his. I understand adventure, but his urge to travel to far flung locations is baffling to me.

"What time is it there?" I ask.

"It's about midnight," he says. He tells me about their trip — the deep lakes in New Zealand, the shrines in Japan, biking through Egypt.

I update him about cleaning out the house.

"What are we going to do with the Cadillac?" he asks. I think that since he's living out of a single backpack taking on a convertible the size of a Chevy Suburban is daunting.

"Jack is going to take it. He'll find storage near his house and get a new top for it and new tires. Maybe even install better seatbelts so he can put the car seat in the back for Gavin." I have a fleeting image of the car, shined up to its former glory sitting in the parking lot of their local ice cream stand.

"What about everything else?" asks Carm.

"We'll sort through it, Donate a lot, sell some stuff. I'll put aside anything that's yours."

"I'm sorry I'm not there to help," he says.

"Me too, but you can't leave the trip of a lifetime to do this. Really, we both want you to finish your trip. You'll be back before the closing ."

We talk more about his travels and he promises to send more pictures.

"I miss you," I say.

"I miss you guys, too." As we're saying goodbye he puts his fingertips up to the screen.

I pull boxes out of the closet and sit cross-legged on my old bedroom floor and start sorting through them. I find the plastic box with the flip-top handle packed with my two Barbies and one Ken. They are stacked on one another half naked and nestled in a pile of clothes. I almost laugh out loud at the thought of them stuck in this box in a twenty-five-year-long ménage à trois. I slip some clothes onto them for decency and then put the whole box into the pile going to Goodwill.

Next, I find a Kangaroo shoebox filled with clothes for my imitation Cabbage Patch doll I got the Christmas that parents were getting in fistfights in Toys R Us to get them, and wealthy parents were flying to France to get them for their little girls. I was so disappointed when I opened my imitation Vegetable Patch Kid on Christmas morning. But I bit my lip, thanked my parents profusely, and named her Cindy after the prettiest girl in my class. A year later when the mania died down, I did get a real Cabbage Patch doll for my birthday—a coveted Preemie no less—and came to love both dolls equally. Cindy became the big sister to little Sally Glorina. They were the central characters to all of my pretend games about home: house and tea party and garden party and restaurant.

My Barbies were so different. They were more my action figures, and I took them into the woods to play camping adventure and GI Joe–style war games. Cindy and Sally Glorina always stayed at home, tucked into scrap pieces of flannel I took from Mom's sewing box or sat politely in front of a neatly laid out tea service for days on end.

I fold up all of the Cabbage Patch clothes back into the box and add it to the growing pile of "I don't know what to do with this." It's the question I keep running into with all my childhood things. I know I won't use them again. But what if I have a daughter someday? Unlikely she'll have any interest in playing with my old toys. No doubt she'll instead want the pink plastic whatever that is all the rage at the time. I run my hands over the scraps of flannel and the lace around the edges of the tiny dresses.

Be brave, I think. *Be brave. Keep the feeling, but let go of the thing.*

But the problem is that I don't even know what the feeling is here. Is it security or comfort or a sense of home? Or maybe it's a hope that they will be used again by someone, someday. It's a longing for something I don't seem to have and can't seem to muster: a mountain of courage and faith and hope beyond reason. I sigh and pick out one small flannel blanket to keep, then put the entire box into the giveaway pile.

For the last task of the day, Jack and I tackle the filing cabinet in the office and easily sort through twenty years of tax records, filling a trash bag. In the second-to-last drawer, we find neatly folded blueprints and copies of the family trees and the genealogy study Dad did a year before he got sick.

There's one for each of us—our names written on the front in Dad's neat block printing. I remember this, but haven't seen it in twenty years. Jack hands mine to me. It's the only letter I have from Dad. The words are shaking until I rest my hands on my knees to read. I read it once quickly, then again slower, taking in each word. I look up at Jack who is reading his own letter. We swipe at our tears and smile through wet faces.

"Can I read mine to you?" I ask.

He nods and I make it through half before my voice cracks.

My Dear Daughter,

This genealogy effort took many years of gathering material and asking questions of relatives. As I finally got to the point of putting this information in final form, I got a question from you as you looked over my shoulder. You (at age 9) asked what I was doing, spending hours at the dining room table. You saw that most of these people were dead, and wanted to know if I would be alive when you had children. Where would we put your children? So I put lines at the bottom and we named your children. Sally Glorina (your Cabbage Patch doll's name), Matthew (one of your classmates), and Teddy (your new cousin from Alice's marriage)!

Gwen's grandmother, Gaynor was called Gay. Ellen is your mother's middle name. I don't care what you name your children, though Sally Glorina will take some getting used to. I love you for your independent, strong-willed, artistic nature, but mostly for just being you.

Your Father,

David Huntress, Jan. 1987

His block printing and the words and the fact that he took the time to write a personal letter to each of us resonates with the message—the one that should be everyone's birthright.

You are loved.

You are wanted.

You matter.

The older I get, the more I see what a rare and wonderful gift this is. Not everyone gets a message like that from her parents. I know that now. Most people don't get what they need at all. Not even close. I wonder what to do with that gift. What does one do with a love like that? What does one do with a happy childhood? For a long time, I thought I should have a family of my own. What better way to honor my parents than by passing on the same message to my own children?

James and I have been having conversations about having children. One of the things I think I will miss the most if we don't have children is the opportunity to understand my parents more. I know that becoming a mother would bring with it questions that have no answers and resurface the feelings of her absence acutely. I think it would also bring some more understanding and joyful connections with both of them that I may not discover otherwise.

Carm says he and his wife will have children in a few years. I'm inordinately glad Jack and his wife chose to be parents. I love this amazing little boy who is related to me by blood and that there'll be more on the way. I'm awed by the fact that Gavin begins the next generation of our family. His very existence seems like something of enormous significance. Maybe the existence of all of us is significant; it just takes somebody to notice.

There's an old photo of Jack and my grandfather on the back porch on a summer day, sitting in the sunlight, surrounded by hanging plants. On the back of the photo, in my father's writing, are five words: "Bespeaks a quality of life." My parents knew how to live. But more importantly, they knew how to love.

All these years later, I'm still surprised that Mom was right. She did her job, her "mission" as she called it, and we were fine. For a third of their lives, Mom and Dad poured everything they had into being our parents. They set up a community network that would hold us and sustain us long after they were gone. It all seemed orchestrated in such a way that all these years later I can't help but see the hand of grace in it all. Now, I marvel at all the people in Hardwick who looked out for us, who showed up with meals and favors, and how my college community got me through the most difficult years.

⸺⸺

I'm sorting through a box of kitchen things and deciding what would be useful or beautiful; those are my criteria. I've decided to only keep the things that are useful, and by that I mean something that can be used right now—within the next few weeks. If it's something that will be stashed away in a box because someday it might be useful, it doesn't qualify. For something to qualify as beautiful, it has to move me. This is harder to quantify, and often it defies aesthetics completely. I try not to get too exact about it, but I can't help thinking about what the equation might be. It might be current aesthetic taste plus quality craftsmanship multiplied by the amount of memories attached to the object, squared, equals beauty.

But there is no way I could prove that theorem, because I keep finding things that defy all criteria, and still I feel compelled to keep them.

So far I've inexplicably saved a stained pot holder with a lobster on it and a lopsided coffee mug from the resort in Minnesota where we spent a few summers before going to Wisconsin.

I sigh as my "to keep" pile grows. I ask Jack if he sees anything he might want.

"Nope," he says, standing over the box.

Then he says, "Mouse."

"Mouse," he says again.

"What?" I ask.

"Mouse. There's a mouse in that box."

I turn to look where he's pointing, and since my brain hasn't yet caught up with the words, I scream and jump back. The mouse has a similar reaction and scurries to the wall and disappears into a hole in the barn floor.

I shudder once, then start laughing, and I can't stop. I double over, and even Jack cracks a smile. *What is it about being terrified that can sometimes be so funny?*

I collect myself and kneel down in front of the box again, shuddering. I don't really want to stick my hands back inside.

Jack sees me staring into the box. "Do you want me to unload it for you?" he asks.

"Oh, would you? That would be great."

He sits next to me and hands me items in bubble wrap, one by one.

Earlier in the day, sandwiched in between books, we uncovered a black-and-white photo of the two of us standing in the field in the summer. The picture is labeled 1980, so he's five and I'm three. Our faces are squinted into the sun, and he has one arm around my shoulders.

Even then I knew he would protect me from mice.

He hands me a jumble of yellow plastic—a set of Tupperware measuring cups that were in the kitchen drawer along with the pot holders and rubber bands for as long as I can remember. I learned from Mom that only baking required measuring. Everything else could be approximated.

I move them into the Goodwill pile and then remember that my current kitchen doesn't have any measuring cups in it. It's partly because I hardly bake anything, and it's partly because I've been trying to be a minimalist for so many years. James and I went through a period of just having one plate and one bowl each in order to keep things simple.

Now, I have, without really trying, acquired everything a fully-stocked modern kitchen has. But I don't have any measuring cups. I nest them into one another and consider them. These are ugly, and although I'm sure they still measure everything accurately, they are not a fine tool. I should buy some sleek stainless steel ones that would have a certain weight to them, like real silver spoons or a steel-handled hammer. I turn them around in my hands. These *were* the measuring cups used for all of the Christmas cookies, banana breads, birthday cakes, and Dad's anadama bread. These stupid yellow plastic measuring cups move me, and I put them in the pile with the lobster pot holder.

A week later I tackle the boxes from the attic. There is so much detritus of life in the boxes. It is four generations' worth of diplomas and yearbooks, photos, paperweights, and Christmas cards.

There's no order to any of it. In one box I find "Welcome, Baby" cards for Jack's arrival, church committee meeting notes, information about clinical trials, light and sound therapy brochures, obituaries for people I don't even know, two journals, and an entire photocopied yoga manual from 1972. It's not just one person's life in that box: it's an entire family's. My family's. And there are fourteen more boxes just like it. I cram the boxes into my small home office so there are little paths between them and start sorting. The room looks disturbingly like where a hoarder might live.

I wish I were the type of person who could just throw it all into the dumpster and be done with it. But I have to sort through every scrap of paper; I'm compelled to. It feels like I'm looking for something, but I don't know what. Occasionally I do find a treasure: a love letter or a journal or notes written in the margin of a book. And the feeling I get when I find them lets me know that this is what I'm looking for. More than anything, I want to know my parents in a different way. I want to know them in the objective way that I imagine adult children get to know their parents. I don't know if that sort of thing can be gleaned from fourteen boxes of papers and a houseful of leftover possessions, but I'm going to try.

Now, in the world of digital everything, I wonder what I will leave behind. Maybe similar electronic files of junk. The whole process of sorting through and seeing what is left of a life has made me question the legacy I'm leaving. *Am I also leaving virtual boxes of junk?* I think, as I carry another load out to the dumpster.

On my way back through the barn, I kneel in the corner in front of our handprints from 1979. I press my palm against the concrete outlines of our hands—Mom's and Dad's and Jack's and mine. Carm isn't an idea yet in 1979, so it's just the four of us. My hand is larger than Mom's print, a bit smaller than Dad's. I cover Jack's and then finally my own hand. I still can't believe I was once so small.

At one time I dreamt that I would raise my own children here, and they would play with their cousins in the backyard and run through this barn. I know now that won't happen. But maybe it will happen somewhere else.

Later in the afternoon, I am going through the books and pulling out my favorites from the bookshelf to save. A lot of them are the ones that I loved and read over and over when I was a girl, but a lot are just good children's books that filled the shelves when I was growing up.

I end up with a huge, ridiculous pile of books that I certainly won't ever read again. I can't imagine picking up Pippi Longstocking or the Bobbsey Twins to reread. I go through them again and try to save only my real favorites but find it impossible to cull any. I keep putting them into the giveaway pile, then grabbing them out again and ending up with more than I started. It doesn't make any sense. I love books, but I'm usually not a book saver. I gladly pass them along and only keep a few shelves of my favorites in the house.

I consider the teetering stack of children's books.

Damn it, why am I saving all these books?

Then I realize I want to share the books with someone else. I want to share them with my own child someday, or someone's child. Out of all the things I've been sorting through, I don't know why it's the collection of books that is bringing this out in me. I want to curl up in front of the woodstove with someone and read to them, read them to sleep, read them to adventure, read them to the same love of the same books.

Jack joins me on the floor amid the stacks of book and leans his back against the doorframe.

"How are you doing?"

I sigh. "I'm having trouble figuring out which books to keep. I want them all, and it's ridiculous." I lie back and put my hands behind my head on the rug so I'm looking up at the ceiling. "I just realized the truth is that I'm saving them for someone who may not ever be born. Part of me wants to be a mother so badly, and part of me is just so scared."

I sit up and ask, "How did you decide to have children so easily? Don't you ever feel like it's impossible? Like you can't ever be as good as them?"

"They weren't perfect, Gayle. They made a lot of mistakes as parents. Sometimes it's hard to remember, but they did."

I consider his words.

"I don't remember much about that. I know I idealize them in a lot of ways."

Jack picks up one of the books at his feet and turns it over in his hands, running a thumb over the binding.

"Do you remember how Mom overcommitted herself to all sorts of volunteer activities?" he says. "She was barely home. Sometimes we needed her, too, and she wasn't always here. And how she threw herself into her work when she took up teaching again?"

It was true. For most of my teenage years, she was harried and tired and incapable of saying "no" to the next big project or committee or church group. Now I know she was running from something by trying to fill every waking minute with some activity, but then I just wished she'd stay home more. Then, I thought of Dad and what his flaws were.

"I guess I do remember how Dad would get in a silent stewing anger sometimes and not talk much. He only blew up a couple of times, but when he didn't, there was a feeling of awful tension in the house."

Jack nods. "Don't ever be afraid of not living up to something," he says. "They were just people, sis. Just people."

In the barn I keep finding box after box of party supplies: paper plates and napkins by the gross, party hats, twinkle lights. I find the boxes of blue and silver candles we used for all the New Year's parties and an industrial-sized box of votive candles. There's enough to start a small catering company. It's all still usable, so I save most of it. The twinkle lights will look good in my backyard. I have a brief image of them lining the top of the fence and wrapping around the banisters of the back porch as our family and friends dance in the backyard. These lights fit into another category of things I'm saving: the category of possibility.

In one of the boxes, I find a collection of photos, and there we are: Jack and Carm in suits, Lynn and Kenli and me in heels and short dresses, Jonathan with one arm around me. And the photo that happened when someone said, "Now just us." Then, Carm and Beth and Jack and I lined up together in front of the shelves in the kitchen where the light was good. We put our arms around each other's shoulders and looked straight into the camera with the widest smiles we had. Even then, we knew that each passing year was reason enough to dress up, invite friends, and celebrate.

There are still some of Mom and Dad's clothes left in the closet. I managed to go through most of them over the years, but still there are a few feet of old sweaters, coats, and shirts. I pull them out one by one and bury my nose in fabric; after all this time, I doubt any scent is left, but maybe. I used to come into the closet and stand in between the hanging clothes and inhale. For years there was still a lingering smell of Mom. It smelled like Evinrude perfume and hand lotion and something else that was just her. I'd stand perfectly still, sandwiched in between the clothes, and breathe.

Now, it just smells like dust and mothballs, and I'm relieved. It makes it easier to put everything into the black trash bags going to Goodwill. The one thing I do keep is the purple coat. It's a floor-length wool duster with hand-painted squares in different colors. It is something one might wear to an art opening. Mom saw it in a store window when we were vacationing when I was a teenager, and she went back multiple times during the week to visit "her" coat. She'd just stand on the street outside the store and admire it. It was outrageously expensive. On our last day there, she bought it and surprised us by sweeping into the room wearing it, turning in circles for us to see. She walked like royalty, with an enormous smile on her face. Both she and the coat were in full color. I love thinking of her on that day.

In the closet, I take it off the hanger and slip it over my shoulders. It fits me fine but is the antithesis of the sensible earth tones I usually wear. I'm going to save it anyway. I'm going to wear it—to potluck dinners or the grocery store or the movies or out to get the mail; it doesn't matter. It's the reminding me to do things in full color that matters.

James strains on the crowbar, and the stone pulls out of the grass. It's been sitting on the edge of the driveway for thirty years and has been partially covered by grass and soil. He's going to plant it in the front yard of our new house. I love things like this: taking the old and incorporating it into the new. Three of his friends work with him with a crowbar to ease the enormous stone onto the truck lift.

Back inside the house is a flurry of activity. Teams of friends are planted in each room, packing and moving boxes. We need to be out in a few weeks, and so I asked for help. I'm overwhelmed at how many people showed up. There's no way we could have done this ourselves. It's my new community helping me move out of my old one. Somebody once said, "Keep only those friends that help you move." This group has now helped me move two houses in less than four months, so I think that qualifies them for life.

⟋

The night before our last day, I dream of a morning in summer, and in the dream I am standing on the back porch. There's high golden grass in the field, and there's a single path cut through the grass, leading away from the house. The path is just wide enough for two people to walk side by side. In the dream I know I have to walk down the path, so I go down the stone steps, and just before the path bends, I turn around to look back at the house. It looks good in the morning light, and all of the landscaping is how it once was, lilies and edged gardens and manicured bushes everywhere. I know this is my last look at it, and I know I will miss it. When I turn back to the path to walk away, I wake up.

It is strange to walk through the house. I have never seen the rooms so empty. The walls are bare, and the wood floors are swept clean. The library is cleared of all the books I remember, the shelves dusted and quiet. The house is now just a shell, and I want it not to feel like mine anymore, but it still does. Maybe nothing can take away the feeling of ownership in a home that was loved.

Doug and Sal from next door come over to say good-bye and take a photo so we can all be in it. It's a group shot with us and our spouses standing in front of the house. Beth is holding Gavin, and his hat is crooked. Since there's no way to name their relationship, he calls her "GrandBeth." Someone makes a joke about us standing here, being the typical American family, and we all laugh. It's my favorite picture from the set.

Later, we all walk to the stone fire pit behind the house. James lights the tinder and adds kindling. We pull the stumps of wood close to the stones to sit on. The fire grows, and we pass around the wood block, the one that was our toothbrush holder in the bathroom as long as I can remember. I've been saving it. It is just a block of wood, cut roughly and with twelve holes drilled into the top. On three sides, it has a scribbles in black Magic Marker. On the other, in Dad's neat printing, it says "Father's Day 1980."

No matter how many people were living in the house, it always was full of toothbrushes. During the Camp Huntress years, I would periodically carry the holder around the house and make everyone point to their own toothbrush so I could throw the rest out. Within a few months, it would be full again.

Jack places the block in the flames, and we watch it smoke and then catch fire.

I think about how we took care of this house and how it took care of us back. It gave us a purpose and a common goal at a time when there was no clear path of how to continue. It was our home and the place where our fierce loyalty and love was forged—and that strength is boundless and not tied to place. It's a part of us now, embedded even deeper than the place where memories reside. And the memories and grief and loss are intertwined with all that boundless joy in the tangled, beautiful mess that is life.

My eyes keep filling, and I can't help the tears that slide down my cheeks. They are not sad tears. Instead, I feel grateful in a way that is alternately crushing and expanding in its force. The gratefulness comes in a wave for these people sitting around the fire with me. Then it comes for the house behind us. And outward beyond that to all the people in Hardwick who rallied around us when we needed them most and who will continue to connect us to this small town.

Our spouses and Beth stand and, as if on cue, walk back towards the house. Just the three of us are left. We huddle and wrap our arms around each other, pressing our foreheads together at the center of the circle. The smoke from the ashes of the fire drift around us. The clouds clear, and the sun comes out. We stand like that for a long time.

With one final squeeze, Jack lets go and we stand in a line facing towards the warmth of the sun. Then Jack turns, and we fall into step beside him, arms around each other for one last walk up the hill to the house.

We join Beth and our spouses in the kitchen for a toast from the bottle of whiskey I found while cleaning in the back of the cabinet. It is made of porcelain and shaped like a duck. Its neck comes off to reveal the bottle opening and potent Canadian bourbon whiskey. It is covered in dust and is older than all of us.

The liquor is rich and brown in the mismatched glasses. We clink them together offering toasts: to Gwen and David, to our new families, to each other, to our community, to Camp Huntress.

"We did it," I say.

And it's true. Everything is done. We processed forty years' worth of stuff, moved it, cleaned it, and made the decisions about every piece and processed the emotional residue that was leftover. I think I may have kept too many things and will have to shift things around to make space. It's a useful metaphor, I think.

We exchange hugs in the kitchen one more time and wave Jack's family out of the driveway. Beth leaves next, and then Carm and Nicole. We'll be together soon for holidays and birthday parties and those precious and ordinary family dinners, but I cry anyway when I hug them good-bye. I can't help it. This is a closing chapter and celebration for our family, and I feel the weight of it. I can't believe this is over. I'm not sure I know how to leave. There's no template for how to do this.

I remember my conversation with June about how to mark a transition. "Sometimes this sort of thing you can't plan," she said. "Just try to tap into what you need in the moment; you'll know if you really stop to listen."

And when I listen, I have a clear image of how I want this to end. The image I have is that I will close the door and I will walk down the driveway, the gravel crunching under my feet. I'll turn around to look at the house where gravel meets pavement next to the big evergreen that was the limit of how far I could venture out of the yard when I was small. I'll go past it and walk up the hill with the house behind me and turn once more at the top of Sessions Road for a final look. Then I will get into James's waiting truck, and I'll ask him to take me home, to our home.

I find him outside packing the last of the boxes.

"James, I need more time," I say. "I need to do a final walk-through by myself. Will you take the truck and wait for me at the top of the hill so I can leave by foot?"

He puts his arms around me.

"Take as long as you need."

I hear the truck leave, and I enter the house and stand for a moment in the kitchen, inhaling deeply to remember the smell. I thought it would feel empty and sad or even devastating to someday be at this juncture of leaving home for good. But instead it feels more like a quiet rest—a time of waiting. I can feel the silent house. It's clear, with all the memories ordered, waiting for the next family to come and fill it with laughter, with tears, with the hard and the good that is life.

I realize this is my greatest wish: I wish that another young family will live here. I imagine a couple will look out the back porch in the waning light in the evening when the sky just above the tree line lights up with the last colors of the day. They will make love during the cool nights of fall, with the smell of wild grapes in the air. They will fill the house with children who will walk outside barefoot on summer mornings to dewy grass in the front yard, to adventures waiting in the field and the woods. They will grow and grow and know this place as their own. A million joys and a million sorrows and a million ordinary moments that fill up the time that constitute a life will continue to happen within these walls. "My bedroom," the children will say of the room that smells of wood and looks out to the lone streetlamp at the top of the hill. "My backyard," they will say of the field and woods that stretch out enormously to their tiny legs and slope down to the stream, growing smaller to them with each passing year. "My town," they will say of the stone library and ball field and the tree-lined triangle of the grass common. "My house," they will say of the place they will always know as home no matter how many years pass.

I think of all of this in the quiet. The rooms echo as I move through the house, taking one last look at the empty rooms, closing doors for the last time. I walk out the front door and shut it very gently behind me, resting my hand on its frame. I know with certainty it is the last time I will shut it, and I take an extra moment to run my fingers over the cool metal of the latch and the twisted wire to hold it open.

As I'm standing there, I hear a tapping sound, and there is a dragonfly beating against one of the windowpanes in the shed. The sound is as regular as a metronome or a heartbeat. Over and over it taps out its rhythm against the windowpane. It is iridescent in the afternoon light.

Every shade of blue is represented on it somewhere, with highlighted flecks of orange. When it lands and rests, I scoop it up in cupped hands and take it outside, pulling the door shut with my foot. I stand under the maple tree, open my palms to the clear blue autumn sky, and let it go.

Acknowledgements

I love the acknowledgements section in books. It's where writers get to admit that any writing project never gets completed alone. I've been blessed with a wide network of friends, family, and supporters along the way.

First, to the community of Hardwick who supported our family and saw us through. I see how much love was given to me for no other reason than I was at the right place at the right time in the middle of a small community that cared. I hope you see yourself on the pages and realize that the story itself is a "thank-you" to you and your kindness. I am so grateful.

For the late Steve Buttner, who lent his cabin in the Adirondacks for a writing retreat where the seed of this story was born. To the Thursday Group and the rest of the Writing It Up In the Garden crew at the Big Yellow House who sat through my early tries at poetry, essays, and two unfinished novels that were the precursors to this work. To my early readers: Liz Bedell, Mike Biegner, Tammi Goddard, Sarah McNaughton and John Popsun. To Nerissa Nields-Duffy for your unfailing enthusiasm and encouragement; I never would have started or continued without you. To Jennifer Fronc; from the Roller Derby track to discovering our shared love of writing, you saw me through all sorts of writer's crises and endless cups of excellent coffee.

To all my friends and family who kept asking "How's the writing going?" and then listened to my answers no matter how elusive, abstract, or whiney. A special thanks to Jack, Carm, and Beth and your excellent additions: Heather, Nicole, Gavin, and Wesley. How lucky I am to have you as my family. Thanks for allowing me to share our story on the page. To my parents, Gwen and David Huntress; I hope this story has honored them and the legacy they left. And finally to James for loving me so well, giving me ample space to write, and providing "home" in every sense of the word.

Author's Notes

For my readers who know me well, you'll notice some discrepancies between this book and "real life." I've altered the order of events and changed names in some places to protect the privacy of others, filled in details where my memory draws a blank, and made one composite character out of the therapists who were instrumental in my healing for the sake of the story. "June" isn't a single person but a blend of many who helped me along my way. Memoir writing is an imperfect science, and where I've gotten the facts all wrong, I hope I've gotten the spirit just right.

Finally, in the spirit of giving back, twenty percent of the proceeds from the sale of this book will be donated to hospice and to Comfort Zone Camp. In my experience, hospice is staffed entirely by angels masquerading as caregivers, and they bring such compassion to the families they reach. Comfort Zone Camp is an organization that was created in the wake of 9/11 to help children and their families cope with the losses of that day. Now, it continues to serve multitudes of children around the country who have experienced loss and to support families in their grieving. I've seen firsthand the healing that this amazing organization brings to children and their families. On their behalf, thank you for buying this book.

To learn more about the charitable donations or the author's upcoming projects please visit www.gaylehuntress.com.

Made in the USA
Charleston, SC
15 April 2014